POLITICAL JUSTICE: THE USE OF LEGAL PROCEDURE FOR POLITICAL ENDS

POLITICAL JUSTICE: THE USE OF LEGAL PROCEDURE FOR POLITICAL ENDS

Dr. Chester Alexis C. Buama

SOCIETY Publishing

www.societypublishing.com

Political Justice: The use of Legal Procedure for Political Ends

Dr. Chester Alexis C. Buama

Society Publishing
224 Shoreacres Road
Burlington, ON L7L 2H2
Canada
www.societypublishing.com
Email: orders@arclereducation.com

ISBN: 978-1-77469-886-0 (Hardcover)

ABOUT THE AUTHOR

Hon. Chester Alexis C. Buama, PhD, is a College Professor at Laguna State Polytechnic University under the Faculty of College of Arts and Sciences and currently serving as Regent of the LSPU Board of Regents the highest policy-making body of the university. He previously served as the College Research Coordinator and Coordinator of Curriculum, Instruction Quality Assurance, A Consultant of the Department of Education Central Office for Learning Assessment, and National Trainer of the Commission on Higher Education for General Education Courses. He is also a member of local and international organizations: he is a Fellow and Senior Member of the Royal Institute of Management and the Royal Institute of Educators, Singapore, Reading Association of the Philippines, and International English Learners Training Institute. He was a Philippine Youth Ambassador to ASEAN countries and Japan which was sponsored by the Cabinet Office of Japan and Office of the President of the Philippines in 2010. He has a Master's degree in Management major in Public Administration and a Bachelor's degree in Journalism. He was conferred a Doctorate Degree in Philosophy major in Public Administration in 2016 and graduated with a Doctorate Degree in Philosophy major in Business Management in 2018. At present he is teaching Human Behavior in Organization, Social Philosophy, Principles of Management and Organization, Good Governance and Social Responsibility, Business Communication, Macro and, Micro Economics and Philippine History and Constitution both in the undergraduate and graduate levels. Moreover, he has actively participated in the Civic Activities of the Global Cooperation Society International, Philippine National Chapter, and is often invited as a resource speaker in various management and research writing seminars. Recently, he was awarded the Ambassador Seal of Excellence for Education as Research Practitioner and as the 2018 Outstanding Premier College Professor and Humanitarian Service Excellence Award by the Asia Pacific Excellence Council, Inc.

TABLE OF CONTENTS

LIST OF FIGURES

SUMMARY

Political justice is the impartial application of the criminal justice system to the disadvantage of particular individuals or groups because of their perceived non-constitutional activities. Meanwhile, political rights allude to a person's capacity to participate in a country's civil activities without constraint and are closely related to citizenship status.

This volume states that there are no universally legal standards for political activity as differentiated from other forms of social action. Something is political if it relates in an incredibly rigorous way to the interests of a community. Each dominant class, group, or individual will develop criteria based on which reprehensible acts, when sufficiently severe, will necessitate public action, according to its estimates and needs. Consequently, an infinite number of "political" factors could be included, excluded, and re-entered into the formal definition of a political crime.

PREFACE

This volume is a definitive analysis of the use of legal processes to settle political conflicts. Generally, something is political if it relates uniquely to the community's interests. This volume argues that there are four unique forms of political justice: procedural (deciding how reasonably individuals are treated), distributive (deciding who gets what), restorative (which seeks to re-establish individuals/communities to "rightness.") and retaliatory (based on crime being punished).

Instead of the legal system, the political process and institutions are typically responsible for resolving conflicts in a society with competing group demands and incompatible values. According to this perspective, political institutions' decisions are delicate, complex, and require significant insight. They involve those directly responsible to individuals whose welfare they promote or jeopardize.

Prosecuting one or more individuals for committing criminal offenses is part of the political trial. Common crimes or illegal acts against the state, like treason and sedition, could be the charges. Modern security legislations protect the political system from propagandist, intellectual and organizational activity focused toward revolution. Nevertheless, the volume argues that a distinction between fact obscures genuine political criticism and wish.

As a tool for gaining and maintaining political authority, political trials take an event from its historical context and shine an intense spotlight on it to divulge its smallest detail. As a potential resource in the struggle for political dominance, the past is restructured for the benefit of the future. The trial needs a "section of history" to be remade. While previous events may be part of a current conflict, the appointed authority can "dismiss its current factors and treat the political case as a previous incident."

According to the volume, in political trials, it is necessary for witnesses to re-enact their roles, or else the political message that the problem was meant to convey will be lost. The use of legal processes to suppress dissenting groups from an established system "has been channeled against small groups of minor significance in domestic operations. Open suppression will undoubtedly miss the objective and induce resistance when the oppressed groups take the role of a mass movement, commanding large portions of the voters.

The level of agreement of a society on a single value structure or the heterogeneity of a general public as far as its sharing of values and needs are concerned constitutes its political-legal system. The importance of political justice consciousness in a heterogeneous society subsequently has exceptional challenges. Assuming no casual agreement exists on community issues, the judges can't take their traditional roles in understanding and guiding the community value structure about the unique issues.

CHAPTER 1

What is Justice

Contents

1.1. INTRODUCTION

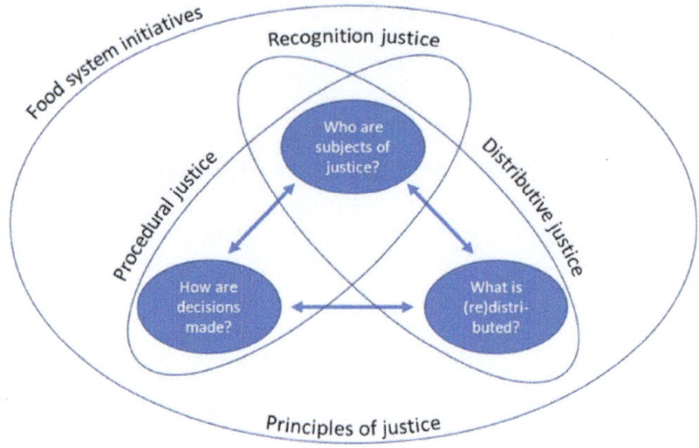

Figure 1.1. Framework to analyze conceptualizations of justice.

Source: Bruin, Annemarieke & Boer, I.J.M. & Faber, Niels & Jong, Gjalt & Termeer, Katrien & De Olde, Evelien. (2023). Easier said than defined? Conceptualising justice in food system transitions. *Agriculture and Human* Values. 1–18. Scientific Figure on ResearchGate. Available from: https://www.researchgate.net/figure/Our-framework-to-analyse-conceptualisations-of-justice-the-interactions-between-them_fig1_371908067 (accessed on 22 September 2023)

1.1.1. Understanding Justice in Various Contexts

Understanding justice is paramount in various contexts, as it influences the fabric of society and shapes human interactions (Figure 1.1). It serves as a guiding principle for ethical decision-making, promoting fairness, and reducing inequalities. By comprehending justice, individuals can engage in constructive dialogue, advocate for human rights, and work towards building a more just and inclusive world (Schwettmann, 2016).

A deep understanding of justice helps develop and improve legal systems in the legal domain. It allows policymakers and legal practitioners to design laws and policies that uphold the principles of justice and protect individual rights. Moreover, it enables citizens to participate actively in their legal systems, ensuring that justice is accessible and applied equitably.

In the social realm, it is understood that justice aids in recognizing and addressing societal injustices and inequalities. It prompts individuals to advocate for marginalized groups, challenge discriminatory practices, and strive for equal opportunities for all members of society. By comprehending the importance of justice, individuals can work towards creating a more equitable and inclusive community that upholds human dignity and respects individual rights (Selznick, 2020).

Ultimately, understanding justice in its various contexts empowers individuals to actively contribute to the pursuit of a fairer and more just world. It encourages critical thinking, empathy, and a commitment to uphold the principles of justice in personal, professional, and societal interactions.

1.2. THE PHILOSOPHICAL PERSPECTIVE ON JUSTICE

The concept of justice has undergone remarkable historical development, with diverse philosophical perspectives contributing to its understanding. Exploring the historical evolution of justice allows us to appreciate the complexities and nuances associated with this fundamental idea (Schwettmann, 2016).

1.2.1. Ancient Greek Philosophers and Justice

The ancient Greek philosophers made profound contributions to the concept of justice, shaping its understanding for centuries to come. Among these philosophers, Plato and Aristotle stand out as key figures.

Plato's Theory of Justice (Plato)

In his seminal work "The Republic," Plato put forth a comprehensive theory of justice that continues to influence philosophical thought. According to Plato, justice was not only a virtue within society but also within the individual. He posited that a just society could be realized when individuals performed their respective roles in alignment with their natural abilities and talents. Plato envisioned a hierarchical social structure led by philosopher-kings with wisdom and virtue. For Plato, justice was the harmonious interplay and equilibrium that emerged when every part of society fulfilled its designated function, creating a balanced and flourishing community. His theory laid the foundation for discussions on the nature and attainment of justice, offering valuable insights into the organization and functioning of just societies (Selznick, 2020).

Aristotle's Concept of Justice (Aristotle)

Aristotle, a student of Plato, presented a unique viewpoint on justice in his renowned work "Nicomachean Ethics." He perceived justice as a virtue that resided in finding the middle ground between extremes. Aristotle delineated two fundamental forms of justice: distributive justice and corrective justice. Distributive justice revolves around the equitable allocation of resources and honors in society, ensuring that each individual receives what is fair and appropriate. On the other hand, corrective justice deals with rectifying wrongs through punishment and restitution, aiming to restore balance and harmony. Aristotle underscored the significance of equity, fairness, and proportionality in attaining justice, highlighting the need for harmonious relationships and balanced distribution to pursue a just society. His perspective expanded the discourse on justice, providing a nuanced understanding of its various dimensions and implications (Schwettmann, 2016).

1.2.2. Roman and medieval philosophers' views on justice

During the Roman and medieval periods, philosophical thought on justice continued to develop, incorporating elements from Greek philosophy and religious teachings.

- Stoic philosophy and justice (stoicism)
- Natural law theory and justice (natural law)

In the medieval era, natural law theorists such as Thomas Aquinas endeavored to establish a profound link between justice and the natural order. According to natural law theory, justice is founded on objective moral principles inherent in human nature and the divine order. Advocates of natural law argued that just laws and systems must align with these principles, prioritizing the common good and safeguarding individual rights. Within the framework of natural law, justice was perceived as a manifestation of an overarching moral order that transcended human constructs. This perspective emphasized the moral dimensions of justice and the need to uphold universally valid principles grounded in the natural order. The natural law theory contributed significantly to discussions on justice, fostering an understanding of justice as an essential component of a harmonious and morally upright society.

1.2.3. Modern Philosophers' Contributions to the Concept of Justice

In more recent times, modern philosophers have expanded their understanding of justice, considered the complexities of society and grappled with ethical dilemmas.

Immanuel Kant and Justice (Kantian Ethics)

Immanuel Kant, a prominent philosopher, put forward a deontological ethical theory known as Kantian ethics, highlighting the significance of moral duties and principles in guiding human behavior. Within Kantian ethics, justice was pivotal in treating individuals as ends in themselves, recognizing their autonomy and inherent dignity. Kant emphasized the universality of moral laws and proposed the concept of the categorical imperative, which required individuals to act based on principles that could be universally applied. According to Kant, justice entailed that individuals adhere to moral codes that could be rationally justified and upheld in all circumstances. By emphasizing the importance of moral duties and the universal application of principles, Kantian ethics contributed to understanding justice as a fundamental aspect of ethical behavior and pursuing a just society (Schwettmann, 2016).

John Stuart Mill and Justice (Utilitarianism)

John Stuart Mill's ethical framework of utilitarianism presented a consequentialist viewpoint on justice. Utilitarianism posits that actions should be assessed based on utility to maximize happiness and minimize suffering. Within this framework, Mill argued that justice entails the promotion of the greatest good for the greatest number of people. He emphasized the significance of equality, fairness, and the consideration of the well-being of all individuals in decision-making processes. Mill advocated for a just society where the happiness and welfare of the majority were prioritized while also recognizing the importance of protecting the rights and interests of minority groups. Utilitarianism contributed to the understanding of justice by emphasizing the consequences of actions and the ethical imperative of promoting overall well-being in pursuing a just society.

These philosophical perspectives on justice have shaped our understanding of the concept throughout history. They provide diverse frameworks and ethical principles that continue to inform contemporary debates on justice and guide our moral and ethical choices in various aspects of life. By examining these philosophical perspectives, we gain insights into the complexities of justice and its significance for creating fair and equitable societies (Selznick, 2020).

1.3. DIFFERENT THEORIES OF JUSTICE

Justice is a complex concept that has led to various theories aimed at understanding and achieving fairness in different contexts (Figure 1.2). These theories offer different perspectives on justice, emphasizing distinct principles and approaches to address societal inequalities and promote a just society (Schwettmann, 2016).

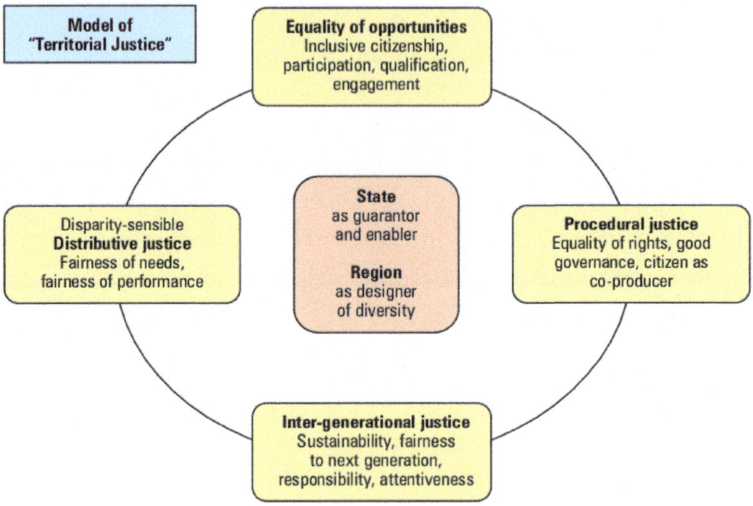

Figure 1.2. Model of four dimensions of territorial justice. Based on theories of justice and empowerment.

Source: Magel, H. (2017). Territorial justice for urban and rural regions? About the responsibility and role of the Bavarian Academy for rural areas. *Geomatics, Land management and Landscape*, 65–79. https://www.semanticscholar.org/paper/Territorial-justice-for-urban-and-rural-regions-the-Magel/97c16a0b3bf2e105bd8bb1e99c2166ecafc26e47

1.3.1. Distributive Justice

Distributive justice concerns the fair distribution of resources, opportunities, and benefits within a society. It focuses on how individuals and groups should allocate wealth, income, and other goods. Two prominent theories within distributive justice are Rawlsian justice and entitlement theory.

John Rawls and Justice as Fairness (Rawlsian Justice)

John Rawls put forth the theory of justice as fairness, which aimed to tackle social and economic inequalities within society. According to Rawls, a just society is one in which resources and opportunities are distributed to benefit the least advantaged members. He introduced the concept of the original position, a hypothetical scenario in which individuals make decisions about societal arrangements without knowledge of their social position. Rawls' theory emphasizes the importance of equal fundamental liberties, fair equality of opportunity, and the difference principle. The difference principle allows for inequalities only if they improve the well-being of the least well-off members of society. Rawlsian justice provides a framework for addressing and rectifying social and economic disparities, promoting a more equitable and just society. (Selznick, 2020).

Robert Nozick and Justice as Entitlement (Entitlement Theory)

Robert Nozick presented entitlement theory as a contrasting perspective to Rawls' theory of justice. Nozick argued that justice lies in upholding individuals' rights to acquire, transfer, and possess property through voluntary transactions. According to entitlement theory, a just society permits wealth accumulation through just acquisitions and voluntary exchanges, regardless of resulting inequalities. Nozick's theory strongly emphasizes individual liberty and rejects the notion of redistributive measures to achieve economic equality. In this view, justice is achieved through respect for property rights and voluntary interactions, allowing individuals the freedom to determine their financial outcomes. Nozick's entitlement theory challenges conventional notions of distributive justice, providing an alternative perspective on the principles underlying the just distribution of resources within society. (Schwettmann, 2016).

1.3.2. Retributive Justice

Retributive justice focuses on punishment for wrongdoing, aiming to restore balance and uphold the moral order. It considers how individuals who have committed offences should be held accountable and the appropriate penalties that should be imposed.

Jeremy Bentham and utilitarian approach to justice (utilitarian justice)

Jeremy Bentham, a prominent utilitarian philosopher, espoused the concept of practical justice, which centers on maximizing overall happiness or utility. According to the practical perspective, punishment is justified if it results in greater societal satisfaction. Bentham advocated for a system of punishment that serves multiple purposes, including deterring future crimes, rehabilitating offenders, and safeguarding society. In this view, the severity of punishment should be proportionate to the harm caused, considering both the deterrence effect and the potential for rehabilitation. Bentham's practical approach to justice highlights the consequentialist aspect of justice, prioritizing promoting overall well-being and societal happiness as the ultimate goal of a just punishment system. (Selznick, 2020).

Restorative justice and the healing approach (restorative justice)

Restorative justice offers a distinct perspective by prioritizing the repair of harm caused by criminal behavior and promoting reconciliation between offenders, victims, and the community. This approach centers around dialogue, accountability, and the restoration of relationships. Restorative justice seeks to address the needs of victims, provide opportunities for offenders to take responsibility for their actions, and foster healing and community engagement. Restorative justice transforms the traditional punitive system into a more collaborative and rehabilitative process by focusing on repairing the harm done and addressing the underlying causes of the offence. It emphasizes the importance of restoring individuals' dignity, improving relationships, and promoting community responsibility for preventing future harm. Restorative justice offers an alternative vision of justice that strives to address the needs and well-being of all parties involved, promoting healing and building more robust, more connected communities. (Schwettmann, 2016).

1.3.3. Procedural Justice

Procedural justice focuses on the fairness of the processes used in making decisions and resolving disputes. It emphasizes the importance of fair procedures and the perceived fairness of decision-making mechanisms.

Fair process and Impartiality (Procedural Fairness)

Procedural fairness strongly emphasizes fair processes and impartiality as essential elements of justice. It asserts that individuals have the right to appropriate treatment, respectful dialogue, and the opportunity to present their case. Proper procedures ensure that decisions are made without bias, relying on reliable evidence and through transparent and inclusive processes.

Impartiality is crucial in procedural fairness, requiring decision-makers to approach cases without favoritism or prejudice. The principle of neutrality ensures that judgments are based on the case's merits and not influenced by personal interests or external factors. It upholds the idea that justice should be impartial and free from discrimination or unfair advantage. Fair process, on the other hand, encompasses the procedures and mechanisms employed in legal and administrative proceedings. It guarantees that individuals can be heard, present evidence, and challenge opposing arguments. The fair process ensures that decision-making is transparent, consistent, and subject to review, providing individuals with confidence in the justice system.

By upholding fair process and impartiality, procedural fairness promotes trust in the legal system, enhances the perception of justice, and safeguards individuals' rights. It emphasizes the importance of fairness in the procedures and mechanisms through which justice is administered, contributing to a just and equitable society. (Selznick, 2020).

John Rawls' theory of justice as fairness (Rawlsian justice)

John Rawls' theory of justice as fairness incorporates aspects of procedural justice into its framework. Rawls argued that fair procedures are crucial for establishing and maintaining a just society. He emphasized the significance of inclusive and equitable decision-making processes allowing individuals to shape society's rules and principles. According to Rawls, just procedures ensure that the outcomes of these processes benefit all community members and are not skewed in favor of particular interests or groups.

Rawls' theory highlights the importance of fair and inclusive procedures in upholding justice. By involving individuals in the decision-making process and ensuring that their voices are heard, approaches contribute to the legitimacy and fairness of the outcomes. This notion aligns with procedural justice principles, emphasizing the importance of transparency, inclusivity, and the opportunity for individuals to shape decisions that affect them. (Schwettmann, 2016).

1.3.4. Commutative Justice

Commutative justice, or corrective justice, focuses on justice in transactions and exchanges between individuals. It deals with the fair treatment of individuals in contractual agreements and interactions involving mutual obligations.

- Equality and mutual benefit (commutative justice)
- Contractual agreements and justice (contractual justice)

Contractual justice refers to the fair and just enforcement of contractual agreements. It entails that individuals honor their commitments, fulfil their obligations, and respect the agreed-upon terms. Contractual justice ensures that individuals receive what they are entitled to base on their voluntary agreements and promotes trust and stability in economic and social interactions.

These different theories of justice provide frameworks for understanding and addressing societal inequalities and ethical dilemmas. Each theory offers distinct perspectives on the principles and approaches necessary to achieve justice in different contexts. Understanding these theories deepens our appreciation of the complexities of justice and informs discussions on how to create fairer and more equitable societies.

1.4. THE LEGAL PERSPECTIVE ON JUSTICE

The legal perspective on justice delves into how justice is understood and applied within legal systems. It encompasses theories, principles, and the role of judges in ensuring fairness and upholding the rule of law (Schwettmann, 2016).

1.4.1. Justice Within Legal Systems

Justice within legal systems refers to applying legal principles and norms to ensure fair outcomes in legal proceedings. Legal systems vary across jurisdictions, but pursuing justice is a fundamental objective in all legal frameworks. Legal positivism and natural law theory are two key perspectives on justice within legal systems.

Legal Positivism and Justice (Legal Positivism)

Legal positivism is a philosophical theory that advocates for the separation of law and morality. According to legal positivism, rules are valid from their creation and recognition by a legitimate authority, such as legislation or the judiciary. Legal positivists contend that the primary function of law is to maintain social order and enforce established norms, irrespective of whether those norms align with moral principles (Selznick, 2020).

From the perspective of legal positivism, justice is understood as the correct application and interpretation of the law. It emphasizes the adherence to legal principles, procedures, and precedents as the basis for determining justice in a given legal system. In this view, justice is not necessarily tied to moral considerations or subjective notions of fairness but instead is rooted in the objective application and interpretation of existing legal rules.

Legal positivism highlights the importance of legal certainty, consistency, and the rule of law in achieving justice within a particular legal framework. While it may not directly address moral or ethical concerns, legal positivism provides a framework for understanding justice as the proper functioning and application of the law within a given legal. system.

Natural Law Theory and Justice In Law (Natural Law)

In contrast to legal positivism, natural law theory asserts that the foundation of law should be rooted in inherent moral principles. Natural law theorists contend that a connection exists between law and morality, and just laws must align with higher ethical standards. According to natural law theory, justice is not solely determined by legal rules but also by the underlying moral principles that guide those rules. In this view, legal systems should strive to promote justice by adhering to universal natural, ethical principles.

Natural law theory recognizes that pursuing justice extends beyond mere adherence to legal norms. It emphasizes the importance of moral considerations and principles that transcend specific legal systems. By aligning legal rules with universal ethical principles, natural law theory suggests that legal systems can contribute to a more just society by ensuring that laws reflect and promote moral ideals (Schwettmann, 2016).

Natural law theory offers an alternative perspective on justice within the legal context, underscoring the interplay between law and morality. It posits that justice is not confined solely to legal rules but extends to the moral foundations that underpin those rules. By integrating ethical principles into legal systems, natural law theory promotes the pursuit of justice in a broader sense, aiming to establish a legal framework that aligns with fundamental moral values (Selznick, 2020).

1.4.2. The Role of Judges in Delivering Justice

Judges play a crucial role in the delivery of justice within legal systems. Their responsibilities include interpreting and applying the law impartially, ensuring due process, and making decisions that align with the principles of justice. The actions of judges can significantly impact the fairness of legal outcomes.

Adjudication and the Pursuit of Justice (Adjudication)

Adjudication refers to resolving legal disputes and determining the rights and obligations of the parties involved. Adjudication aims to arrive at just decisions that consider the merits of each case and uphold the rule of law. Judges are responsible for impartially hearing arguments, evaluating evidence, and applying legal principles to render fair judgments. Adjudication seeks to give individuals access to justice, allowing them to assert their rights and obtain redress for grievances.

Judicial Activism and Justice (Judicial Activism)

Judicial activism is a controversial concept that refers to judges' active interpretation of the law beyond its literal meaning. Proponents argue that judicial activism is necessary for promoting justice in cases where existing laws may be inadequate or unjust. Judges can ensure fair outcomes and protect individual rights by broadening interpretations or addressing gaps in the law. However, critics argue that judicial activism may infringe on the separation of powers and undermine democratic decision-making.

1.4.3. Equality and Justice in Law

Legal equality and justice are vital to a fair and just legal system. They ensure that all individuals are treated equally under the law and that the principles of justice are upheld. Within this framework, two significant aspects to consider are equal protection under the law and justice application within the criminal justice system (Selznick, 2020).

Equal Protection under The Law

Equal protection under the law is a fundamental principle that guarantees that all individuals are treated equally by the legal system, irrespective of their race, gender, religion, or other protected characteristics. This principle aims to eliminate discrimination and ensure fairness in applying laws and legal processes. Two critical aspects of equality and justice within the legal system are civil rights and laws addressing discrimination (Schwettmann, 2016).

Civil rights and justice (civil rights): Civil rights encompass the fundamental rights and freedoms individuals are entitled to, protected by law. Civil rights ensure equal opportunities, protections, and benefits under the law. The pursuit of justice in civil rights involves challenging discriminatory practices, advocating for equal treatment, and striving for social and legal equality. Prominent examples of civil rights movements include those that fought for racial equality, gender equality, and LGBTQ+ rights.

Discrimination and justice (anti-discrimination laws): Addressing discrimination is crucial to achieving equality and justice. Anti-discrimination laws prohibit unfair treatment based on protected characteristics such as race, gender, religion, disability, or age. These laws aim to eradicate discriminatory practices, promote equal opportunities, and provide legal remedies for those who have experienced discrimination. By enforcing anti-discrimination laws, the legal system plays a crucial role in upholding justice and ensuring all individuals are protected from unfair treatment.

1.4.4. Criminal Justice System and the Principle of Justice

Justice within the criminal justice system entails ensuring fair treatment for individuals accused of crimes, victims, and society. This involves safeguarding the rights of the accused, promoting fair trials, and considering the principles of justice in punishment and rehabilitation.

Fair Trials And Justice (Right To A Fair Trial)

The right to a fair trial is a fundamental principle of justice within the criminal justice system. It encompasses various rights, including the right to legal representation, the presumption of innocence, the right to confront witnesses, and the right to an impartial jury. Fair trials ensure that the accused are treated justly, evidence is presented and evaluated properly, and judgments are based on legal standards and principles. The right to a fair trial upholds the principles of justice by preventing arbitrary or biased outcomes (Selznick, 2020).

Punishment and Rehabilitation (Punitive Justice)

The principle of justice in the criminal justice system extends to the determination of appropriate punishment and the pursuit of rehabilitation. Punishment serves the purpose of retribution, deterrence, and incapacitation. However, justice also requires that punishment be proportionate to the offence's severity and consider individual circumstances. On the other hand, rehabilitation focuses on addressing the underlying causes of criminal behavior and facilitating the reintegration of offenders into society. Pursuing justice within the criminal justice system involves striking a balance between punishment and rehabilitation, ensuring that the goals of accountability and restoration are met (Schwettmann, 2016).

Equality and justice in law are essential components of a fair and just legal system. Equal protection under the law ensures that individuals are treated equally, free from discrimination. Pursuing justice within the legal system involves safeguarding civil rights and addressing discrimination through anti-discrimination laws. In the criminal justice system, justice is upheld through fair trials that protect the rights of the accused. The principle of justice is also applied in determining appropriate punishment and promoting offender rehabilitation. By supporting equality and justice in law, legal systems can foster a more just society where individuals are treated fairly, and their rights are protected.

1.5. SOCIAL JUSTICE: EQUITY AND FAIRNESS

Social justice is a concept that focuses on equity and fairness in society. It seeks to address systemic inequalities and promote equal opportunities for all individuals. Within social justice, key aspects to explore are the concept of social justice, the importance of equality and equity, and the intersectionality of social justice (Figure 1.3).

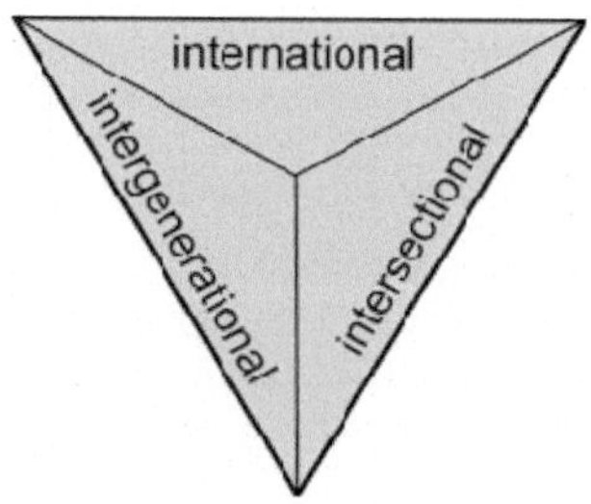

Figure 1.3. Three domains of responses to sustainability challenges available for the state.

Source: Jerneck, Anne & Olsson, Lennart & Ness, Barry & Anderberg, Stefan & Baier, Matthias & Clark, Eric & Hickler, Thomas & Hornborg, Alf & Kronsell, Annica & Lövbrand, Eva & Persson, Johannes. (2011). Structuring sustainability science. *Sustainability Science.* 6. 69–82. Scientific Figure on ResearchGate. Available from: https://www.researchgate.net/figure/Three-domains-of-responses-to-sustainability-challenges-available-for-the-state_fig3_220041282 (accessed on 22 September 2023)

1.5.1. Social Justice in Society

Social justice is pursuing fairness and equity in distributing resources, opportunities, and privileges. It involves addressing societal inequalities and creating a more just and inclusive society that upholds the dignity and rights of all individuals. Understanding the concept of social justice and its significance is crucial in striving for a more equitable world (Selznick, 2020).

The Concept of Social Justice

Social justice embodies the principles of fairness, equality, and the equitable distribution of wealth, income, and opportunities within society. It addresses the systemic barriers that impede individuals from realizing their full potential and seeks to dismantle social, economic, and political structures that perpetuate inequality. Social justice acknowledges every person's inherent worth and dignity and advocates for removing barriers that prevent individuals from accessing the same rights, resources, and opportunities, irrespective of their background or circumstances (Schwettmann, 2016).

At its core, social justice strives to create a society where all individuals can thrive and flourish. It recognizes that race, gender, socioeconomic status, and other forms of social identity should not limit or determine one's access to basic needs, education, healthcare, employment, and other essential resources. Social justice calls for creating inclusive policies and institutions that address systemic inequities, promote equal opportunity, and challenge the structures perpetuating disadvantage and discrimination.

Pursuing social justice requires collective action, advocacy, and policy changes to address societal disparities and promote a more equitable distribution of resources. It calls for recognizing and redressing historical injustices, eliminating systemic biases, and creating inclusive and just systems that foster social well-being and equal opportunities for all members of society.

Equality and Equity in Social Justice

Equality and equity are core principles within the realm of social justice. While both concepts strive for fairness, they approach it from different perspectives. Equality ensures everyone is granted equal opportunities, rights, and treatment without discrimination or favoritism. It aims to create a level playing field where everyone starts from a similar position.

Equity, however, recognizes that individuals have different starting points and face varying barriers due to historical disadvantages or systemic inequalities. It acknowledges that achieving true fairness may require providing additional support or resources to individuals based on their unique circumstances. Equity recognizes the need to address existing disparities and actively redistributes resources to offer more significant opportunities for historically marginalized or disadvantaged (Selznick, 2020).

In the pursuit of social justice, both equality and equity are essential considerations. While striving for equality ensures everyone is treated with equal respect and dignity, equity recognizes that not everyone starts from the same position and requires additional support to achieve fairness. By addressing historical disadvantages and implementing redistributive measures, social justice aims to create a society where all individuals, regardless of their background, have an equal opportunity to thrive and reach their full potential.

Achieving social justice is an ongoing process that requires a commitment to dismantling systemic barriers, challenging discriminatory practices, and advocating for policies that promote equality and equity. By embracing both principles, social justice aims to create a more inclusive and just society where fairness and opportunities are accessible to all (Schwettmann, 2016).

Redistribution of resources and justice (resource redistribution): Redistribution of resources addresses economic and social disparities to promote social justice. It involves policies and programs to allocate resources more equitably, such as progressive taxation, social welfare programs, and public investments in education and healthcare. Resource redistribution seeks to ensure that all individuals have access to the necessities of life and the opportunities needed to thrive.

Affirmative action and justice (affirmative action): An affirmative action is a policy approach that addresses historical inequalities and promotes diversity and inclusion. It involves proactive measures to provide opportunities to historically marginalized groups, ensuring representation and equal access to educational and employment opportunities. Affirmative action recognizes the need for targeted efforts to overcome systemic barriers and achieve social justice.

Intersectionality and Social Justice

Intersectionality recognizes that individuals experience multiple forms of oppression and discrimination based on their intersecting identities, such as gender, race, class, and sexuality. Intersectionality highlights the importance of considering the unique experiences and challenges individuals with multiple marginalized identities face (Selznick, 2020).

Gender justice (gender equality): Gender justice is a vital social justice component dedicated to attaining equality and fairness for all genders.

It endeavors to challenge and overcome gender-based discrimination, stereotypes, and societal barriers that restrict opportunities based on an individual's gender identity. Gender justice seeks to establish a society where all genders are treated with equal respect, have equitable access to resources, and can actively participate in all aspects of social, economic, and political life. Gender justice recognizes that individuals should not face disadvantages or be limited by societal norms and expectations related to their gender. It aims to dismantle systemic gender inequalities, addressing the gender pay gap, gender-based violence, gender discrimination in education and employment, and unequal domestic and caregiving responsibilities distribution. Gender justice advocates for the empowerment of marginalized genders and the amplification of their voices in decision-making processes.

By promoting gender equality and challenging oppressive gender norms, gender justice builds a society that values diversity, inclusion, and equal opportunities. It calls for recognizing and respecting individuals' rights and autonomy, irrespective of gender identity or expression. Gender justice is essential in creating a world where all individuals can thrive and live free from discrimination, enabling a more equitable and just society for everyone.

Racial justice (racial equality): Racial justice aims to eliminate systemic racism and achieve equality for all racial and ethnic groups. It addresses discriminatory practices, biases, and disparities in education, employment, criminal justice, and healthcare. Racial justice seeks to create a society where individuals are not judged or mistreated based on race or ethnicity and have equal opportunities to thrive (Schwettmann, 2016).

Social justice revolves around the principles of equity and fairness in society. It encompasses the concept of social justice itself, the importance of equality and equity, and the recognition of intersectionality. Achieving social justice requires addressing systemic inequalities, redistributing resources, and promoting equality and inclusion for all individuals, regardless of gender, race, or other identities. By striving for social justice, societies can create a more equitable and just world that upholds the rights and dignity of every individual. (Selznick, 2020).

1.5.2. Economic Justice and Fairness

Economic justice and fairness focus on creating equitable economic systems that address income inequality, wealth redistribution, and global economic disparities. Understanding these concepts and their impact on society is essential for promoting economic justice.

Income Inequality and Economic Justice

Income inequality refers to the unequal income distribution among individuals or households within a society. Economic justice addresses income inequality and promotes fairness in allocating financial resources.

Wealth redistribution and justice (wealth redistribution): Wealth redistribution is a strategy to address economic disparities by reallocating wealth from the wealthy to the poor or disadvantaged individuals. It involves the implementation of policies and programs that promote a more equitable distribution of wealth and resources within society. Through progressive taxation, social welfare programs, and targeted investments, wealth redistribution ensures wealth is more fairly distributed, providing opportunities and resources to historically disadvantaged people.

The concept of wealth redistribution is rooted in the principle of economic justice, which recognizes the need to address systemic inequalities and ensure that individuals have access to essential resources and opportunities regardless of their socioeconomic background. By redistributing wealth, societies can strive for a fairer distribution of resources, reducing the disparities between the rich and the poor.

Wealth redistribution promotes social cohesion, reduces poverty, and fosters greater economic mobility. It aims to create a more just society by addressing the structural barriers perpetuating inequality and providing individuals with the means to meet their basic needs and access quality education, healthcare, and other essential services (Selznick, 2020).

Critics of wealth redistribution argue that it may discourage innovation and individual effort while undermining personal property rights. However, proponents say rectifying historical injustices and creating a more equitable society is necessary (Schwettmann, 2016).

Minimum wage and justice (minimum wage laws): Minimum wage laws serve as a mechanism to ensure that workers receive a fair and livable wage. These laws establish a minimum hourly rate that employers are legally required to pay their employees. Minimum wage laws contribute to economic justice by preventing exploitative practices and striving to uplift workers out of poverty by setting a floor on wages. They promote fairness by ensuring that individuals are compensated adequately for their work and can meet their basic needs.

Minimum wage laws are crucial in addressing income inequality and providing economic stability for low-wage workers. They aim to bridge the gap between workers' earnings and rising living costs. By ensuring a minimum standard of compensation, these laws promote a sense of fairness by recognizing the value of labor and protecting workers from exploitation.

Advocates argue that minimum wage laws promote social justice by reducing income disparities, improving worker well-being, and stimulating local economies. They assert that fair wages increase consumer spending power, fostering economic growth and benefiting communities.

Conversely, critics contend that minimum wage laws may have unintended consequences, such as potential job losses or reduced hiring. They argue that market forces should determine wage rates rather than government intervention.

Global Justice and International Fairness

Global justice focuses on addressing economic disparities and promoting fairness internationally. It recognizes the global nature of economic interdependence and the need to create a more just and equitable world economy (Selznick, 2020).

Global poverty and justice (global poverty): Global poverty represents a pressing challenge that demands a lens of economic justice. It encompasses the stark disparities in income, resources, and living conditions between regions and countries worldwide. Addressing global poverty necessitates the implementation of policies and initiatives aimed at alleviating poverty, fostering sustainable development, and ensuring access to necessities for all individuals across the globe (Schwettmann, 2016).

Achieving global justice requires recognizing the inherent dignity and worth of every human being, regardless of their geographic location or socioeconomic status. It entails a commitment to tackling systemic barriers and inequalities that perpetuate poverty on a global scale. This includes addressing limited access to education, healthcare, clean water, sanitation, and economic opportunities in disadvantaged regions.

Efforts to combat global poverty should encompass strategies that promote inclusive economic growth, enhance social protection systems, and facilitate equitable distribution of resources. This involves addressing the root causes of poverty, such as structural inequalities, unfair trade practices, and insufficient social welfare programs.

Global justice necessitates international cooperation, collaboration, and solidarity among nations, organizations, and individuals. It calls for recognizing shared responsibility in eradicating poverty and creating a more just and equitable world. Efforts should focus on empowering marginalized communities, promoting sustainable development, and creating opportunities for individuals to break free from the cycle of poverty.

By prioritizing global justice and addressing global poverty, societies can work towards building a more equitable and inclusive world. This requires recognizing the interconnectedness of global issues and actively engaging in initiatives that promote economic justice and improve the well-being of all individuals, irrespective of their geographical location (Selznick, 2020).

Trade and economic justice (trade justice): Trade justice aims to establish fair and equitable trade practices that benefit all nations, focusing on countries in the global South. It recognizes the need to address the unequal power dynamics inherent in international trade and the detrimental effects of exploitative trade practices. Trade justice advocates for implementing fair trade policies, increasing market access for developing countries, and protecting workers' rights and environmental standards. Promoting economic justice ensures that trade benefits are distributed more equitably among nations and contribute to sustainable development (Schwettmann, 2016).

Trade justice acknowledges that the current global trade system often disadvantages developing countries, perpetuating economic inequalities and hindering their ability to achieve self-sufficiency and economic growth. It calls for fairer trade rules, reduced barriers to market entry, and the inclusion of marginalized countries in decision-making processes related to trade agreements.

Furthermore, trade justice advocates for protecting workers' rights and the environment in trade practices. It recognizes the importance of ensuring decent working conditions, fair wages, and environmental sustainability in global trade activities. By promoting these principles, trade justice seeks to address the negative social and ecological impacts of exploitative trade practices and foster economic justice on a global scale.

Efforts towards trade justice require international cooperation, transparency, and a commitment to fair and equitable trade policies. By fostering a more just trade system, trade justice aims to contribute to poverty reduction, sustainable development, and more equitable global economic relations (Selznick, 2020).

In summary, throughout this chapter, we have explored the concept of justice from various perspectives, delving into its philosophical, legal, and social dimensions. We began by understanding the background and significance of justice, followed by its definition and importance in different contexts. We then examined the philosophical perspective on justice, tracing its historical development and exploring the theories proposed by influential philosophers such as Plato, Aristotle, Kant, and Mill. Moving on to the legal perspective, we discussed justice within legal systems, including the principles of legal positivism, natural law, and the role of judges in delivering justice. We also explored the concepts of equality and justice in law, encompassing equal protection, civil rights, and the criminal justice system. Additionally, we examined social justice, highlighting its focus on equity, fairness, and the intersectionality of different identities. Lastly, we discussed economic justice, income inequality, wealth redistribution, and global justice. (Schwettmann, 2016).

The Ongoing Debate on the Nature of Justice

The concept of justice continues to be a subject of ongoing debate and philosophical discourse. Scholars, thinkers, and policymakers grapple with questions such as the balance between equality and equity, the role of morality in law, and the implications of justice in diverse social, economic, and political contexts. The nature of justice is complex and multifaceted, with differing perspectives shaping the discourse.

Importance of Justice in Personal, Legal, and Societal Contexts

Justice holds immense importance in personal, legal, and societal realms. At a personal level, justice ensures that individuals are treated fairly and have equal opportunities to succeed. In legal systems, justice protects rights, the fair administration of laws, and the resolution of disputes justly. In broader societal contexts, justice promotes social cohesion, equality, and the well-being of communities. It addresses systemic inequalities, protects marginalized groups, and creates a more just and inclusive society. (Selznick, 2020).

Call to Action for Promoting Justice in Various Spheres of Life

Understanding the concept of justice and its significance calls us to action. We are called to promote justice in our personal lives, ensuring fairness, empathy, and respect for others. In the legal realm, we are encouraged to advocate for equal protection under the law, access to justice, and eradicating discriminatory practices. Moreover, in societal contexts, we are called upon to challenge systemic injustices, work towards social equality, and contribute to the betterment of our communities. Promoting justice requires collective efforts, policy changes, and an ongoing commitment to creating a more equitable and just world (Schwettmann, 2016).

Justice is a complex and multifaceted idea that transcends various domains of human existence. It holds significant importance in personal, legal, and societal contexts, shaping our understanding of fairness, equality, and the well-being of individuals and communities. The ongoing debate on the nature of justice reflects its complexities and the need for continuous reflection and action. By recognizing the importance of justice and working towards its promotion, we can contribute to creating a more just and inclusive world for all. (Selznick, 2020).

CHAPTER 2

The Standpoint of Political Justice

Contents

In terms of political justice, we define it as fair and equitable societal governance. It consists of the principles, ideals, and frameworks that govern how authority, assets, and opportunities are distributed within a political framework. A just political system adheres to various viewpoints, theories, and philosophical tenets, all evaluated in terms of political justice. It investigates issues concerning fairness, equality, rights, and the role of institutions in fostering a just society. By studying various theories, such as utilitarianism, liberalism, libertarianism, communitarianism, egalitarianism, and Rawlsian justice, we thoroughly understand how different schools of thought define and interpret political justice. This investigation allows us to critically evaluate the advantages and disadvantages of each point of view, illuminating the intricate relationships that exist between the pursuit of a just political order, societal well-being, and individual rights (Eriksen, 2016).

2.1. THEORIES OF POLITICAL JUSTICE

Theories of political justice are fundamental frameworks that examine the nature and tenets of justice in a political context. These theories provide conceptual tools for understanding and evaluating political institutions' equality, fairness, and legitimacy. Philosophers and political theorists have developed various theories of political justice, each of which offers a unique perspective on how authority, resources, and opportunities are distributed in multiple societies (Schmoller, 2016).

2.1.1. Utilitarianism

Utilitarianism, as a theory of political justice, provides a consequentialist framework that prioritizes maximizing society's overall happiness or well-being. Political justice prioritizes the interests of the most significant number of people while balancing the benefits and drawbacks of various political systems and policies to achieve the best possible results (Figure 2.1).

Fundamentally, utilitarianism holds that political justice is defined by advancing public welfare and alleviating suffering. Decisions and policies, according to the theory, should be evaluated in terms of their effects, specifically the overall net improvement in happiness or well-being they bring about for the vast majority of people in society. In utilitarianism, the maximization of general utility, frequently measured as pleasure, joy, or preference satisfaction, takes precedence over rejecting absolute moral rules or rights (Eriksen, 2016). Utilitarianism sees political justice as primarily promoting the common good. It seeks to create a society that maximizes happiness while minimizing suffering, regardless of personal freedoms or rights. This viewpoint holds that the ability of a political system to increase overall satisfaction among its citizens determines how just it is. Political justice is impossible to achieve without institutions and policies that promote general social welfare, economic growth, and basic needs satisfaction.

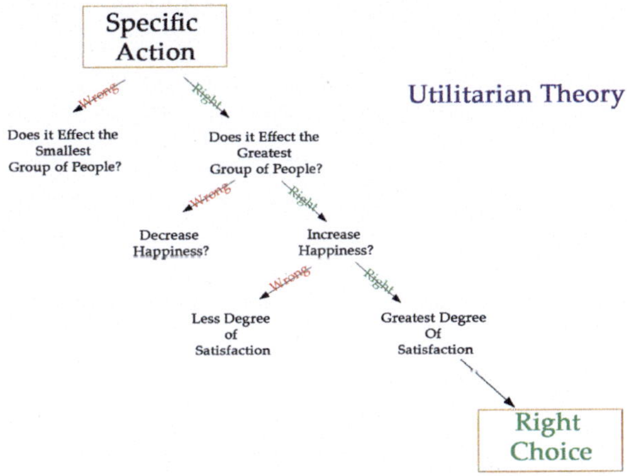

Figure 2.1. Illustration of utilitarian theory.

Source: Pace, Ronnie. (2016). Relationship of Institutional Characteristics to CACREP Accreditation of Doctoral Counselor Education Programs. Scientific Figure on ResearchGate. Available from: https://www.researchgate.net/figure/Illustration-of-utilitarian-theory-The-basic-idea-behind-the-need-to-make-a-decision_fig3_342106096 (accessed on 22 September 2023)

Utilitarianism interprets political justice through the utilitarian calculus, which involves weighing the benefits and drawbacks of various courses of action, governmental regulations, or resource allocations. This calculation requires considering the degree, duration, and scope of happiness or suffering caused by multiple options. Even if they may cause some short-term or localized harm, utilitarian thinkers advocate for laws and choices that maximize utility over time (Schmoller, 2016).

When making decisions, utilitarianism encourages a neutral and inclusive viewpoint. It treats everyone's happiness or well-being equally valuable without favoring any particular group or person. As a result, utilitarianism frequently supports initiatives aimed at reducing social and economic disparities, improving public health and education, and addressing structural injustices that undermine happiness as a whole. However, there are objections and difficulties with utilitarianism in the context of political justice. Critics argue that it may disregard the rights and interests of minority groups and individuals whose well-being may be sacrificed for the greater good. Furthermore, defining happiness or well-being can be complex and subjective, sparking debate about the appropriate metrics for calculating utility.

In its definition and interpretation of political justice, utilitarianism emphasizes maximizing overall happiness or well-being for the most significant number of people. It prioritizes the common good and works to balance advantages and disadvantages through political systems and policies. Utilitarianism's consequentialist approach to political justice focuses on the outcomes and consequences of decisions to build a society that promotes social welfare, economic development, and the alleviation of suffering.

2.1.2. Liberalism

Liberalism, a theory of political justice, provides a comprehensive framework for comprehending and interpreting the concept of justice in a political context. Individual rights and liberties are strongly emphasized as the cornerstone of political justice in liberalism, which has its roots in the writings of significant philosophers such as John Locke, John Stuart Mill, and Immanuel Kant (Eriksen, 2016).

Liberalism defines political justice as defending and protecting individual liberties and rights. It contends that people have inalienable rights that should be respected and upheld by the government and other societal institutions. These liberties frequently include freedom of expression, religion, assembly, and property ownership. Political justice, according to liberalism, is achieved when people are given the freedom to choose their paths and achieve their own goals as long as they do not violate the rights of others.

Liberalism views political justice through the lens of fairness and equal opportunity (Figure 2.2). It promotes a similar opportunity environment where everyone can access opportunities regardless of social status, race, gender, or other characteristics. This interpretation emphasizes the importance of meritocracy, which rewards people for their abilities and efforts rather than their social standing or inherited privileges. By ensuring equal opportunities, liberalism seeks to prevent systemic discrimination and create a society where people can thrive and realize their full potential. (Schmoller, 2016).

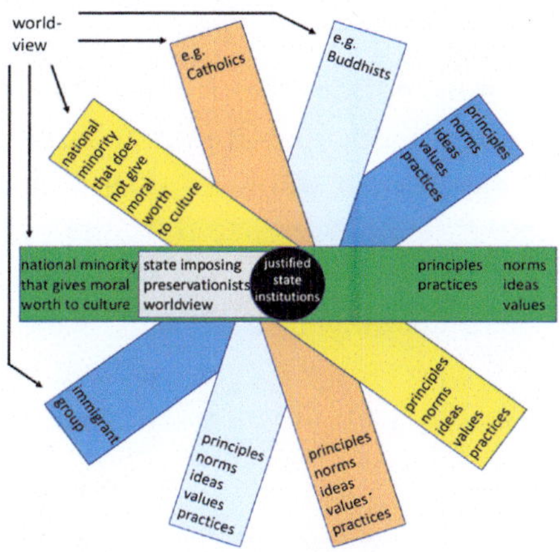

Figure 2.2. Just policies, according to liberalism.

Source: Goemans, Piet. (2023). Normative Principles and Non-Territorial Autonomy. Scientific Figure on ResearchGate. Available from: https://www.researchgate.net/figure/Just-policies-according-to-liberalism-are-based-on-the-lowest-common-denominator-of_fig2_370933581 (accessed on 22 September 2023)

Private property rights defense is critical to liberalism's interpretation of political justice. Liberals argue that the state owes individuals the right to own and manage property. Private property is an essential component of economic and individual liberty. The acquisition of personal property allows people to exercise their freedom of choice, make independent financial decisions, and pursue their interests, according to liberalism.

Furthermore, liberals see political justice as inextricably linked to the rule of law. The practice of law ensures that political decisions and actions are governed by transparent and fair laws rather than being dictated by arbitrary or discriminatory laws. It advocates for the principle that everyone should be subject to the same laws and court processes regardless of status. Liberalism aims to protect individual rights and liberties by upholding the rule of law and preventing abuse of authority (Eriksen, 2016).

Liberalism also recognizes the importance of striking a balance between a person's rights and society's overall well-being. Liberalism values individual liberty but realizes that restrictions and laws may be necessary to protect others or maintain social order. This delicate balancing act is made possible by democratic governance and the establishment of institutions that reflect popular preferences and interests.

2.1.3. Libertarianism

Libertarianism, as a theory of political justice, provides a unique perspective that prioritizes personal freedom and minimal government involvement (Figure 2.3). Political justice is defined as the defense of individual freedoms and rights with little interference from the government, according to libertarianism, which has its roots in the writings of philosophers such as Robert Nozick, Friedrich Hayek, and Ayn Rand. It emphasizes the importance of individual liberty, open markets, and voluntary interactions as essential components of a just political order. (Schmoller, 2016).

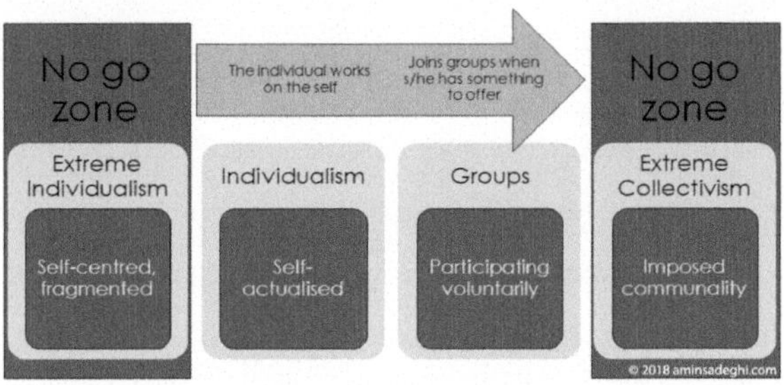

Figure 2.3. The scope of Libertarianism emphases where it starts and where it ends; and where it does not venture.

Source: Sadeghi, Amin. (2018). Libertarian Theory: A graduate student's interpretation. Scientific Figure on ResearchGate. Available from: https://www.researchgate.net/figure/The-scope-of-Libertarianism-emphases-where-it-starts-and-where-it-ends-and-where-it-does_fig1_329973226 (accessed on 22 September 2023)

The principle of self-ownership, which holds that people have inherent rights over their bodies, labor, and the products of their work, is at the heart of libertarianism. According to this viewpoint, people are free to pursue their own goals and engage in voluntary interactions as long as they respect the rights of others. Negative rights, which primarily imply non-interference, are the foundation of libertarian political justice.

According to libertarianism, the best way to achieve political justice is through a small government that upholds the rule of law, defends individual rights, and supports contracts. Libertarians believe the state's role should be reduced to its bare minimum, primarily focusing on maintaining social order and protecting individual liberties. Libertarians argue that excessive government involvement, particularly in economic matters, leads to inefficiencies, stifles personal freedom, and distorts market processes

(Eriksen, 2016). Libertarians believe in free markets and oppose government regulations and interventions that limit economic liberty and individual freedom of choice. They argue that the most effective resource distribution results from voluntary exchanges based on mutual consent and free of coercion. According to this viewpoint, property rights and commercial transactions are critical components of political justice, and any violation of either is considered unfair.

Libertarianism's detractors point out the flaws in this theory of political justice. They argue that unrestricted free markets will lead to income inequality, exploitation, and the concentration of power and wealth in the hands of a few. Another issue critics raise is the ability of a purely libertarian system to address collective goods such as environmental protection, healthcare, and education, which they argue require collective action and public intervention (Schmoller, 2016).

Individual liberty, little to no government interference, and free markets are central to libertarianism's view of political justice. It emphasizes the importance of personal freedom and unalienable rights as fundamental components of a just political order. Although libertarianism provides an internally consistent and coherent theory of political justice, its applicability in dealing with complex societal issues remains debatable.

2.1.4. Communitarianism

The importance of shared values and community in defining and defining a just society is a significant focus of the communitarian theory of political justice. It seeks to resolve the conflict between individual rights and the common good by viewing political justice as a balance between personal autonomy and people's duties to their communities (Eriksen, 2016).

The central claim of communitarianism is that people are not self-contained entities but are part of social contexts and communities. According to communitarian thinkers such as Alasdair MacIntyre and Michael Sandel, political justice cannot be separated from the shared norms, customs, and moral principles that define a specific community. These principles foster a sense of community, identity, and social cohesion.

According to communitarianism, political justice results from developing civic virtues and pursuing the common good. It argues that people are responsible for participating actively in their communities, contributing to their well-being, and upholding the shared standards and values that keep them alive. According to this viewpoint, political justice entails not only defending individual rights but also upholding social duties and advancing the general welfare of the community (Schmoller, 2016).

The idea that communities have the right to self-determination is central to communitarianism's understanding of political justice. According to communitarian theory, communities should have the freedom to establish and uphold their standards of behavior, but only within certain limits. They support decentralized decision-making procedures that involve active participation and discussion among community members to advance inclusivity and democratic governance.

Communitarianism recognizes the importance of social solidarity and cohesion in pursuing political justice. It contends that to live in a just society; citizens must put the common good ahead of their interests when necessary. This perspective rejects other theories' overemphasis on individual liberties and rights, arguing that a thriving community depends on shared accountability and group effort.

Regarding public policy effects, communitarianism favors programs that strengthen interpersonal ties and advance social welfare. It advocates for policies prioritizing the provision of public goods, spending on healthcare and education, and preserving social and cultural institutions that contribute to a thriving and cohesive sense of community. Communitarianism also emphasizes the importance of civic education because it believes that informed, active citizens are essential to maintaining a fair and flourishing society (Eriksen, 2016).

However, communitarianism has been accused of limiting diversity and personal freedom within communities. Some argue that emphasizing local values and norms may silence dissenting voices and marginalize minority groups. Furthermore, there is an ongoing debate about how to resolve value conflicts between various communities in multicultural societies and the precise boundaries of districts. (Schmoller, 2016).

2.1.5. Egalitarianism

Egalitarianism, as a political justice theory, strongly emphasizes promoting fairness and equality in society. It seeks to address and remedy systemic disparities and inequalities by promoting equal opportunities, resources, and outcomes for all people. Egalitarianism aims to create a just political system by reducing or eliminating social, economic, and political hierarchies that give some groups unfair advantages or disadvantages (Figure 2.4).

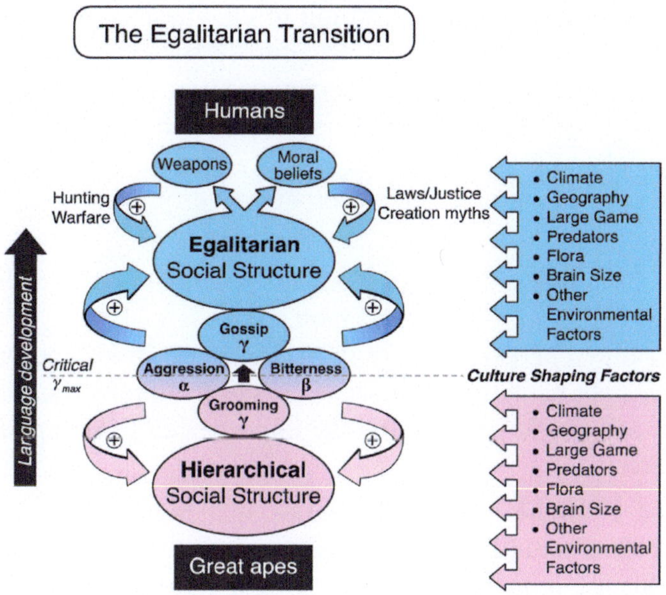

Figure 2.4. Factors underlying the egalitarian transition as language develops in early humans.

Source: Calmettes, Guillaume & Weiss, James. (2017). The emergence of egalitarianism in a model of early human societies. Scientific Figure on ResearchGate. Available from: https://www.researchgate.net/figure/Factors-underlying-the-egalitarian-transition-as-language-develops-in-early-humans-In_fig4_321192143 (accessed on 22 September 2023)

Egalitarianism defines political justice as the goal of treating all members of society equally and distributing opportunities, resources, and goods equally. It opposes discrimination and preferential treatment based on race, ethnicity, socioeconomic status, or other factors. According to egalitarianism, political justice requires a level playing field in which everyone has an equal opportunity to succeed and thrive (Eriksen, 2016).

Egalitarian theories employ various approaches to achieving political justice, but they all seek to reduce inequality and advance social equality. John Rawls' theory of justice as fairness is a well-known egalitarian viewpoint. The original position is a Rawlsian theory in which people make decisions about how society is structured while being obscured by a "veil of ignorance" that prevents them from being aware of their own social standing or individual characteristics. In this fictitious scenario, people would choose just principles that ensure equal access to fundamental freedoms and address socioeconomic inequality in a way that benefits society's most vulnerable members (Schmoller, 2016). According to egalitarianism, political justice necessitates redistributive policies to address socioeconomic disparities. This includes progressive taxation, welfare programs, and affirmative action to level the playing field and provide equal opportunities. Egalitarians argue that interventions to promote greater equality are required because unequal opportunities and resources can exacerbate poverty cycles and stifle social mobility.

Egalitarians are chastised for having the potential to undermine personal freedom and motivation to work hard. They argue that strict equality enforcement may decrease private initiative, innovation, and productivity. Furthermore, opponents of egalitarianism say it diminishes the variety of skills and goals people possess and the importance of merit and individual accountability.

However, egalitarian advocates argue that racial and socioeconomic inequality and structural barriers to equal opportunity must be addressed if political justice is to be achieved. They argue that promoting equality benefits society by reducing social tensions, increasing social cohesiveness, and creating a more equitable and inclusive environment (Eriksen, 2016).

Equality of opportunities, resources, and outcomes for all members of society is critical to egalitarianism as a political justice theory. Egalitarianism seeks to create a more just and equitable political system by removing unfair advantages and disadvantages, ensuring that everyone has an equal opportunity to succeed and contribute to society as a whole.

2.1.6. Political Justice According to Rawls

The comprehensive theory of political justice, known as Rawlsian justice, developed by political philosopher John Rawls, aims to establish fairness and equity as guiding principles in societal structures. A tenet of Rawls' theory, "justice as fairness," provides a framework for defining and interpreting political justice by focusing on the distribution of social and economic goods and the fundamental freedoms that should be protected for all people. Let us look at the basic ideas of Rawlsian justice, such as how it defines and conceptualizes political justice.

The concept of a fictitious social contract, a thought experiment that establishes justice's guiding principles from an unbiased standpoint, is central to Rawlsian justice. According to Rawls, people should imagine themselves hidden behind a "veil of ignorance," unaware of their unique characteristics and social standing. People are motivated to build a just society because they are unaware of their social status, wealth, capabilities, or specific interests. This ensures that the basic concepts of justice are derived from a just and impartial standpoint (Schmoller, 2016).

According to Rawls, people would try to establish two fundamental principles of justice in this fictitious situation: equal access to basic liberties and the direction of just equality of opportunity.

According to the concept of equal fundamental freedoms, everyone has the right to the broadest range of freedoms and rights compatible with an identical degree of ownership for everyone else. These fundamental liberties include the right to due process, the right to private property, and the freedoms of speech, assembly, and the press. Rawls emphasizes the defence of individual autonomy and self-determination, which he sees as necessary for political justice (Eriksen, 2016).

According to the principle of fair equality of opportunity, all people should have equal access to social and economic positions under impartial and unbiased conditions. According to Rawls, a just society should provide equal opportunities for social advancement, employment, and education. While acknowledging that different circumstances and innate talents will result in some inequalities, Rawls believes these inequalities should be tolerated only if they benefit society's most vulnerable members. In other words, the most vulnerable and marginalized people should benefit the most from unequal wealth and resource distribution.

Rawls also proposed the "difference principle" to address socioeconomic disparities. Inequalities may be acceptable under this principle if they benefit the most vulnerable people. This allows for differences as long as they benefit society's most vulnerable citizens. Rawls contends that this strategy provides a justifiable basis for some income and wealth redistribution to ensure a fair distribution of resources.

Rawlsian justice defines political justice in terms of fair equality of opportunity, equal fundamental liberties, and the difference principle to create a just society that upholds individual rights, fosters equal opportunities and addresses socioeconomic disparities. It values personal freedom and individual autonomy while prioritizing the welfare of society's most vulnerable citizens (Eriksen, 2016).

Rawlsian justice provides a comprehensive framework for understanding political justice, emphasizing fairness, equality, and the defence of individual rights. It is a powerful tool for assessing political systems and policies because it inspires a more equitable distribution of opportunities and resources. Rawls' theory has significantly influenced political philosophy, and it continues to influence discussions of justice and fairness in current politics discourse.

2.2. SOCIAL CONTRACT THEORY IN POLITICAL JUSTICE

Political justice debates have long been based on the concept of the social contract. It is a theoretical framework that postulates an implicit agreement between people and the state to explain government legitimacy and power. People voluntarily enter into a social contract in which they give up some of their freedoms and submit to governmental authority in exchange for safety, the protection of their rights, and the advancement of the general welfare, according to the social contract theory. The origins of the social contract theory can be traced back to influential thinkers such as Thomas Hobbes, John Locke, and Jean-Jacques Rousseau, who each offered their interpretations of the social contract (Schmoller, 2016).

Thomas Hobbes, an English philosopher, developed the social contract theory to shed light on the origins and nature of political power. In "Leviathan," Hobbes argued that people in a fictitious state of wildlife live in constant conflict and self-interest. To escape this chaotic situation, people enter into a social contract and give up their rights and freedoms to a centralized authority. According to Hobbes, this sovereign ruler establishes order, security, and protection, ensuring political justice by maintaining peace and protecting humanity from the triumph of its destructive nature.

Another crucial English philosopher, John Locke, made significant contributions to the social contract theory. Everyone has the right to their own life, liberty, and property, according to Locke. In his seminal work "Two Treatises of Government," Locke argued that the government aims to defend these inalienable rights. People voluntarily enter into a social contract that establishes a limited government and their consent to be governed. According to Locke, the primary responsibility of the government is to protect individual rights. Locke proposed that the people have the right to revolt and form a new social contract if a government fails to fulfil this duty.

A Swiss philosopher, Jean-Jacques Rousseau, provided a unique interpretation of the social contract theory. In his influential book "The Social Contract," Rousseau emphasized the importance of the common good and the group's will. In his opinion, people are naturally free but subject to socially imposed moral and political restraints. Rousseau advocated for people to band together as a single entity and agree to be governed by the community's collective will. According to Rousseau, the social contract secures political justice by advancing the common good and protecting individual freedom within the constraints of the group's will (Eriksen, 2016).

German philosopher Immanuel Kant helped advance our understanding of political justice by morally analyzing the social contract. In "Perpetual Peace," Kant argued that people are responsible for forming a social contract to create a just and peaceful society. Kant believed that to achieve political justice, a republican government founded on liberty, equality, and the rule of law was required. He emphasized that the social contract must reflect people's moral obligations to uphold justice and that political institutions must be founded on ethical principles and reason.

These thinkers have significantly impacted our understanding of the social contract and its role in political justice. Their ideas influenced subsequent generations of philosophers, political theorists, and policymakers as a foundation for discussions on the legitimacy of political authority, individual rights and obligations, and the rules governing just governance. (Schmoller, 2016).

2.3. FAIRNESS AND EQUALITY IN POLITICAL JUSTICE

Equality and fairness are fundamental elements of political justice because they serve as guiding principles for developing and evaluating just political systems. Equality refers to equal treatment, opportunities, and rights for all members of society. Conversely, fairness refers to the concepts of impartiality, justice, and the absence of bias or discrimination in resource and advantage allocation.

Political justice is a field in which equality can manifest itself in various ways. The principle of equal treatment before the law states that everyone should be subject to the same rules and held to the same accountability standards. This principle ensures that no one will be unfairly treated or discriminated against because of race, gender, religion, or socioeconomic status (Eriksen, 2016).

Opportunity equality is another critical component of political justice. It emphasizes that everyone should have an equal opportunity to succeed and achieve their goals, regardless of social background or birth circumstances.

This principle promotes access to opportunities for high-quality education, healthcare, and employment by advocating for removing structural barriers that prevent people from reaching their full potential.

Equality can also be applied to the distribution of wealth and resources within a society. This viewpoint, which is frequently associated with egalitarianism, emphasizes the reduction of disparities and the promotion of a more equitable distribution of financial resources. Proponents of political justice argue that addressing wealth and income disparities is necessary to ensure a fairer society where everyone has a decent standard of living.

Political justice emphasizes impartiality and the absence of bias in decision-making processes. It entails being fair to people and ensuring that laws, policies, and decisions are made and implemented just and impartially. To avoid an excessive concentration of power and to promote democratic participation, fairness requires openness, responsibility, and the consideration of various viewpoints in political processes (Schmoller, 2016).

A critical fairness component is distributive justice, which concerns how resources and benefits are distributed in society. It calls into question the equitable distribution of resources, opportunities, and burdens among individuals and groups. Diverse distributive justice theories advance guiding principles, such as egalitarianism, which promotes equal distribution, and meritocracy, which contends that opportunities and resources should be distributed based on each person's effort and success.

Political justice can be difficult to reconcile because different theories of justice may contradict one another. The pursuit of total equality may be incompatible with the belief in individual liberty or the promotion of merit-based rewards. Political theorists and decision-makers frequently engage in complex debates to balance upholding equality and fairness and considering the diverse needs and aspirations of people in a society (Eriksen, 2016). Equality and fairness are the foundations of political justice. They serve as blueprints for creating just political structures that promote equality of opportunity, treatment, and resource allocation. To strike a harmonious balance between these principles, careful thought and dedication to addressing systemic biases and inequalities, advancing equal opportunities, and fostering a society where every person has the opportunity to thrive are required.

2.3.1. Concepts of Equality in Political Justice

Different conceptions of equality have a significant impact on how fairness is perceived as well as how resources and opportunities are distributed in society, influencing discussions of political justice. The three main ideas are equal opportunity, equal results, and the meritocracy principle.

Equal opportunity. The pursuit of a level playing field for all people, regardless of social status or birth circumstances, is referred to as equal opportunity. According to its tenets, everyone should have an equal chance to succeed and realize their dreams. In terms of political justice, equal opportunity aims to eliminate institutionalized prejudice and barriers to accessing good jobs, healthcare, education, and other necessities. Individual outcomes should be determined by effort, talent, and personal choices in society rather than social advantages or disadvantages.

Equal outcomes: Achieving political justice, according to the concept of equal outcomes, entails working toward equal outcomes as well as equal opportunities. To address societal inequalities, this viewpoint focuses on redistributing wealth and resources to achieve a more equitable distribution. According to proponents, true political justice requires closing the wealth and poverty gap, ensuring that everyone has access to necessities like food and shelter, and fostering a more egalitarian society. Equal outcomes may include policies such as progressive taxation, social welfare programs, and wealth redistribution to reduce inequalities and support a more equitable distribution of resources.

Meritocracy: The meritocracy principle states that rewards for hard work, talent, and accomplishments should be used to determine political justice. According to the meritocracy theory, positions, opportunities, and rewards should be distributed by each person's skills and contributions to society. Supporters argue that a meritocratic system fosters competition, rewards excellence, and fosters a sense of fairness because people are recognized and rewarded based on their merits. Political justice is achieved through meritocracy when people have the opportunity to advance and succeed based on their efforts and abilities (Eriksen, 2016).

These conceptions of equality, which reflect various approaches to political justice, highlight the complexities and trade-offs involved in promoting fairness in societies. Every picture has benefits and drawbacks and may have different policy implications. There are disagreements about which principle should take precedence and how to balance them.

Political theorists and policymakers frequently need help finding the ideal combination of these conceptions because they can be challenging to reconcile. If systemic barriers are removed, and a level playing field is maintained through policy, equal outcomes and meritocracy can coexist with the pursuit of equal opportunity. Similar effects and meritocracy can sometimes be contradictory because focusing on comparable results can undermine the concept of merit and individual achievement.

Finally, how society views equality regarding political justice is determined by its values, priorities, and specific problems. To strike the right balance between equal opportunity, equal outcomes, and the principle of meritocracy, careful consideration of people's various needs and aspirations and the more general objectives of creating a just and equitable society is required. (Schmoller, 2016).

2.4. SOCIAL JUSTICE, EQUALITY, AND POLITICAL JUSTICE

Understanding the dynamics of social justice and equality necessitates investigating the distribution of opportunities, wealth, and resources within political systems. The distribution of these critical components significantly impacts how well-off, prosperous, and successful people are in a society. Examining this distribution sheds light on the justice and fairness of a political system by highlighting potential inequalities and areas for improvement.

Resource allocation refers to distributing necessary goods, services, and resources within a society. This includes access to necessities such as food, water, shelter, medical care, and education. A key component of resource distribution research is determining whether these resources are equally accessible to all societal members, regardless of socioeconomic status, race, gender, or other factors. Unequal resource distribution can result in significant inequalities, giving some people advantages and disadvantages.

The main focus of wealth distribution is the unequal distribution of material and financial resources. Money, property, investments, and savings are all examples of assets. Understanding wealth distribution necessitates an examination of the concentration of wealth among various societal groups. Wealth disparities, income inequality, and the availability of economic opportunities for all people are all considered in this analysis. Social stratification and the cycle of poverty can be exacerbated by a lack of socioeconomic mobility and unequal wealth distribution (Eriksen, 2016).

This refers to the distribution of opportunities for social, professional, and personal advancement, education, and employment. A key component of opportunity distribution research is determining whether people have equal access to good education, job opportunities, social networks, and upward mobility. Systemic barriers, discrimination, and unequal access to resources can all lead to disparities in opportunity distribution, reducing some people's or groups' chances of success and full participation in society.

A political system's distribution of opportunities, wealth, and resources reflects its values, priorities, and policies. Different political theories and ideologies present different perspectives on addressing these distributions. Other points of view may tolerate or even support some levels of inequality based on merit or financial incentives, but egalitarianism emphasizes equal distribution and works to reduce disparities (Schmoller, 2016).

Just a few of the factors that go into analyzing the distribution of resources, wealth, and opportunities include studying measures of income and wealth inequality, looking at rates of educational attainment, evaluating statistics on social mobility, and taking into account taxation, social welfare programs, and affirmative action policies. This investigation requires a thorough understanding of societal structures, economic systems, and the effects of political decisions on distributional outcomes (Eriksen, 2016).

By examining how resources, wealth, and opportunities are distributed within a political system, we can learn about its fairness, equity, and justice. It enables us to identify potential intervention areas that will aid in reducing inequality and advancing an inclusive and just society. Such research can also help shape policy debates and the development of plans for more equitable distributions, thereby promoting a culture that values social justice and equality of opportunity.

2.4.1. Theories of Distributive Political Justice

Various theories of distributive justice, such as egalitarianism, libertarianism, and Rawls' theory of justice as fairness, offer different perspectives on how resources and opportunities should be distributed within society. Analyzing the implications of these theories for political structures and societal well-being is possible.

Egalitarianism promotes a society in which all community members have equal access to opportunities and resources. It emphasizes the importance of reducing inequality and ensuring everyone can access necessities such as healthcare, education, and other essential goods and services. Egalitarian principles frequently call for redistributive policies such as progressive taxation and social welfare programs to address systemic disparities. The goal is to promote social justice while providing a safety net for society's most vulnerable citizens. A just political system prioritizes the reduction of social and economic inequalities because it increases fairness and societal well-being from an egalitarian standpoint.

Libertarianism, on the other hand, places a strong emphasis on individual liberty and minimal government involvement. It maintains that everyone has a right to hard work and private property and that any redistribution of resources done under duress violates this right. According to libertarian principles, a just political system respects individual autonomy and allows people to exchange and accumulate resources freely. The emphasis is on voluntary exchanges, open markets, and minimal government intervention. According to libertarian theory, such a system fosters personal liberty, innovation, and prosperity, which leads to societal well-being (Eriksen, 2016).

According to Rawls' theory of justice as fairness, distributive justice can be viewed in various ways. According to Rawls, a just society should be built on values; people would choose if they were hidden behind a "veil of ignorance" or were unaware of their social standing, wealth, or prowess. The liberty principle ensures everyone has the same fundamental liberties, whereas the difference principle only allows for inequalities if they benefit society's most disadvantaged members. These are the two justice principles proposed by Rawls. Rawls' theory advocates redistributive measures to address inequalities and establish a fair distribution of resources and opportunities. By emphasizing the welfare of the least fortunate, Rawls seeks to build a just and equitable society for all its members.

These various distributive justice theories profoundly affect political structures and societal well-being. When applied correctly, egalitarian principles can help create a more just society by reducing poverty and increasing social cohesion. However, concerns have been raised about the viability of maintaining high levels of redistribution and potential disincentives to individual effort and innovation (Schmoller, 2016).

Despite focusing on individual liberty and minimal government intervention, libertarian principles may result in wider economic disparities and potential disparities in access to essential opportunities and resources. Critics argue that such a system would ignore the needs of society's most vulnerable citizens.

Rawls' justice as fairness theory aims to balance individual liberty and equality. It seeks to address social and economic disparities while preserving individual rights by prioritizing the well-being of the least fortunate. Putting Rawls' ideas into practice may result in a more just and inclusive society.

Still, deciding how resources should be allocated and what qualifies as benefiting the least can be challenging advantaged.

2.5. POLITICAL EQUITY AND INDIVIDUAL LIBERTIES AND RIGHTS

Any just and equitable society must consider how political justice interacts with individual rights and liberties. Political justice establishes a system where the government and its institutions uphold and protect individuals' rights and freedoms.

Individual rights and liberties encompass a wide range of fundamental freedoms that belong to everyone. These include but are not limited to the rights to privacy, due process, equal legal treatment, and freedom of expression, religion, assembly, and association. Both happiness and human dignity are viewed as being dependent on these rights.

To be political justice, the government must protect and uphold these rights and liberties. It recognizes that people have inalienable rights that should not be violated or unfairly limited. As stewards of political justice, governments are obligated to create and maintain an environment that supports and defends these liberties (Eriksen, 2016).

When political justice is upheld, people can freely express their thoughts, convictions, and identities without fear of censorship or retaliation. They have the right to peacefully assemble and protest, to practice any religion they want or none at all, and to participate in political activities. The equal treatment principle also prohibits discrimination based on race, gender, religion, or other protected characteristics.

Individual rights and liberties must be recognized and protected for a just political system to function. These rights act as a deterrent to authority usurpation and arbitrary rule. They provide people with a sense of security, independence, and agency in their society.

However, there is a complicated relationship between political justice and individual rights and liberties. Striking a balance between competing rights and resolving disputes involving multiple people or groups can be difficult. Individual requests may occasionally clash with the interests of the group or the rights of others. Finding the right balance is a constant challenge that necessitates careful consideration and the development of legal frameworks that outline precise guidelines for the boundaries and justifiable limitations on individual rights (Schmoller, 2016).

In addition, for political justice to exist, the government must ensure that those whose rights have been violated have access to justice and legal redress. It calls for a fair and impartial judicial system capable of resolving disputes and defending people's rights against interference from the government or others parties.

2.5.1. Human Rights and Civil Liberties

Human rights and civil liberties are central to discussing a just political system. Human rights are fundamental freedoms and entitlements that are inherent in all humans. They include many values, such as the rights to life, liberty, equality, and freedom of expression. On the other hand, civil liberties are specific rights and freedoms recognized and protected by law within a specific political jurisdiction.

There is a conflict between upholding individual rights and promoting the common good because individual rights are not absolute and may conflict with society's more extensive interests and welfare. A just political system strives to balance protecting individual rights and advancing the common good.

On the one hand, defending individual rights is critical to preserving people's liberty, autonomy, and dignity. Human rights and civil liberties must be recognized and upheld to ensure justice and fairness in a society. These liberties allow people to express themselves, participate in politics, pursue their goals, and live without unjustified interference or discrimination. They defend marginalized groups, promote social equality, and serve as a check on repressive regimes (Eriksen, 2016).

A just political system, on the other hand, recognizes the importance of the common good and society's overall well-being. It acknowledges that there are times when some limitations on individual rights are necessary for the greater good of humanity. For example, restrictions on free speech may be imposed to prevent hate speech or violent incitement. Personal freedom restrictions may be acceptable in situations involving public health emergencies, such as temporary travel restrictions during a pandemic.

Finding the balance between individual rights and the common good can be difficult. It is difficult to determine the boundaries of individual rights and when their exercise may infringe on the rights and well-being of others or the larger social fabric. Different political structures and societies may interpret this tension differently, resulting in differences in how highly individual rights are valued relative to group interests.

A just political framework seeks to resolve this conflict by establishing judicial and institutional frameworks that protect individual rights while ensuring the welfare of society. To accomplish this, a system of checks and balances, a separate judiciary, and democratic procedures that allow for public deliberation and decision-making are frequently required. It also calls for a commitment to inclusive policymaking, the elimination of structural disparities, and the equitable distribution of the benefits of societal advancement (Schmoller, 2016).

Human rights and civil liberties are critical in a just political system. While individual rights are essential for maintaining personal autonomy and freedom, they must be balanced against the common good. To create a society that respects and protects the rights of individuals while promoting the welfare of all its members, careful consideration, effective institutions, and a commitment to fairness and justice are required.

2.6. THE RULE OF LAW AND GOVERNMENTAL INSTITUTIONS

The rule of law, a fundamental pillar in political justice, ensures a just and fair society. It provides a framework for how individuals, organizations, and the government act. The rule of law establishes norms and procedures that promote impartiality, institutional accountability, and equality before the law, all of which contribute to the overall goal of achieving justice.

First, the rule of law promotes equality before the law. It ensures that no individual or group is exempt from the reach of the law. Regardless of social standing, financial means, or level of influence, everyone is held to the same legal standards and receives equal protection and treatment. This egalitarian principle fosters an unbiased and blind sense of justice, resulting in a society that upholds the idea that everyone is similar in the eyes of the law (Eriksen, 2016).

Furthermore, the rule of law ensures that the law is applied and interpreted relatively. It requires that legal decisions be based on clear-cut, objective statutes rather than subjective opinions or arbitrary judgments. This impartiality helps to reduce favoritism, discrimination, and power abuse. It establishes a system in which justice is influenced by fairness principles and the merits of each case rather than by political or personal agendas.

The rule of law is also critical to ensuring institutional accountability. It establishes a system in which those in positions of authority must account for their actions. The government is one of the institutions that must follow the law and account for the people it is responsible for protecting. This accountability creates a system of checks and balances, allowing individuals or institutions to have their deviant behavior scrutinized, challenged, and corrected. By holding institutions accountable, the rule of law protects against corruption, power abuse, and political justice deterioration (Schmoller, 2016).

The rule of law also provides predictability and stability to society. People can have faith in the legal system when laws are consistently applied and upheld. Because of this predictability, people can plan their lives, conduct business, and settle disputes reasonably and efficiently. It fosters social cohesion and the peaceful resolution of conflicts by instilling trust in the legal system.

The rule of law must be upheld at all costs to achieve political justice. It provides a framework that ensures institutions' impartiality, equality before the law, and accountability. By keeping these values, the rule of law creates an equitable society where people are treated fairly, institutions are held accountable, and justice ideals guide everyone.

The judicial system, legislative bodies, and law enforcement agencies are just a few of the institutions necessary for a society to maintain political justice. These organizations promote good governance by defending individual rights, upholding the rule of law, and fostering impartiality and fairness. They continue to face challenges and prejudices that make it difficult to carry out their responsibilities successfully (Schmoller, 2016).

The judiciary, an institution that interprets and applies the law, must uphold justice. Its duties include resolving disputes, maintaining constitutional principles, and ensuring that justice is administered fairly. However, judicial independence, political interference, and judicial bias can make it difficult for the judiciary to render fair verdicts. Safeguards must be implemented to ensure that the court is impartial and unbiased. Clear appointment procedures, strong legal safeguards for judicial independence, and channels for dealing with judicial misconduct are among these safeguards (Eriksen, 2016).

Legislative bodies, such as parliaments or congresses, are in charge of enacting legislation that reflects societal values and goals. They are critical in developing legal frameworks and policies that promote political justice. However, partisan politics, lobbying, or undue influence from special interest groups may cause problems in legislative bodies. These factors may lead to legislation that favors some groups over others and is thus biased. Campaign finance reform, transparency in legislative procedures, and strict ethics rules are critical strategies for ensuring the fairness and integrity of legislative decision-making.

Law enforcement organizations are responsible for upholding the rule of law, defending citizens' rights, and stopping and investigating criminal activity. However, biases and abuses of power within the criminal justice system can seriously impact political justice. Racial profiling, excessive use of force, and corruption are examples of issues that can erode public trust and perpetuate injustice. To address these issues, strategies such as comprehensive training programs, community policing programs, and effective oversight mechanisms are required to ensure that law enforcement organizations act reasonably, are held accountable, and respect individuals' rights (Schmoller, 2016).

Several strategies can be employed to ensure the fairness and impartiality of these institutions. To begin with, encouraging diversity within these institutions can reduce biases and provide a variety of perspectives. This can be accomplished by employing inclusive hiring practices and allowing underrepresented groups to participate in decision-making. Second, solid checks and balances can help prevent abuses of power and hold organizations accountable for wrongdoing. Independent oversight bodies can be included in these checks and balances. Transparency and accountability measures such as public reporting and external audits can also boost public trust in these institutions.

Programs for ongoing education and training can address biases, encourage moral behavior, and increase the professionalism of those who work in these institutions. These programs should cover topics like unconscious bias, cultural sensitivity, and human rights to foster a culture of fairness and respect. (Eriksen, 2016).

CHAPTER 3

Importance of Political Institutions

Contents

3.1. INTRODUCTION

Political institutions are the entities within a government that create and enforce laws. They typically function as dispute mediators, make (governmental) economic and social policy decisions, and represent the public differently. Political institutions are not perfect because humans manage them, and people are imperfect. Within the confines of civil society, however, political institutions are critical to preserving and promoting human progress. Human development is the process of increasing people's freedom and opportunities while also enhancing them. Human development is all about the space that ordinary people have to determine who they are, what they do, and how they live. Human development attempts to expand the richness of human existence rather than only the riches of the economy where people live (Cook, 2012).

The political structures and procedures of a country have a direct influence on its commercial environment and activities. A clear-cut political system, for example, that stimulates citizen involvement in politics is constantly developing and is laser-focused on the welfare of its people and benefits the local economy. Every society needs some form of political framework to allocate resources and carry out ongoing activities effectively. A political institution creates the laws that a law-abiding society must follow and eventually determines and enforces the rules against those who break them. Presidential (headed by a president) and parliamentarian (guided by a parliament) are the basic democratic political systems. Unicameral or bicameral legislatures—two chambers, such as a Senate and a House of Representatives or a House of Commons and a House of Lords are intended to back up regimes. Party systems can be two- or multi-party, depending on the degree of internal coherence among the parties, and the parties themselves can be powerful or weak. Political institutions are the bodies that comprise the complete framework of modern government parties, legislatures and heads of state. Political institutions include (legal) courts, unions, and political party organizations. The term "political Institutions" may also refer to the established framework of norms and ideals that the organizations above adhere to, which includes concepts such as the right to vote, accountable governance, and accountability. (Mallick, 2017).

3.1.1. Types of Political Systems

In addition to politics and government, the political system comprises law, economics, culture, and other social structures. The most well-known political systems that we are familiar with may be reduced to a few simple essential notions. There are various political systems with similar ideals or fundamentals, but the bulk revolves around the following concepts:

- Democracy is a type of government in which all eligible citizens or inhabitants of a state participate, often through elected representatives.
- Republic: A non-monarchical state in which the people and their elected representatives have ultimate authority and the president is selected or elected by the people.
- Monarchy: A system of government in which only one person, usually a monarch or queen, rules. A crown, also known as power, is usually passed down via families.
- Communism is a system of government in which the government directs and regulates the financial sector. When an authoritarian party is in control, state limitations are typically imposed.
- Dictatorship: A form of government in which one person has complete power and makes decisions without consulting anybody else (Cook, 2012).
- Coleman established the three main responsibilities of a political system:
- To develop regulations to keep society cohesive.
- To change and adapt components of social, economic, and religious institutions as needed to achieve shared (political) goals.
- To protect the integrity of the political system from external threats.

The principal purpose of the two major political parties in contemporary American society, for example, is seen as a way of representing their followers and constituents and crafting policies with the fewest feasible possibilities. The objective is to make it easier for people to understand and participate in legislative processes. Institutions can address collection action problems. For example, while reducing carbon emissions is in the common interest of all governments, acting in the interests of a single actor could be more economically sound. As a result, the federal government must determine the legal consequences. However, the primary objective of a political institution is to build and maintain stability. This is made possible by the "veto players," as American political scientist George Tsebelis refers to them. Tsebelis believes that the number of veto players—individuals who must approve a change before it can be implemented—significantly influences how easy it is to make changes.1 Wide changes to the status quo are complex, with too many veto players and wide ideological disparities between them. Agenda setters are veto players who may say, "Take it or leave it." They must, however, submit ideas to the other veto players that they feel will earn their favor (Cook, 2012).

3.2. RIGHTS AND LIBERTIES PROTECTION: HUMAN DEVELOPMENT

Protecting individual rights and freedoms is made possible by political institutions. They draft and uphold laws safeguarding individuals' fundamental liberties, including the right to free speech, assembly, and religion. Effective political institutions prevent the misuse of power and stop human rights breaches. Civil rights are known as governmental safeguards for political participation, equality, and equal treatment under the law. Civil liberties protect from government action. State policies and institutions determine how well human rights are protected and understood. Each nation's ability to exercise its human rights depends on the national laws, policies, practices, and processes in place. Therefore, human rights must be incorporated into national constitutional and legal systems, judicial professionals get training on implementing human rights norms, and human rights abuses be denounced and punished. Compared to regional and international standards, national standards have a more immediate impact and are easier to understand. Where, after all, do universal human rights begin (Mallick, 2017)?

In remote locations that are near to home yet so small that they cannot be shown on any map of the globe. The area where he lives, the school or college he attends, and the factory, farm, or office where he works all represent the universe of the particular person. These are the areas where every man, woman, and child pursues unrestricted equality of justice, opportunity, and dignity. These rights are meaningless if they don't apply there. The responsibility of the State to uphold rights is thus paramount, and that of regional or international tribunals is only relevant when the State is willfully or repeatedly infringing on them. We all have examples of when acknowledging that breaches at the national level have necessitated the use of regional and international structures. Regional or international help or concern may serve as the impetus for domestic rights protection, but only after all domestic options have been explored and exhausted (Cook, 2012).

When governmental authority gets disproportionately broad, political institutions harm human growth. People's freedom and liberties are constrained in such circumstances, and the government adopts coercive measures to encourage corruption. Because an expansive and centralized government restricts people's options and possibilities, most cultures with this type of government are more economically impoverished and have a lower quality of life than civilizations where government authority is constrained and governed by law. And because of this constraint on their freedom, individuals could not improve their welfare. The proper operation of political institutions depends on political freedom. According to Nobel Prize-winning economist Milton Friedman, political freedom cannot coexist with economic freedom. Political freedom and the effective management of political institutions depend on financial freedom. This implies that political institutions function better and more effectively to promote human development in a market-based economy than in a command-based economy since a market economy allows people to express their freedom of choice. Political freedom is one of the options that people can employ at their discretion since they are, by nature, free. Each person has the right to choose the form of government and policies they think would best advance their well-being. Political institutions can only serve as a legal framework that protects people's rights and freedoms and expands their options and opportunities to better their welfare if it aims to improve people's living conditions and promote human development. The government's duty is constrained by nature, and extending its purview of authority hinders the advancement of society. As a result, we forecast that the influence of six political institutions on human development would be good in market-based economies and negative in countries with weak political institutions (Cook, 2012).

3.3. PARTICIPATION AND REPRESENTATION

Political institutions offer ways for people to participate in and be represented in politics. They provide citizens the opportunity to express their choices, pick their leaders, and participate in decision-making through institutions like elections, political parties, and legislatures. Strong political institutions make sure that various interests and points of view are taken into account and included when formulating policy. Beyond just casting a ballot in an election, political engagement and representation symbolize the right of citizens to free speech and the ability to organize to influence policy.

Together, they make sure that democratic institutions and democracy itself represent the will of the people. Promoting and guaranteeing equitable political participation and representation remain problems for today despite their basic relevance to democracy. Democracy is not always able to offer equal chances for all people to participate in and be represented in politics. Many people are losing faith in the current political structures and procedures, which are perceived as being controlled by a small number of organizations or elites, in both more mature and younger democracies. The globe still has unequal representation and engagement chances for men and women. Minorities continue to be unable to engage in democratic institutions and processes or to voice their interests there (Mallick, 2017).

3.4. POLICY DEVELOPMENT AND EXECUTION

Political institutions fundamentally influence the creation and execution of policies. They lay down the procedures for developing, debating, and carrying out governmental policies. Informed decision-making, evidence-based policymaking, and the capacity to handle social issues and satisfy population demands are all fostered by effective institutions. Public policies shape institutions, and institutions, in turn, shape public policies. In addition to having their views on what makes for excellent policy, institutions may organize the flow of information and ideas from the environment. The process of implementing procedures is formative. At the nexus of politics, policy, and the general public, it dictates the shape and impact of policy. Implementing a policy takes place inside a specific institutional framework. It calls for a particular structure and organization, both distributing decision-making authority and defining specific responsibilities in the process. However, contemporary implementation research frequently ignores that power is impacted by and exerted through implementation arrangements. This special issue uses several implementation options to highlight the essential but little-known implementation polity (Cook, 2012).

Institutions also contribute to the durability of public policy and the credibility of governmental commitment (Figure 3.1). An institution's administration of policies shapes not just how it operates but also how it interacts with other organizations and players in its environment. Individuals are not atomistic under an institutionalist view of political conduct or policymaking; they are entrenched in various institutions. These institutional linkages provide the individuals with indications for their conduct and meanings for their political actions. The institutions give guidelines for action and may also impose punishments on those who fail to live up to their expectations. Those signals may take the shape of incentives or disincentives or be more normative. Lutes will define the institution and, consequently, the policies that that organization is developing. While many institutional principles are substantive, some may be procedural, such as how choices are made. When someone joins the institution, they are taught these substantive and procedural principles, which operate as guides for their behavior while a member of the institution. Because of this, players in this method follow a "logic of appropriateness" and act in ways consistent with their membership in the institution and the principles they have learned. (Mallick, 2017).

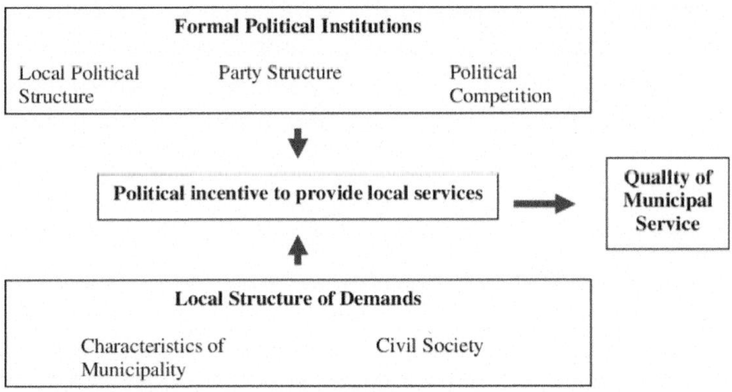

Figure 3.1. Interaction of national political institutions and local incentive structure.

Source: Kauneckis, Derek & Andersson, Krister. (2008). Making Decentralization Work: A Cross-national Examination of Local Governments and Natural Resource Governance in Latin America. Studies in Comparative International Development. 44. 23–46. Scientific Figure on ResearchGate. Available from: https://www.researchgate.net/figure/nteraction-of-national-political-institutions-and-local-incentive-structure_fig1_225652389 (accessed on 22 September 2023)

This logic of appropriateness defines what kinds of policy decisions are acceptable to the institution and its members (Figure 3.2). Given the above, one benefit of the rational choice approach to institutionalism is that changing institutions is relatively easy. To modify the behavior of the institution's participants, all the institution's prospective designers need to do is adjust the rules or incentives. This contrasts with the normative approach, where altering the institution would need changing the values held by its constituents. While a crude definition of rational choice institutionalism could make such a strong assumption, this viewpoint has been evolving in response to criticism. It has started to incorporate assumptions about values and learning in addition to the purely practical theories of behavior at its core. Policy is the substantive component of the recognized solution, and polity is the structural aspect of decision-power distribution in politics, which is seen as the answer to social problems. Power, defined as the ability of an individual or collective authority to persuade a target population to act in a way that they would not have without the authority's orders or interventions, is a critical component of policymaking in general and implementation in particular because public policy is the exercise of state power over target groups to solve societal problems. However, the application of the polity viewpoint needs to be better discussed. However, how this power is significantly distributed affects implementation. The special issue this article introduces is focused on implementation arrangements or the politics of performance. The seven contributions of this work provide light on the many functions that implementation arrangements perform when implementing policies. (Cook, 2012).

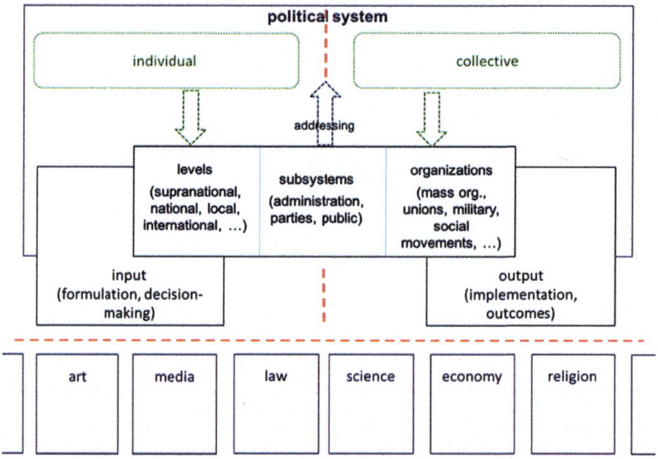

Figure 3.2. Inclusion points and patterns in the political system and its sub-systems.

Source: Ahlers, Anna & Stichweh, Rudolf. (2017). The Bipolarity of Democracy and Authoritarianism: Value Patterns, Inclusion Roles and Forms of Internal Differentiation of Political Systems. Scientific Figure on ResearchGate. Available from: https://www.researchgate.net/figure/Inclusion-points-and-patterns-in-the-political-system-and-its-sub-systems_fig2_318211455 (accessed on 22 September 2023)

3.5. CONFLICT RESOLUTION

Political institutions offer procedures for amicably and methodically handling conflicts and disagreements. Institutions contribute to reducing violence and advancing social cohesiveness through courts, arbitration panels, and other conflict resolution processes. They create a framework for discussions, agreements, and consensus-building, which lessens the possibility of social tensions turning violent. Do political institutions explain why some post-conflict nations relapse into conflict? On the one hand, many people think that inclusive political structures are essential for preventing conflicts (Mallick, 2017).

On the other hand, the scholarly research so far, which has concentrated chiefly on the influence of regime type in general, has yet to uncover any consistent effects. It is not evident that more democratic governments will face fewer future conflicts. Operations for maintaining the peace negotiate and facilitate peace accords and aid in ensuring that they are carried out as planned. They aid in preserving peace and communication between conflicting parties that have yet to reach a sustainable peace deal. Connecting local-level mediation to national political actors and procedures fosters trust between local populations and conflict players. This search for long-term political solutions guides the planning and execution of peacekeeping missions. Partners in peacekeeping work together at the local, national, regional, and international levels to advance security, national reconciliation, the rule of law, human rights, and sustainable development (Cook, 2012).

The possible list of institutions that might be crucial for preventing conflicts is extensive: For instance, SDG 16 asks for "responsive, inclusive, participatory, and representative decision-making at all levels" and "effective, accountable, and transparent" institutions. To identify two sets of elements that should be particularly important for conflict avoidance, the study dissected the critical justifications for why democracy should be conflict-reducing. These two sets of criteria are political involvement and executive restraints. First, institutional controls like parliaments or high courts should forbid electoral winners from marginalizing or escalating election losers or other key political parties, preventing the emergence of fresh complaints during the post-conflict era. Second, it should be able to resolve prospective conflicts peacefully rather than violently if previous rebels and potential future rebels are given avenues to engage in the political system, such as political parties, civil society, or municipal elections (Mallick, 2017). Various environmental, economic, and social crises frequently strike nations, necessitating an urgent, persistent policy response from its political leadership. Multiple problems that civilizations worldwide have historically experienced include large-scale natural catastrophes (cyclones, tsunamis, droughts, etc.) and health and humanitarian crises (such as epidemics, ethnic clashes, etc.). Furthermore, it is suggested that the frequency and magnitude of such problems may rise due to climate change (IMF, 2017). Do nations with various political structures react to these unfortunate situations differently? If so, how do these reactions differ from one another? These inquiries are vital for international organizations and learning how to lessen the effects of a disaster.

3.6. ECONOMIC DEVELOPMENT AND STABILITY

Political institutions have a substantial impact on the development and stability of the economy. Every government aspires for peace; without institutions, a democratic political system cannot operate. Rules are required for systems to select political candidates. Leaders must understand the principles of political institutions, and there must be rules for making authoritative decisions. Institutions restrain political actors through punishments for bad behavior and rewards for excellent behavior. Institutions that are open and responsible promote a favorable economic climate, draw investments, and encourage entrepreneurship. They offer legal protection for property rights and guarantee fair competition. Maintaining investor confidence and macroeconomic stability depends on stable political institutions. It isn't easy to evaluate how political systems affect economic performance (Cook, 2012).

All of today's national institutions and economies have been influenced by long-standing, deeply ingrained political and social issues. Similar political structures in two separate nations might affect each economy differently. Additionally, political differences between the two nations' systems might cause those nations to fare economically similarly. What explains these erratic and distinctive results? What impact do political institutions have on the state of the economy? Economic institutions (such as property rights, regulatory institutions, institutions for macroeconomic stabilization, institutions for social insurance, institutions for conflict management, etc.) have already been shown to be a significant factor in economic growth across nations. Financial institutions significantly impact investments in human and physical capital, technology, and industrial output, among other things. Economic institutions are crucial for resource allocation and play a vital role in economic growth. Because of the distribution of resources and the previous economic conditions, specific groups or people will be able to profit more than others. In other words, financial institutions are endogenous and represent a constant conflict of interest over selecting economic institutions and allocating resources among different groups and people (Mallick, 2017).

Therefore, the distribution of political power among elite groups heavily influences the institutional framework of economic organizations. The restrictions and incentives that significant participants in a particular society must contend with are determined by the official and informal political institutions. Given the endogenous nature of political institutions and the strategic distribution of power they offer, well-selected institutions can aid in creating reliable mechanisms that can reduce the likelihood of opportunistic conduct on the part of political and economic actors. In other words, political institutions must consistently motivate politicians to uphold them.

In low-income nations, political institutions are crucial for economic development. Notably, the party system becomes more fragmented the longer the same elite holds power; the more parties make up the ruling coalition, and the more party-centered the election system is, the less economic progress low-income nations will see. Conversely, political polarization and federalism aid impoverished nations in achieving better financial performance the more significant the district magnitude and the more pluralized the election system is. For autocracies and democracies, the impacts of political and institutional factors are not the same. Economic development tends to increase under democratic regimes when a political leader is in office for longer; in contrast, this impact is the opposite in autocracies. Both democratic and authoritarian governments experience an adverse effect from political division. While this factor does not aid in the economic performance of authoritarian regimes, it has a favorable impact on favors democratic administrations (Cook, 2012).

Even autocratic regimes may have reasonable economic performance as long as certain political rights are allowed. This is because political institution characteristics frequently reflect a certain degree of political rights. Additionally, it can imply that in an authoritarian system, political institutions serve as a stand-in for democracy and spur economic expansion. In other words, political institutions provide a way for autocracies to vary from one another. There are no appreciable variations in economic development depending on the political system, whether in democracies or dictatorships. It is crucial to identify which type of democracy and autocracy is considered within the analysis controlling for its specific political institutions to avoid simply comparing the various types of regimes as a single "package" (democracy versus authoritarianism). We must look beyond the dichotomy between democracy and non-democracy to comprehend how various political institutions impact economic decisions and progress. Even if establishing a democratic system alone won't result in higher economic development, democracy with sound institutions just could (Mallick, 2017).

3.7. INTERNATIONAL RELATIONS

Political structures influence how a nation interacts with the outside world. They create diplomatic relations, bargain for agreements, and advocate their country's interests abroad. Strong institutions improve a nation's reputation, impact its status abroad, and promote international collaboration. However, from the public policy standpoint, international relations is normative in its investigation, guiding decision-makers toward acts that can improve the globe. Public policy, broadly defined, is a collection of guidelines for how the executive branch of government implements the law; it, therefore, describes what "should be" in terms of state activity, not what is.

Consider the problem of nuclear weapons. The number of atomic weapons in the world and the nations that possess them may be determined objectively using an academic and positivist methodology. However, from a policy standpoint, international relations offers a platform from which several policy recommendations are made, such as how to reduce the threat posed by nuclear weapons in the global environment or how to prevent some rogue actors from obtaining nuclear weapons. Realist, liberal, and regime theories have positivist foundations, and international relations theory has historically been positive. However, post-positivist theories (such as constructivist, Marxist, and feminist IR theories) have become a significant area of study in the sub-discipline. The three positivist (realism, liberalism, and institutionalism) and one post-positivist (feminist IR theory) international relations theories will be covered in detail below (Cook, 2012).

Realism Theory

The absence of a centralized authority that controls the international system is the foundation of realist international relations theory. In summary, anarchy prevails in the international environment as governments seek either force or permission to advance their interests in the global order while being sovereign in their own right. As long as nations preserve their sovereignty and independence from one another, there cannot be a genuinely governing international authority to regulate state behavior in a global setting. Because state survival and preservation is the guiding principle in a realist setting, power is the only tool to sustain preservation under anarchy. Realist theory holds that international institutions like the United Nations are formalized ways for nations to exert pressure on other states and project power. Realist philosophy has that conflict, not collaboration, is the norm. For the realist, collaboration is simply a way to exercise power. Military, economic, or diplomatic power can all be projected, but they are all intended to have a coercive impact that pushes other actors to comply (Mallick, 2017).

The four underlying presumptions of realism theory. First, realism theory's primary goals are survival and preservation. Foreign invasion and occupation are constant threats in anarchic systems. The state's principal objective is to reduce the danger by projecting strength so that other states are warned not to mess with you. States will always act in a way that minimizes any threats to their existence because they are rational players in this anarchic environment and are aware that there are no governing standards in the international system and that survival is the only important factor. State actors are aware of all the information available, can arrange their preferences, and act in ways that advance those preferences. Third, states must assume that no state knows what other nations will do, just that they will behave rationally and that other states have a certain amount of military, economic, or diplomatic power that they are willing to project into an international system. Fourthly, based on the hypotheses above, it is legitimate for state actors to hypothesize that the more power you possess, the more probable it is that you will influence international agreements and the general course of the global environment. In other words, considerable Power politics is the norm in an international setting—the decisive and dominating activities in the world are those of the big nations.

The two main points of contention among IR realists are the hegemonic approach and the balance of powers method. However, there is considerable overlap. The hegemonic system assumes all of the premises above and contends that state actors should attempt to dominate the international environment and become the dominant power that decides the majority of the course and features of the global system. Hegemonic realists assert that because someone must consolidate power and rule the world system, it may as well be you. On the other hand, the balance of forces approach contends that pursuing a position of hegemony can harm state interests by inciting more hostility and conflict than necessary. States can best achieve the realist goal of survival by attempting to strike a balance between competing powers that will deter state actors from engaging in interstate conflict. Balance-of-power realists contend that while anarchy may be the rule in the international system, governments should nevertheless strive for stability by mutually assuring a balance of power globally (Cook, 2012).

Liberalism Theory

Realists view the world as defined by conflict and anarchy, whereas liberals view it as characterized by collaboration and the desire for peace. Liberalism also highlights that while nations are autonomous and frequently pursue their interests, individuals, private parties, international organizations, and multinational businesses play significant mediating roles in the world that realists all too frequently neglect. The United Nations is a global worldview based on collaboration and peace, not just a crude representation of self-interested governments (Mallick, 2017).

Although international relations as a discipline tends to stress the positivist method, significant post-positivist theories criticize this approach and offer an alternative view, such as IR feminism. Furthermore, IR, as a public policy issue, must finally provide recommendations on how to enhance interactions between state actors on a global scale. It is crucial to have a firm understanding of foreign policy and the instruments and goals that influence how foreign policy operates (or fails to operate!) daily when studying international relations. We conclude by outlining four critical theories of international relations—concepts that guide what interactions may and should occur in a global setting. Realism, liberalism, and institutionalism, three of those ideologies, are positivist in outlook and offer fundamental premises for what controls the global environment. On the other hand, post-positivist feminist IR theory contends that positivist theories undervalue the significance of how governments are built on specific value systems (Cook, 2012).

3.8. GOVERNANCE AND THE RULE OF LAW

Political institutions set the foundation for these two concepts. They offer guidelines, processes, and methods for making decisions, ensuring that authority is used in a planned and responsible manner. In a civilization, this promotes stability, predictability, and order. The rule of law upholds the notion of the separation of powers. The practice of law serves two purposes: first, it ensures that all individuals are treated equally before the law, and second, it ensures that people's rights and freedoms are preserved. As a result, it is a fundamental and necessary component of a successful government. The separation of powers is adequately upheld when the rule of law is (Mallick, 2017).

Because of this, the state's capacity to supply these institutions heavily influences how people act in markets and how well markets work. Providing such institutions successfully is frequently referred to as "good governance."1 With establishing, defending, and enforcing property rights, the potential for market transactions is greatly expanded. It also entails the establishment of a regulatory framework that cooperates with the market to foster competition. Additionally, it involves implementing solid macroeconomic policies that support market activity. Corruption may undermine policy objectives and the legitimacy of the public institutions that underpin markets. Therefore good governance also entails its absence. Growth and the eradication of poverty are impacted by good management. Strong correlations between per capita income and indicators of the durability of property rights and the lack of corruption have been shown in several studies. This partially reflects the higher ability of wealthy nations to build strong institutions. However, new research indicates that more robust governance significantly impacts development outcomes.

There is proof that heavy regulation retards economic development. Additionally, there is proof that weak macroeconomic policies and trade restrictions harm a nation's ability to expand.3 Thus, reducing poverty fundamentally depends on effective governance due to its significant impacts on total economic growth. Additionally, several aspects of lousy government, notably corruption and excessive inflation, impose costs that disproportionately affect low-income people. For the impoverished, improvements in these aspects of governance may be especially crucial. To implement policies and create institutions, one must have the authority to do so, even if it means alienating a significant portion of the populace. Public officials can only enforce such rights with the power to prosecute, adjudicate, and punish people who violate property rights. Without the ability to tax people and businesses to generate public funds, the state cannot offer expensive public goods. Public authorities can only foster competition with the ability to enforce laws against monopolistic practices. They cannot guarantee a stable macroeconomic climate without the ability to ensure that the state's policies are carried out; in the evolution of the modern state, there is a conflict between making sure that public officials have enough authority to provide effective governance and making sure they are restrained from using this authority arbitrarily for the benefit of a privileged few. When unrestrained, they are less able to offer the institutions that underpin markets by boosting competition, providing access to information, and upholding agreements. This is crucial when preserving property rights because, without a genuine governmental commitment to support and enforce such requests, the formal existence of those rights has little impact (Cook, 2012).

Political institutions establish limits on the arbitrary use of power by politicians and bureaucrats. They do this by defining the boundaries of private and public property rights and providing for their enforcement. A historical illustration of this is provided by the modifications made to political structures in 17th-century England, which restricted the Crown's ability to confiscate property and enhanced the security of private property. The degree of competition in the political process and the degree to which this competition holds politicians responsible for their actions are also influenced by political institutions. For instance, delegating authority to local governments might affect the incentives for competition across jurisdictions to deliver better public goods. This chapter examines a wide range of political structures that influence public officials' conduct, among other things. Political institutions of formal democracies, which make up an increasing percentage of the world's nations, include election laws that specify how governments are chosen and removed from office. They also include the constitutional provisions that dictate how the legislative and executive arms of government are split up and how much authority each has. Political institutions and traditions in every nation outline the separation of powers between the central and local governments and the delegation of duties to various departments within the executive branch. These institutions might be explicit (like electoral laws) or informal (like the influence of standard political party views on conduct). Political institutions interact in significant ways as well. For instance, how much other political institutions restrict the ability of governments to revoke the agency's independence in the future will determine how credible autonomous agencies are (Mallick, 2017).

The state will be better able to establish institutions that promote broad-based markets if institutions that restrict its power to take arbitrary action are in place. But in many of the world's poorest nations, the lack of adequate controls on public officials hinders the state's capacity to build institutions that support the market. This exemplifies the overarching issue of complementarities across institutions that permeates this Report: policymakers must modify institutional designs to account for these complementarities. For instance, independent regulatory institutions will only be separated in name if there are no adequate checks and balances in the political process. Simpler, less discretionary regulation is less likely to be eroded by corruption when governmental capacity is inadequate. The anticipated advantages of further decentralization and competition across jurisdictions could not be realized when central government oversight is insufficient. Innovation is crucial because only some political institutions can properly support market institutions everywhere and at all levels of growth (Cook, 2012).

Development depends on the state's capacity to provide institutions that promote economic expansion and eradicate poverty (often called "good governance"). Incomes stagnated, and poverty persisted in nations that failed in this regard. The relevance of political institutions in motivating governments to practice sound governance is emphasized in this chapter. Political institutions that successfully restrain state officials from arbitrary action include constitutional rules, the division of power among levels of government, independent agencies and mechanisms for citizens to monitor public behavior and laws that discourage corruption. As a result, good governance is likely to flourish. There has yet to be a plan for changing political institutions to promote effective management. Different political and socioeconomic influences can influence a country in different ways. However, the form of political institutions and how public servants engage with their constituents determine the kind of policy advice most useful in a particular nation and impact the implemented policies. It is crucial to consider public officials' motivations while developing specific government systems. Institutions can influence these incentives by assisting in the behavior observation of public servants. Institutions impact how responsive governments are to social and economic issues as well as to a wide range of persons in society. They achieve this through providing information, fostering more competition, and articulating and upholding rights between the state and its citizens and other government entities (Mallick, 2017).

When constructing specific structures, this must be kept in mind. For instance, it is essential to balance the present popularity of policies like increased decentralization or greater formal autonomy for tax or regulatory agencies with the knowledge that the success of these innovations depends much on supportive political and social institutions. These organizations will only be independent in name if governments lack the more extensive checks and balances that would prevent them from interfering in independent agencies. The advantages of decentralization could not be fully realized if there are no political structures that match local government incentives with national goals and if local governments are no more responsible to their citizens than central governments. Furthermore, the sorts of operations that can be decentralized successfully may need to be improved by local capability and overall literacy levels. At both the municipal and regional levels, some experimentation and competition can aid in identifying viable political structures. This process can be facilitated by open information exchange, public discussion; information flows between regions and between public and private entities. It has the potential to influence public officials' motivations and to intensify pressure for change.

3.9. ACCOUNTABILITY AND TRANSPARENCY

Political institutions set up procedures for making government employees answerable for their deeds. They offer checks and balances to stop corruption and the misuse of authority. Transparent institutions encourage transparency and public scrutiny so that citizens can see how decisions are made and how public resources are used. To ensure excellent governance in the public sector, transparency and accountability are essential. Without a doubt, responsibility requires transparency. Accountability and transparency go hand in hand and are mutually beneficial (Cook, 2012).

In general, transparency is believed to lead to improved government, more accountability, and decreased corruption. Transparency is built on the open exchange of information. Every person has a right to knowledge regarding State policies that impact them, including legislative actions, policy-making, legal requirements, policy enforcement, administrative budgets, public spending, and other pertinent political data. Additionally, accountability and actual involvement depend on transparency. The amount of good governance increases with more openness. Responsibility entails that officials and administrative bodies must fulfil the duties and obligations associated with their employment. Decision-makers in the public, corporate, and civil sectors must be held to the same standards as institutional stakeholders. Because accountability is strongly tied to the need to eradicate corruption, which is often viewed as a significant failing in governance, the government must be held accountable at all levels. For the public service delivery system to be effective, transparency is necessary. To guarantee that public services are provided to the 'intended' beneficiaries satisfactorily and effectively, it is not enough to merely be aware of entitlements and who is accountable for fulfilling them (Mallick, 2017).

- The fairness and justice of their government are the top concerns of citizens in a healthy civil society. A government's governance structures and subsystems must be effective in terms of efficiency, economy, ethics, and equity.
- The legislative procedure must also be fair, rational, just, and user-friendly. To accomplish these and other attributes and good governance, the administrative structure must be responsible and responsive in addition to encouraging openness and public engagement.
- Transparency makes certain that the public is aware of what is happening and the justifications for the decisions taken by the government or its representatives at various levels. A public servant must be held accountable to the government, society, and the people for all of their actions and inactions as well as the results of those actions.
- In all democracies, civil employees are responsible for ensuring that policies are implemented in a responsive, open, and honest manner and that services are provided to the public. Holding public officials responsible for their outputs and outcomes is a complicated process, making it challenging to ensure accountability for performance in government.
- Setting and achieving performance goals are simpler for service delivery organizations, especially when the delivered service is tangible and can be measured as a unit, but for many public organizations where the output is related to policy and is, therefore, less concrete, performance evaluation becomes significantly more difficult.
- The lack of a connection between authority and accountability and the distribution of responsibility and authority across levels of government both contribute to a system where plausible justifications for non-performance are common, especially for tasks that cross departmental boundaries or different functional divisions within departments.

Accountability of the executive branch of government to Parliament and the people is a crucial aspect of a democracy. Accountability mechanisms in every nation are defined as those placed within and outside the state

(Cook, 2012). In conclusion, political institutions are essential for good administration, the defence of rights, citizen involvement, the creation and execution of policies, resolving disputes, economic growth, and international relations. They offer the framework, accountability, and legitimacy required to guarantee stable and functional societies. Political institutions do have a significant impact on how people grow. However, this function fosters human growth when, as we have postulated, the authority of these organizations is restrained by the law. The primary purposes of constitutions are to define the government's powers and provide the legal protection of individual rights. Poor economic freedom, restricted access to property rights, and very high levels of government corruption are standard in nations with poor human development indices. The Hobbesian method of using political power in these nations undermines individual rights and the rule of law. In this situation, political institutions endanger the advancement of humanity (Cook, 2012).

CHAPTER 4

Principles of Government

Contents

4.1. INTRODUCTION

The governing principles of governance are the fundamental beliefs and values that determine how a government governs its citizens. These principles are a compass for a nation's policies, decision-making processes, and overall orientation. They provide a framework for the formation and management of a government.

Typically, the principles of governance reflect the objectives and aspirations of a society, as well as its historical, cultural, and political context. They provide the framework for interactions among the various branches and levels of government and between the government and its citizens (Ullmann, 2010).

The fundamental principles of government consist of the rule of law, democracy, individual liberties and rights, equality, social justice, openness and accountability, efficient governance, and safety. Although not exhaustive, these concepts are frequently regarded as essential in democratic nations (Figure 4.1).

Figure 4.1. The five principles of good governance adopted in the Project.

Source: Freguin-Gresh, Sandrine. (2014). Mapping institutions that govern Access and Uses of Natural Resources in the Nicaragua-Honduras Sentinel Landscape - Revealing the complexity, issues, and challenges of natural resource governance. Scientific Figure on ResearchGate. Available from: https://www.researchgate.net/figure/the-five-principles-of-good-governance-adopted-in-the-Project-Source-authors_fig6_315553362 (accessed on 22 September 2023)

Governments that adhere to these principles seek to foster an environment that promotes justice, fairness, and the welfare of their citizens. They work to ensure that power is exercised responsibly, with respect for the rights and dignity of the individual, and that decisions are made in the best interests of society.

It is essential to recognize that these guiding principles can be interpreted and applied in various ways, depending on the political system, cultural context, and historical context. Governments may prioritize specific values over others, and there may be ongoing debates and controversies regarding the extent to which these principles are adhered to (Ullmann, 2010).

On the other hand, the governing principles of government provide a framework for analyzing and evaluating its legitimacy, effectiveness, and impact on society. In addition, they are crucial in determining the nature and operation of a government.

4.2. RULE OF LAW

The governing principles of government are the fundamental beliefs and concepts that determine how a government governs its citizens. These concepts determine a nation's policies, decision-making processes, and orientation. They provide a structure for the formation and administration of a government (Jones, 2017).

Governance principles frequently reflect a society's goals and aspirations and its historical, cultural, and political context. These institutions provide the framework for interactions between the numerous branches and levels of government and the government and its citizens.

The rule of law, democracy, individual liberties and rights, equality, social justice, openness and accountability, effective governance, and security are fundamental principles of government (Figure 4.2). Even though this list is not exhaustive, these values are regarded as indispensable in democracies (Ullmann, 2010).

A society that upholds these values endeavors to create an atmosphere that fosters justice, fairness, and the well-being of its citizens. They work to ensure that power is used prudently, with respect for the rights and dignity of each individual, and that decisions are made in the best interests of society.

Recognizing that these guiding principles can be interpreted and implemented differently depending on the political system, cultural environment, and historical context is essential. Governments may place some values above others, and there may be ongoing debates and controversies regarding the degree of adherence to these principles (Ullmann, 2010).

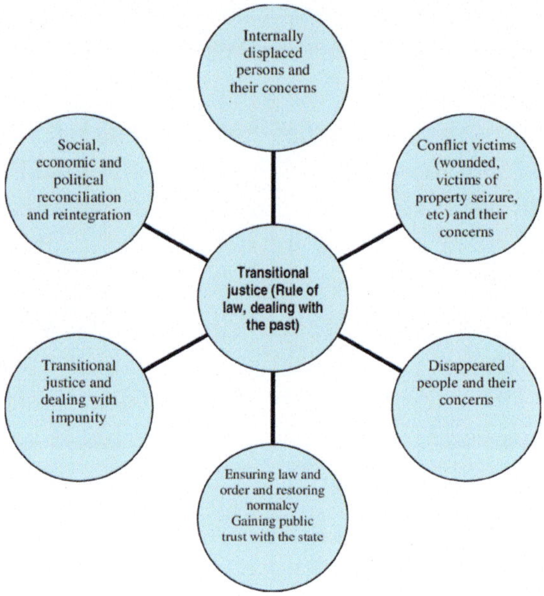

Figure 4.2. Different interrelated components of rule of law and dealing with the past (transitional justice).

Source: Bishnu, Raj & Upreti, Bishnu. (2014). Peace and post conflict reconstruction in Nepal: A bird's-eye view 1. Scientific Figure on ResearchGate. Available from: https://www.researchgate.net/figure/different-interrelated-components-of-rule-of-law-and-dealing-with-the-past-transitional_fig3_269165979 (accessed on 22 September 2023)

On the other hand, the government's governing principles provide a framework for assessing and evaluating its legitimacy, effectiveness, and impact on society. In addition, they play a crucial role in determining the structure and operation of a government (Jones, 2017).

Because it can be pursued in various methods, it is more accurate to consider the rule of law a value or set of values that may influence institutional design rather than a blueprint. On the other hand, the premise that those who judge the legitimacy of the exercise of power should not be the same as those who execute it leads to several extremely straightforward and generalizable institutional conclusions. A regular rule-of-law state, for instance, would institutionalize some means of safeguarding legal authorities from political interference that undermines their independence. Consequently, it is commonly believed that the structural separation of the judiciary from the other branches of government is a crucial element of nations that uphold the rule of law. Additional initiatives to ensure equal access to legal institutions may be essential for rule-of-law systems. In addition, the majority of nations in the world have formal written constitutions because they are believed to uphold the rule of law (Ullmann, 2010).

Although certain institutional traditions, conventions, and written laws may be necessary to ensure that judicial decisions are based on plausible interpretations of existing laws, only some institutional characteristics of a state should be considered necessary or sufficient to achieve the rule-of-law ideal. Although it may be supported more strongly in some nations and by some institutions, the rule of law is not dependent on a particular national history or collection of institutions. Furthermore, it may be difficult to replicate or transplant institutional frameworks that promote the rule of law from one state to another. Due to their unique legal and cultural histories, which inevitably alter the form of their institutions, numerous polities express their judgments regarding how to apply specific rule-of-law standards. For the rule of law to be more than a mere ideal, most people in a society, including those whose duty is to uphold the law, must concur that no individual or group should be exempt from the rule of law (Jones, 2017).

Whoever believes that having the proper individuals in power is more essential than how power should be limited cannot be persuaded of the rule of law's value. Nobody else will if they believe that government institutions are merely the tools of the governing class and should be abolished rather than limited. Nevertheless, most contemporary democratic nations recognize the significance of the rule of law, which requires authorities and citizens to be accountable to the law. In modern society, the liberal tradition prioritizes the rule of law. Liberals view the rule of law as an all-encompassing source of security when defending (and implementing) some form of liberty and averting its threats. Even among liberals, however, there is considerable disagreement over what comprises a genuine application of the term and, when this is specified, how it should be implemented (Ullmann, 2010).

The rule of law is not a precise description of any particular circumstance but rather a problematic ideal that is even more challenging to implement. Therefore, it is permissible to question whether something referred to as the word would necessarily benefit society. For instance, the court's independence is a cause for concern if it is misused to promote sectoral benefits for its employees or to permit unbridled legal interpretations. A preponderance of formal aspects of the rule of law, such as procedural justice, may detract from the substance and consequneces of such laws. According to detractors, a purely formal perspective on the rule of law can lead to excessive legalism and disregard for legal issues' political or practical implications. If exaggerated respect for the law and legal processes prevents impartial social evaluations of the merits of a particular policy proposal, or if the official mandate of "blindness" gives legitimacy to actions carried out "according to the law" even when the majority of people disagree with such activities, it may be too expensive. Moreover, according to some academics, expanding judges' and attorneys' spheres of influence -- i.e., their incursion into areas previously reserved for legislators and the electorate -- entails the loss of many political and democratic assets (Jones, 2017).

In other words, placing excessive emphasis on the procedures for preventing arbitrariness can undermine the administration of justice by what would otherwise be supported by the rule of law, and the legal requirements become an unjustified form of arbitrariness. On the other hand, those who support the negative value of the rule of law oppose more profound interpretations of the ideal because morally elevated aspirations for the ideal risk robbing the concept of its uniqueness and utility. They contend that expanding the definition to include extralegal factors such as substantive justice and larger societal objectives is tantamount to conflating the concepts of "the rule of law" and "the rule of good law," thereby eliminating the distinction between the two. Consequently, the study of the rule of law is only complete with a philosophical examination of the meaning and function of the law (Ullmann, 2010).

4.3. DEMOCRACY

Democracy, which translates to "power of the people," is a form of government based on the people's will. The word "democracy" is derived from the Greek words "demos," which means "people," and "Kratos," which means "power."

Because there are so many distinct varieties of democratic government in existence today, it may be simpler to comprehend the concept of democracy by focusing on what it is not. Consequently, democracy is not an autocracy, despotism, or oligarchy in which one person or a small group of people control. Democracy, as it should be understood, should not be the "rule of the majority" if it implies that the concerns of minorities are entirely disregarded. Theoretically, a democracy is a form of governance in which all citizens are represented and their "will" is implemented (Jones, 2017).

There are as many variants of democracy as democratic countries around the globe. Because no two systems are identical, one plan cannot serve as a "model" for another. Some monarchies are also democracies, presidential and parliamentary democracies, federal and unitary democracies, majoritarian and proportional voting democracies, etc.

Current democratic systems share a characteristic that distinguishes them from the previous model: the employment of representatives of the people. Instead of allowing individuals to participate in the drafting of laws actively, modern democracies use elections to choose representatives who are sent to rule on behalf of the people. In this context, we refer to democracy as representational. It can claim to be "democratic" to some extent because it is founded on the two ideals above of equality for all (one person, one vote) and the right of everyone to some degree of personal autonomy (Ullmann, 2010).

People typically refer to nations as "becoming" democracies when they begin holding predominantly open and transparent elections. However, democracy encompasses much more than just elections; therefore, it makes more sense to evaluate a country's level of democracy based on the concept of popular will than on institutional or electoral arrangements. Rather than being something that either exists or does not, democracy should be viewed as something that can always be attained to varying degrees.

Almost always, democratic institutions can be made more inclusive, reflective of more perspectives, and receptive to their influence. In other words, it is possible to increase democracy's "people" and "power" or "will" components by including more people in decision-making and by delegating greater actual authority to the people. Throughout history, battles for democracy have frequently centered on one or both of these characteristics (Jones, 2017).

In most countries today, women have the right to vote, but this is a recent development. Women were not permitted to compete for office in the legislature until 1919, even though New Zealand was the first country in the world to implement universal suffrage. Many nations have granted women the right to vote before allowing them to vie for political office. In 2011, Saudi Arabia only recently permitted women to vote in elections. Even in today's well-established democracies, there are still groups of people who do not have the right to vote, most notably immigrants, migrant laborers, prisoners, and minors, even though many pay taxes and abide by the law.

4.3.1. Democracy and Participation

The two most prominent methods of political participation are voting and running for office as a representative of the people. However, several additional methods exist to participate in politics and administration; democracy is about much more than just voting. In reality, the efficient operation of democracy depends on the populace's widespread adoption of these other means. The government cannot be considered "by the people" if citizens only vote once every four or five years, do not vote during the intervening years, and do nothing else. Such a system is challenging to describe as democratic. Listed below are a few suggestions that may be the bare minimum required for your legislators to act democratically:

Keep abreast of current events; decisions made "in the name of the people," and, in particular, the decisions and actions of your representative (Ullmann, 2010).

Share your opinions with those working on the issue, the media, and your elected officials. If "the people" are not involved, leaders can only govern by their interests and goals.

Please make an effort to be heard when decisions appear to violate human rights or democracy or when you disagree with them vehemently. This will facilitate the revision of policy. Collaborating with others to amplify your voice may be the most effective approach. Vote whenever you have the chance. Members are effectively unaccountable if no one ballots (Jones, 2017).

4.3.2. Democracy and Human Rights

Without one, the other is inadequate and, in some ways, dependent. Participation in governance is a fundamental human right, alongside equality and autonomy. According to Article 21 of the Universal Declaration of Human Rights (UDHR), "the will of the people shall be the basis of the authority of government"; hence, democracy is the only system compatible with human rights (Figure 4.3).

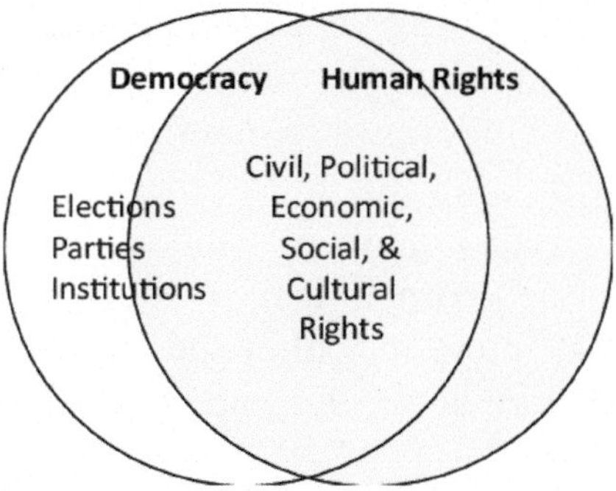

Figure 4.3. Definitions of democracy.

Source: Landman, Todd. (2017). Democracy and Human Rights: Concepts, Measures, and Relationships. Politics and Governance. Scientific Figure on ResearchGate. Available from: https://www.researchgate.net/figure/Definitions-of-democracy-adapted-from-Beetham-1999-p-94_fig1_323236846 (accessed on 22 September 2023)

4.3.3. The Twilight of Social Democracy

This analysis seems to contradict that social democracy emerged in most capitalist nations, where there was a significant redistribution of income due to government intervention, which appropriated nearly half of the national income in some cases and even more in others, particularly in Scandinavian nations.

Due to the connection, it has made between democracy and social struggle, the working-class movement is the driving force behind establishing a social and political democracy; this is the fundamental strength of the social democratic concept. This indicates that democracy cannot exist without the most significant number of individuals adhering to a society's and culture's basic ideals, nor can it live without fundamental social disagreements (Ullmann, 2010).

These two concepts distinguish the democratic perspective from both the revolutionary and liberal views. Nonetheless, the social democratic interpretation of these values is diminishing. This is partially because central societies are transitioning from industrial society to post-industrial society, or a community without a dominant paradigm, and partially due to the triumph of the global market and the decline of state intervention, even in Europe (Jones, 2017). Consequently, Swedish social democracy and most social democratic parties are concerned about the future of mid-century policies. In several nations, the influence and membership of the labor union movement have decreased drastically. This is especially true in France, the United States, and Spain. Still, it is also true in the United Kingdom and ex-communist nations, where trade unions lost their function as an independent social force long ago. Trade unionism abandoned the industrial workplace and transformed into neo-corporatism, a mechanism for safeguarding specialized professional interests within the state apparatus, resulting in wildcat strikes and the formation of competing ad hoc organizations as a reaction.

This brings us to the most critical question regarding democracy: where does it reside in modern society if participation and conflict are necessary but the social-democratic paradigm has reached its end? What is the "positive" aspect of democracy, and what makes democratic action distinctive? To respond, we must first reject any one of the premises. Human liberty is not synonymous with either the universality of pragmatic reason (and, consequently, with interest) or with collective culture. It is challenging to have a democracy that is both exclusively liberal and completely popular (Jones, 2017).

In contrast to revolutionary historicism and utilitarianism, contemporary democratic philosophy begins with an open and unresolved conflict between the two aspects of modern society. On the one hand, there is the liberal aspect of a dynamic organization whose effectiveness depends on the expansion of business and the unrestricted movement of wealth, power, and information. On the other hand, there is the image of someone defying market forces by appealing to their subjectivity, which pertains to a desire for personal autonomy and a reaction to tradition or collective memory. A democratic society can arbitrate between these contradictory demands: the free market and individual and collective humanity, money, and identity.

Current terminology is immensely distinct from the antecedent period, characterized by social democracy and industrial society. We are now more interested in subjectivity and the circulation of symbolic commodities than in wage-earning employees and their employers (Ullmann, 2010).

Despite their apparent abstractness, these concepts are not more abstract than employers or wage-earners. They represent the shared experiences of most people in center civilizations aware of consumer culture and subjective reality. Nonetheless, these opposed aspects of people's lives have yet to find codified political expression, just as it took over a century for the political categories left over from the French Revolution to be supplanted by the class categories unique to industrial society. This political latency is typically why we have a negative view of democracy.

4.3.4. Arbitration

The democratic system is neither thoroughly liberal nor fully participative. Most importantly, adjudication requires understanding a fundamental contradiction between divergent tendencies such as investment and engagement or communication and subjectivity. Is this concept pertinent to the rest of the world, the vast majority, or is it limited to the most prosperous post-industrializing nations and those who control the global system?

A negative response would refute the previous assertion. Nevertheless, safeguarding an individual's or group's identity from being devalued or transformed into an arbitrary ideological construct must be a priority in Third World nations today. Global market exposure is essential for competitiveness.

Consider the preponderance of Latin American nations which are classified as intermediate. They are making a bold (often successful) effort to reclaim their former share of international trade. They participate in mass culture via consumer goods, television programs, production methods, and educational programs. However, they are resisting a suffocating integration into the global economic, political, and cultural system, making them ever more dependent. They strive to be both universalist and particularist, as well as contemporary and loyal to their history and culture (Jones, 2017).

Unless it can mediate between modernity and identity, politics cannot meet the fundamental demand of democracy: representation. As a result, a hazardous rift has developed between grassroots organizations advocating for community autonomy and political parties, which are nothing more than coalitions formed to support a candidate and attain power.

The primary distinction between central and peripheral countries is that in the former, a person is defined primarily in terms of personal freedom and consumer behavior, whereas in the latter, collective identity defence may still be more important, to the extent that there is pressure from abroad to impose a bloodless revolution in the form of mandatory modernization on the pattern of other nations (Ullmann, 2010).

This conception of democracy as a method for resolving social issues goes beyond the concept of majority rule. It requires knowledge of the relationships between each component and the others, as well as the similarities and differences between them. This is where the popular or revolutionary conception of democracy, which typically entails the elimination of minorities or categories hostile to perceived progress, diverges most dramatically from the "arbitral" understanding.

Today, there is an open conflict between ideological commitment and economic modernity, disrupting social order in many regions of the globe. As long as modernity and identity are viewed as irreconcilable, democracy cannot flourish. The foundation of democracy is the partial integration of multiple forces and their ability to balance or reach a compromise. Those who believe that modernity is the devil's work and those who think that progress requires eradicating tradition and the past are enemies of democracy. A democratic society acknowledges both its internal divisions and its sense of unity.

In a democratic society, the rule of law and the concept of justice—the highest degree of unity between the party's respective interests—are crucial. The primary criterion of justice is maximizing liberty for the most significant number of actors. A democratic society strives to produce and value as much diversity as possible, with as many people participating in the community's institutions and consuming its products (Jones, 2017).

4.4. INDIVIDUAL RIGHTS AND FREEDOMS

Individual rights are considered to be of such fundamental importance that they require explicit legal protection. While the United States Constitution guarantees and protects certain individual rights and liberties from government interference, it also divides and limits the powers of the federal and state governments to check their respective authority. The majority of these rights are safeguarded by the Bill of Rights, including the First Amendment's prohibition on government actions that impede the right to free speech and the Second Amendment's guarantee of the right to keep and bear arms. Nevertheless, the Constitution also contains several additional individual rights, such as the right to a jury trial in Article III and the Sixth Amendment, and the Due Process Clause in the post-Civil War Fourteenth Amendment.

Numerous individual rights guaranteed by the Constitution pertain to criminal justice, including the well-known Fifth Amendment protection against self-incrimination and the Fourth Amendment prohibition against arbitrary government searches and seizures. Supreme Court interpretations of the Constitution's sometimes ambiguously worded clauses grant additional individual rights. Group rights, which are founded on the long-term characteristics of a group's members, are frequently viewed as antithetical to individual rights. The right of an indigenous people to have their culture respected is an example of a group right, as is the right of a religious community to freely practice its faith and to have its holy sites and symbols protected from harm (Ullmann, 2010).

4.4.1. Common Individual Rights

The constitutions of all democracies in the world protect the legal and political rights of individuals accused of crimes from unjust or severe treatment by the state. Most democracies, including the United States, assure everyone the right to a legal proceeding when interacting with the government. Additionally, the majority of constitutional democracies safeguard the liberties of all their citizens. Examples of frequently protected individual rights include:

Religion and Belief

The majority of nations protect freedom of religion, belief, and expression. Everyone has the right to practice, proclaim, educate, and spread the religion or belief of their choosing. This includes the ability to practice one's religion and attire accordingly. People have the right to embrace a variety of nonreligious ideologies, such as atheism or agnosticism, satanism, vegetarianism, and pacifism, as well as the freedom to alter their faith or belief. When it is necessary to protect morality, public order, health, or safety, as well as the rights and liberties of others, democracies limit religious freedom (Jones, 2017).

Privacy

The right to privacy is the notion of keeping a person's private information private, and it is acknowledged in the constitutions of over 150 nations. Previously, United States Supreme Court Justice Louis Brandeis referred to it as "the right to be left alone." Personal autonomy, or the freedom to choose whether or not to engage in a certain activity, is commonly understood to include the right to privacy. Private liberties, on the other hand, are often limited to family, marriage, motherhood, reproduction, and parenthood.

The right to privacy, like the freedom of religion, is constantly evaluated against societal needs such as public safety. Even if they are aware that government monitoring is carried out for national security reasons, the majority of Americans favor it.

Personal Property

Personal property rights pertain to the moral and legal possession and use of assets. The overwhelming majority of democracies safeguard the rights of individuals to purchase, retain, transfer, lease, or sell property to third parties. There are two categories of personal property: tangible and intangible. Real estate, animals, goods, and precious stones are examples of tangible property. Intangible assets consist of securities, bonds, patents, and copyrights to intellectual property (Ullmann, 2010).

Unless a higher legal claim or title to the property in question can be established, fundamental property rights permit continued ownership of tangible and intangible products without interference from others. Additionally, they secure the possessor's ability to retrieve any confiscated property.

Rights of Speech and Expression

While the First Amendment of the United States Constitution grants everyone the right to free speech, it encompasses much more than the ability to express oneself. According to how the courts have interpreted the term, "expression" can refer to anything from written publications of opinions to political speech or peaceful protests to religious teachings. In this sense, actions such as burning the American flag, which conveys opinions without using words, are considered forms of free expression (Jones, 2017).

It is essential to keep in mind that the right to free speech and expression protects individuals against the government, not other individuals. No governmental entity, whether federal, state, or local, may take any action that prevents or inhibits individuals from expressing their opinions. However, the right to free speech does not prohibit private entities, including businesses, from regulating or prohibiting particular forms of communication. For instance, it could not be argued that the owners of certain American professional football teams violated the free speech rights of their employees when they forbade their players from kneeling during the playing of the national anthem in protest of police shootings of unarmed Black Americans.

4.5. EQUALITY

Constitutional changes can promote gender equality in a country by incorporating wording on sex-based discrimination and equality or by including measures on election issues or parity democracy. Similarly, improving public administration should consider both men's and women's needs and circumstances, especially in providing equal access to justice and public services. Finally, promoting and researching successful governance must include gender equality as a primary concern.

One of the six goals of the Council of Europe's Gender Equality Strategy 2018–2023 is to achieve equal involvement of men and women in political and public decision-making. The Council of Europe's Committee of Ministers supported Recommendation CM/Rec(2003)3 on the equitable involvement of men and women in political and public decision-making in 2003, with a target of at least 40%. The 2016 Analytical Report on the Third Round of Monitoring of Council of Europe Recommendation Rec (2003) 3 on Equal Participation of Men and Women in Political and Public Decision-Making offers specific information on six decision-making domains. The Council of Europe's Parliamentary Assembly, in a resolution titled Assessing the Impact of Initiatives to Strengthen Women's Political Representation, advised its member states to "consider introducing the principle of parity into their constitution or electoral legislation." In 2016, the Congress of Local and Regional Authorities approved a proposal on women's political engagement and representation at the local and regional levels (Ullmann, 2010).

The Venice Commission (VC), the European Commission for Democracy through Law, has issued several findings and comments on gender equality since 1992. Their 2009 Report on the Impact of Electoral Systems on Women's Representation in Politics, in particular, urged for legislative quotas, and their 2015 Report on the procedures for nominating candidates inside political parties backed up this stance. 2015 the VC hosted a regional conference on election procedures and gender equality. The VC authorized a compendium of gender equality research and opinions in 2016. Furthermore, the VC is looking into how gender equality and anti-discrimination problems are addressed in the constitutions of its 61 member countries. Preliminary findings show that 35 of the 61 bodies analyzed had gender equality/nondiscrimination clauses. In addition to a gender equality component on its website, the VC has formed a subcommittee of gender equality specialists (Jones, 2017).

The European Committee on Democracy and Governance (CDDG) has begun investigating gender mainstreaming problems, particularly those relevant to public administration, as part of its work. The Center of Expertise for Local Government Reform launched the "Leadership Academy" in 2008 to help local leaders improve their abilities. The curriculum addresses gender integration. The current edition of the Public Ethics Benchmarking tool now includes a gender component (Ullmann, 2010).

4.6. SOCIAL JUSTICE

Social justice is the equitable distribution of society's resources, opportunities, and advantages. Originally a theological term, it now refers to the fair arrangement of social systems that provide access to financial benefits. Also referred to as "distributive justice." Social justice is a broad concept whose proponents apply it in various ways. However, social justice theory significantly emphasizes social factors such as racial, economic disparities and unequal access to healthcare. Several social justice-related applications, such as critical race theory, have become political battlegrounds in the United States.

"social justice" originated in Christian theology and was first used in the early 1840s in Luigi Taparelli's Theoretical Treatise on Natural Law. Taparelli was an Italian Jesuit friar during the Risorgimento, the 19th-century Italian nationalist movement, when union negotiations occurred. Throughout its existence, social justice has been a religious concept. Applying justice to social issues was Taparelli's conception of social justice, and he believed that individuals should act morally based on natural theology and religion.

The research on social justice conducted by the American philosopher John Rawls is among the most significant of its kind. Rawls articulated his perspective on social justice, which he referred to as a theory of justice, in A Perspective of Justice (1971), in which he defined "justice as fairness."

According to Rawls, this meant that individuals should consider both the permissible levels of inequality within a community and the criteria for a fair distribution of social benefits. Rawls popularized the "principle of difference," which states that social and economic disparities can be permissible if they benefit society as a whole, and the "veil of ignorance," which is a pretense of ignorance regarding where one would wind up in a given community (Ullmann, 2010).

Fairness is a fundamental criterion, especially regarding access to social resources, also known as "social goods." Even though it may seem impersonal, how social products are distributed has a significant impact. It is essential because the "social determinants" of outcomes are deemed necessary for determining whether a system is just.

In terms of public health, a person's origin may affect their healthcare options and, consequently, their lifespan. Considering this, social justice advocates in healthcare may focus on increasing the likelihood that individuals will remain healthy despite historical and economic resource constraints (Jones, 2017).

4.6.1. Theories of Justice

The earliest philosophical analyses of justice and political authority in the West were conducted by Ancient Greek and Roman philosophers, whose works combined theoretical inquiry with especially keen practical observations (Figure 4.4). Among these works, Plato's Republic, an extensive dialogue-style investigation of justice as a personal virtue and defining characteristic of the ideal political society, was arguably the most significant. According to Plato, justice in the city-state and the human soul is the harmonious operation of their fundamental parts: the rulers, guardians (or soldiers), and producers (such as cultivators and artisans) in the city-state. A balanced process is accomplished when each component pursues or performs the appropriate object or function and does not obstruct other components' pursuits or operations.

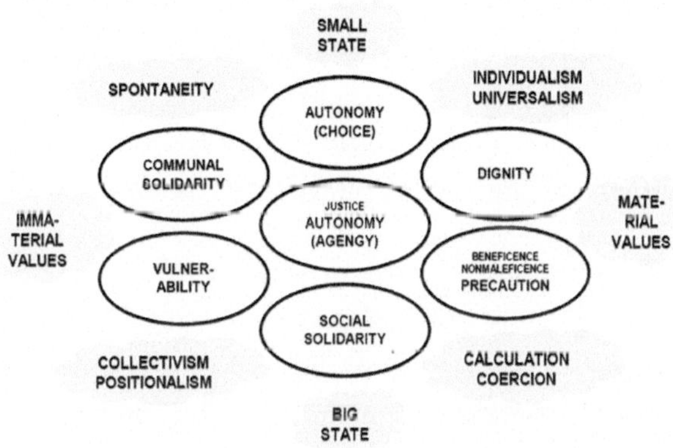

Figure 4.4. Presuppositions of theories of justice.

Source: Hāyry, Matti. (2018). Doctrines and Dimensions of Justice: Their Historical Backgrounds and Ideological Underpinnings. Cambridge Quarterly of Healthcare Ethics. 27. 188–216. Scientific Figure on ResearchGate. Available from: https://www.researchgate.net/figure/Presuppositions-of-theories-of-justice_fig2_323590715 (accessed on 22 September 2023)

Even though Plato's concept of a just society is anti-democratic and class-based, his emphasis on the contribution of social classes to the common welfare became a key component of many later ideas. (It should be noted that Plato believed that men and women were equally able to contribute to the common welfare and, as a result, deserved equal opportunities to do so. He asserted that a democratic republic would have both male and female directors (Ullmann, 2010).

Like Plato, Aristotle viewed justice as both a personal virtue and a characteristic of a faultless (or well-functioning) city-state. Although Aristotle's concept of political justice has been interpreted in numerous ways, the following are universally acknowledged: The pursuit of the common good, the equitable distribution of benefits and burdens among equally deserving or meritorious individuals (distributive justice), and fairness in interpersonal interactions (corrective, commutative, or reciprocal justice). On the other hand, the only individuals who can acquire political desert and merit are those who are virtue-driven and make substantial contributions to the common good. Consequently, even if it is founded on the competent promotion of the common welfare, the just society consists of a hierarchical social order and an equitable distribution of political rights and responsibilities among the higher-ranking members. In this sense, Aristotle's view of political justice is patrician (Jones, 2017).

Aristotle's conception of justice profoundly influenced St. Thomas Aquinas, a Christian philosopher from the Middle Ages. Aquinas concurred with Aristotle that the purpose of political authority is to advance the common welfare and that in a just society, "more prominent" community members would receive proportionally more significant benefits. In the 16th century, the Roman Catholic Church adopted Aquinas' philosophy and theology as official doctrine. His vision of justice influenced the church's gradual social reforms in the late nineteenth and early twentieth centuries (Ullmann, 2010).

In the 17th and 18th centuries, the English philosophers Thomas Hobbes and John Locke and the French philosopher Jean-Jacques Rousseau created influential conceptions of justice founded on the idea of a social contract. According to the social-contract theory, individuals were born into an anarchic "state of nature" from which they eventually desired to flee due to the dangers and anguish it entailed or because they desired to profit from the social order. To accomplish this, they established a society through a compact or agreement delineating several individual rights and responsibilities and several governmental authorities. Consequently, social-contract theories attempt to legitimize and define political power based on individual self-interest and rational consent. Social-contract theory-based conceptions of justice diverged significantly from prior concepts because they viewed justice as a human construction or social construct instead of an ideal founded on objective aspects of human nature and society. Locke's distinctive interpretation of the social compact, which recognized fundamental individual rights that the governing power was obligated to respect, was the intellectual cornerstone of political liberalism.

Due to the vast economic disparities caused by the expansion of industrial capitalism in Europe and the United States during the Industrial Revolution, the English utilitarian philosopher's John Stuart Mill and Henry Sidgwick spent most of the nineteenth century addressing social justice issues. Mill developed a theory to explain and defend, on practical principles, what he perceived to be the essential elements of justice, as reflected in the common usage of the terms just, unjust, and related phrases. Bentham, a practical lawyer, had previously proposed a theory on which activities are morally good or evil in proportion to the quantity of pleasure or unhappiness they engender. Justice requires respect for people's moral and legal rights and their right to attain or receive what they deserve, according to one of the guiding principles. According to Mill, such precepts are justifiable because, in the long run, societies that consistently support them (as laws or moral standards) experience higher happiness for more individuals than those that do not. Mill's conception of a just society is predicated on liberal principles of individual rights (such as the right to life, liberty, and property), democracy, and free enterprise (Ullmann, 2010).

Although utilitarianism was a central social theory in the nineteenth and twentieth centuries and played a significant role in the intellectual reform of social justice, it eventually faced substantial challenges, some of which could be traced back to fundamental problems with practical explanations of the rightness or wrongness of particular actions. Some utilitarian critics, for instance, questioned whether Mill's conception of justice would prohibit any social arrangement in which the exploitation or enslavement of a minority of the population is justified because it enhances the happiness of the majority (Jones, 2017).

John Rawls, an American political philosopher, reignited interest in social-contract principles in the second half of the twentieth century. Rawls addresses the problem above in A Theory of Justice (1971) by criticizing utilitarian interpretations of justice and promoting the concept of "justice as fairness." According to Rawls, rational and autonomous individuals would embrace the fundamental concepts of law and order in an ideal society of equality. To ensure the adoption of equal principles, Rawls imagines a group of people who have been deceived about their social, economic, and historical origins, as well as their fundamental beliefs and objectives, including their conception of the "good life." Behind this "veil of ignorance," any group would be compelled by logic and self-interest to agree that everyone has an equal right to the broadest essential freedom compatible with similar space for others, that social and economic inequalities should be established to benefit the least advantaged. Open positions and offices should be linked to them to ensure fair equality of opportunity.

While the second Rawls principle protects against harmful income and wealth disparities and ensures that everyone has a meaningful chance to run for public office, the first principle guarantees the majority of the fundamental liberties and rights associated with modern liberalism and democracy. Numerous individuals view Rawls's theories as a conceptual model for the capitalist welfare state or free-market social democracy (Ullmann, 2010).

Despite widespread acceptance, conservative libertarians quickly criticized Rawls' liberal egalitarianism, arguing that the society he envisioned was unjust because it would permit (indeed, require) the state to redistribute social and economic goods without the owners' consent, thereby violating their private property rights. According to American philosopher Robert Nozick, an adequately formed social contract could only support a "minimal state," with powers limited to those required to defend citizens from homicide, theft, and fraud. Others argued that Rawls' theory does not adequately explain how a community determines acceptable behavior.

4.6.2. Main Principles of Social Justice

Access

A central tenet of social equity is equal access to social benefits. According to this, everyone in society should have equal access to resources. For instance, many social justice theorists believe everyone should have equal employment, healthcare, and education access. Government employees can promote this method by assuring that everyone has access to these resources (Jones, 2017).

Equity

The concept of equity asserts that everyone should have an equal opportunity to succeed, regardless of past transgressions or institutional bias. This may indicate that resources are allocated to meet the specific requirements of disadvantaged groups or individuals (Ullmann, 2010).

Diversity

According to the diversity principle, government and business leaders should broadly represent the communities they serve. This implies that minorities should be adequately represented in public institutions and that women and people of color should hold leadership positions. Policy-wise, this could mean prohibiting discrimination or offering resources in multiple languages.

Participation

According to the principle of participation, every community member should have a voice in major decisions. In many nations, a few influential individuals must consult the communities they represent to determine public policy. This may erroneously exclude a substantial portion of the population.

Officials can resolve this issue by interacting with minority community advocates and considering their concerns. (Jones, 2017).

4.7. GOOD GOVERNANCE

Under the term "government," all forms of government, as well as the institutions, procedures, and routines used to address and manage matters of public concern, are included. Excellent governance improves the normative or evaluative quality of the governing process. Human rights are primarily concerned with how government institutions manage public resources, conduct public affairs, and assure the fulfilment of human rights (Ullmann, 2010).

Although there is no single definition of "good governance," it may include the following elements: strict adherence to human rights, the rule of law, effective participation, multi-actor partnerships, political pluralism, transparent and accountable institutions and processes, a functioning public sector, legitimacy, access to knowledge, information, and education, political empowerment of the people, equity, sustainability, and attitudes and values that support good governance.

Effective governance is a set of institutional and political activities and outcomes necessary for achieving development objectives. A "good" government is distinguished by its ability to uphold human rights, including civil, cultural, economic, political, and social rights (Jones, 2017).

Effective government and respect for human rights are inextricably linked. Human rights concepts and norms can affect governments and other political and social actors. In addition, they provide the performance criteria that will be used to hold these actors accountable. Human rights concepts impact all aspects of governance, including legislative frameworks, policies, initiatives, funding decisions, and other governance-related endeavors.

In contrast, without effective management, human rights can only be guaranteed for a while. Fulfilling people's goals and requests necessitates the development of a supportive and hospitable environment consisting of fundamental institutions and legal frameworks, as well as political, managerial, and administrative structures.

When human rights values are at their core, enhancements to democratic institutions' effective governance create opportunities for public participation in policymaking through official or informal channels. In addition, they facilitate the participation of numerous social groups in decision-making, particularly at the local level. Finally, they may encourage local communities and members of civil society to communicate their opinions on pressing issues.

Good governance reforms enhance human rights by bolstering the state's capacity to provide public commodities essential for preserving a vast array of human rights, such as the right to sustenance, health, and education. Reform efforts may include public input channels, accountability and transparency measures, and culturally sensitive policy instruments to guarantee that services are acceptable and accessible to all (Ullmann, 2010).

Human rights-aware good governance initiatives strengthen laws and aid institutions such as prisons, tribunals, and legislatures in enforcing the law more effectively. Public education on domestic and international law and advocacy for legal reform may be prioritized on initiatives supporting good governance (Jones, 2017).

To develop anti-corruption measures, initiatives for good governance in the struggle against corruption emphasize concepts such as accountability, transparency, and participation. Initiatives include the establishment of anti-corruption commissions, the utilization of information-sharing platforms, and the monitoring of how governments spend tax dollars and accomplish their goals. (Ullmann, 2010).

CHAPTER 5

Principles of Society

Contents

5.1. INTRODUCTION

Political justice is a concept that encompasses the principles and values governing the distribution of power, resources, and opportunities within society. At its core, political justice seeks to create a fair and equitable social order that upholds the rights and well-being of all individuals. One crucial aspect of achieving political justice is incorporating social principles, which guide the formation and implementation of policies and practices that address social inequalities and promote the greater good.

Social principles in political justice are grounded in the belief that every member of society should have equal opportunities and access to resources necessary for a dignified and fulfilling life (Figure 5.1). These principles acknowledge the interconnectedness of individuals within an organization and recognize the importance of collective well-being. By considering the social implications of political decisions and actions; policymakers can strive to create an inclusive and just community that prioritizes the needs of marginalized and vulnerable groups (Vom Saal, 2012).

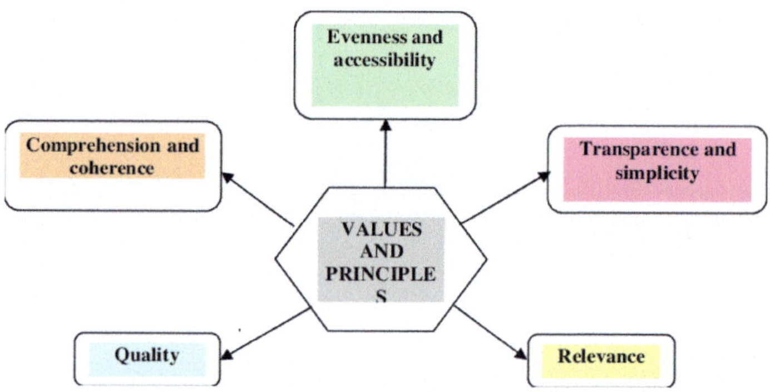

Figure 5.1. Common values and principles needs to be identified.

Source: Dziechciarz, Józef. (2007). Econometric Evaluation of Education Systems. Scientific Figure on ResearchGate. Available from: https://www.researchgate.net/figure/Common-values-and-principles-needs-to-be-identified-a-Evenness-and-accessibility-CNCIS_fig7_301328321 (accessed on 22 September 2023)

Incorporating social principles in political justice requires a comprehensive understanding of social structures, power dynamics, and systemic inequalities. It necessitates recognizing and addressing how social, economic, and cultural factors contribute to disparities in opportunities and outcomes. By embracing these principles, political systems can work towards dismantling unjust systems and fostering social cohesion, cooperation, and solidarity. Furthermore, social principles in political justice emphasize the importance of democratic participation and representation. They encourage the inclusion of diverse voices and perspectives in decision-making processes, allowing for a more comprehensive understanding of societal needs and aspirations. By engaging citizens in the political sphere, these principles foster a sense of ownership and accountability, thereby strengthening the legitimacy of political institutions and ensuring their responsiveness to the concerns and aspirations of the people (Arato, 2016)

This chapter will explore some critical social principles that underpin political justice. Concepts such as equity, social cohesion, inclusivity, human rights, and distributive justice will be explored toto shed light on these principles' essential role in fostering a just and inclusive society. By understanding and advocating for social principles in political justice, we can strive towards a world where fairness, equality, and social well-being are central tenets of governance with a conscious understanding of the principles of the society.

This chapter builds on exploring fundamental social principles by beginning with the renowned Social Contract Theory. This theory, developed by influential philosophers throughout history, examines the reciprocal relationship between individuals and their society, emphasizing the mutual obligations and benefits that arise from this social contract. By examining the principles and dynamics of this theory, we gain valuable insights into the foundation of political justice and its essential role in shaping a harmonious and equitable society. Through a comprehensive understanding of the Social Contract Theory, we can further appreciate the intricate interplay between individuals and their collective responsibilities, paving the way for a just and inclusive society (Vom Saal, 2012).

5.2. THE SOCIAL CONTRACT THEORY

The social contract theory is a philosophical concept that has played a significant role in shaping and developing the principles upon which societies are built. This theory proposes that individuals willingly enter into an implicit agreement or contract with each other and the governing body of a community, surrendering certain rights and freedoms in exchange for the protection and benefits that society provides. The concept of the social contract has profoundly influenced the formation of social principles and the establishment of societal norms (Arato, 2016). At its core, the social contract theory explores the relationship between the individual and the community.

It postulates that individuals in a state of nature agree to unite and form a society to improve their collective lives (Figure 5.2). This agreement is driven by the recognition that living in isolation would be precarious and devoid of the advantages offered by communal living. Thus, The social contract becomes the foundation upon which societies are built, establishing the framework for social order and cooperation.

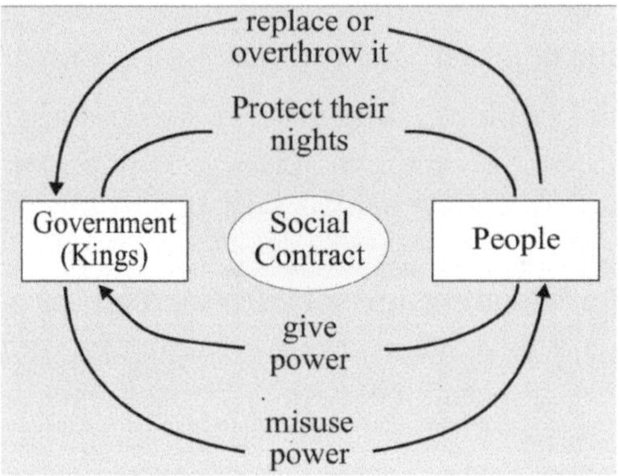

Figure 5.2. Social contract theory.

Source: Ajayi, Olumuyiwa. (2022). Effect of Thinking map on Pupils' Academic Performance in Basic Science in Ilorin South Local Government Area of Kwara State. 23. Scientific Figure on ResearchGate. Available from: https://www.researchgate.net/figure/Social-Contract-Theory-Source-Rousseau-1762_fig1_369243926 (accessed on 22 September 2023)

One of the critical implications of the social contract theory is the notion of consent. According to this theory, individuals willingly give up certain freedoms and submit to the authority of a governing body or state. This voluntary surrender of some individual liberties is predicated on the understanding that the benefits and protections provided by society outweigh the sacrifices made. In this way, the social contract ensures that the rights and responsibilities of individuals are balanced in a manner that promotes harmony and stability (Vom Saal, 2012).

The social contract theory has been influential in developing democratic systems of government. In a democratic society, the government is seen as an agent of the people, entrusted with the responsibility to uphold the terms of the social contract. The consent of the governed is sought through regular elections and active participation in the decision-making process. This democratic framework, derived from the social contract, empowers citizens to shape the principles and policies that govern their society.

Moreover, the social contract theory has also shaped the principles of justice and fairness within societies. The idea that individuals willingly enter into a contract implies that they expect equitable treatment and a just distribution of resources and opportunities. This has led to the development of legal systems and institutions to ensure equal rights and protect against discrimination and exploitation. By recognizing the fundamental equality of individuals, the social contract theory fosters a sense of justice and equality within societies (Arato, 2016).

Furthermore, the social contract theory has provided a basis for discussions on the limits of government power and the rights of individuals. It establishes the idea that the governing body's authority is derived from the consent of the governed, and as such, it is limited by the terms of the social contract. This concept has fueled debates on individual rights, privacy, and the proper role of government in society. By examining the mutual obligations and expectations outlined in the social contract, organizations can navigate these complex issues and balance collective welfare and individual freedom.

Overall, the concept of the social contract has played a crucial role in shaping and developing the social principles that guide our societies. By postulating that individuals willingly enter into an implicit agreement with each other and the governing body, the social contract theory establishes the foundation for social order, cooperation, and collective well-being. It has influenced the development of democratic systems, principles of justice, and discussions on individual rights and government power. However, as societies continue to evolve, the concept of social contract theory becomes biased due to economic disparities, social hierarchies and systematic biases, which undermines the principles of a fair and just society (Vom Saal, 2012).

5.3. EQUALITY AND JUSTICE IN SOCIETY

5.3.1. Examining the Notions of Equality and Justice

In a society that values fairness and harmony, social equality and justice principles form the bedrock of a just and inclusive community. These principles are rooted in the fundamental belief that everyone deserves equal rights, opportunities, and treatment, regardless of background, race, gender, or socioeconomic status. While pursuing social equality and justice is a complex and ongoing process, exploring and understanding the underlying concepts is crucial to create a more equitable society (Arato, 2016). At its core, social equality refers to the absence of discrimination or prejudice and the fair distribution of resources, benefits, and responsibilities across all members of society. It recognizes that everyone has inherent worth and should be treated with dignity, respect, and impartiality. Achieving social equality requires addressing systemic barriers and ensuring equal access to education, healthcare, employment opportunities, and other essential services. It involves challenging and dismantling oppressive structures and norms that perpetuate discrimination and marginalization (Figure 5.3).

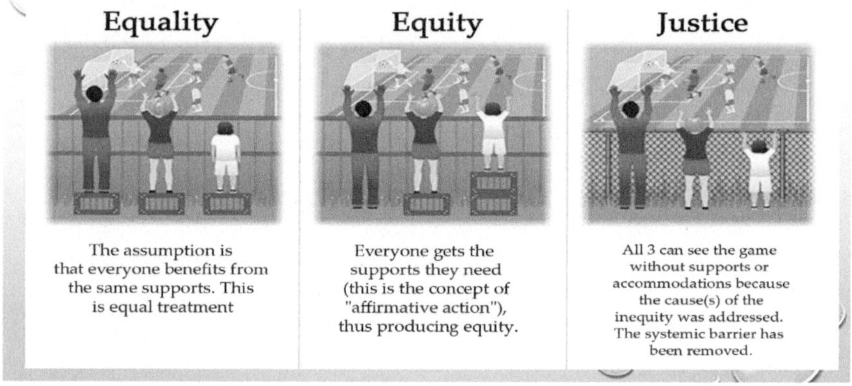

Figure 5.3. Equality, equity, and justice.

Source: Breny, Jean. (2020). Continuing the Journey Toward Health Equity: Becoming Antiracist in Health Promotion Research and Practice. Health education & behavior: the official publication of the Society for Public Health Education. Scientific Figure on ResearchGate. Available from: https://www.researchgate.net/figure/Equality-equity-and-justice_fig1_344204011 (accessed on 22 September 2023)

Conversely, justice encompasses notions of fairness, impartiality, and the just application of laws and regulations. It seeks to ensure that individuals are treated equitably, and that their rights are protected. Justice is not only concerned with the consequences of actions but also with the underlying causes of inequalities. It recognizes that historical injustices and systemic biases can create disparities and strives to rectify them through policies, legal reforms, and social initiatives (Vom Saal, 2012).

To fully understand the notion of equality and justice, it is essential to recognize the interplay between individual and collective responsibilities. Social equality is not merely the absence of discrimination; it requires active efforts to promote inclusivity, diversity, and equal opportunities. Individuals must cultivate empathy, compassion, and a willingness to challenge their biases and prejudices. Moreover, collective action is necessary to address systemic issues, as individuals alone cannot dismantle deeply entrenched inequalities (Arato, 2016).

Social equality and justice go hand in hand. True justice can only be achieved when society recognizes and addresses the historical and ongoing injustices faced by marginalized communities. It involves acknowledging and rectifying past wrongs, empowering disadvantaged groups, and ensuring their voices are heard in decision-making. Justice also requires accountability and holding individuals and institutions responsible for their actions, particularly when perpetuating inequality or discrimination (Vom Saal, 2012).

While progress has been made in advancing social equality and justice, it is an ongoing process that requires collective effort and continuous reflection. Policies and initiatives that promote equal access to education, healthcare, employment, and legal protection are vital in dismantling systemic barriers. Promoting diversity and inclusivity in leadership positions and fostering allyship across different communities can help break down discriminatory practices and bring about transformative change.

5.3.2. Challenges Experienced in the Pursuit of Equality

While pursuing equality is a noble and essential goal, it can sometimes be complicated. Various challenges and controversies arise along the path, often reflecting differing viewpoints and interpretations of what constitutes true equality. These challenges encompass practical and philosophical aspects, and understanding them is crucial for fostering meaningful discussions and progress.

- **Interpreting Equality:** One significant challenge lies in the interpretation of equality itself. Equality can be understood differently, leading to debates about its meaning and application. Some view equality as an outcome where everyone possesses equal resources, opportunities, and advantages. Others emphasize equal treatment and access to opportunities, focusing on fairness rather than absolute parity. These interpretations can lead to contrasting approaches and differing priorities in achieving equality (Arato, 2016).
- **Balancing Individuality and Equity:** Another challenge arises from the tension between valuing individual differences and ensuring equitable outcomes. While recognizing and celebrating

individuality is crucial for fostering diversity and promoting personal growth, it can pose challenges in pursuing equality. Striking a balance between preserving the essence and addressing systemic inequalities requires careful consideration and a nuanced approach (Vom Saal, 2012).

- **Affirmative Action and Meritocracy:** The concept of affirmative action is often a topic of controversy in discussions about equality. Proponents argue that affirmative action is necessary to rectify historical injustices and promote equal opportunities for marginalized groups. On the other hand, critics raise concerns about the potential undermining of meritocracy, where qualifications and achievements are the primary basis for advancement. Finding a middle ground that addresses historical disparities without compromising merit-based systems is complex.
- **Economic Inequality:** Economic disparities present a significant challenge in pursuing social equality and justice. The concentration of wealth and resources among a few can perpetuate systemic inequalities and hinder efforts to create a level playing field. Addressing economic disparities requires comprehensive approaches such as progressive taxation, wealth redistribution, and ensuring access to quality education and healthcare for all.
- **Intersectionality:** An important aspect to consider in the pursuit of equality is intersectionality, recognizing that individuals may face multiple forms of discrimination and disadvantage based on their intersecting identities, such as race, gender, sexuality, and socioeconomic status. Understanding and addressing individuals' unique challenges at intersections of multiple identities is essential for achieving genuine equality (Vom Saal, 2012).
- **Resistance to Change:** Often, societal norms and ingrained biases hinder progress towards equality. Whether conscious or unconscious, resistance to change can manifest in various ways, from overt discrimination to subtle biases that perpetuate unequal treatment; overcoming resistance to change requires education, awareness, and ongoing efforts to challenge and dismantle systemic barriers and prejudices (Arato, 2016)
- **Global and Cultural Contexts:** The pursuit of equality must also consider the global and cultural contexts in which it operates.

Different societies have distinct historical, cultural, and socio-political frameworks shaping their understanding of equality and justice. Recognizing and respecting these diverse perspectives while seeking common ground is essential for fostering global conversations and inclusive approaches to equality.

While social equality and justice are vital principles for a fair and inclusive society, their pursuit is not without challenges and controversies. Interpreting equality, balancing individuality and equity, affirmative action, economic inequality, intersectionality, resistance to change, and global contexts all contribute to this pursuit's complexities. However, understanding and respecting the rights and responsibilities of individuals is the foundation of an equitable and just society. These principles are the foundation for a fair and just society where everyone is treated equitably, regardless of background, characteristics, or circumstances (Vom Saal, 2012).

Rights and responsibilities are intrinsically linked to the notion of social equality. Every individual possesses certain inherent rights, encompassing fundamental aspects such as freedom of expression, liberty, and the pursuit of happiness. These rights are not contingent on wealth, social status, race, or gender. Instead, they are universal and apply to all members of society. Upholding these rights ensures everyone has an equal opportunity to lead a fulfilling and dignified life.

However, more than the existence of rights alone can need social equality. It is essential to recognize that along with rights, individuals also have responsibilities towards society. Duties can vary in nature, ranging from upholding the rule of law to respecting the rights and well-being of others. The fulfilment of these responsibilities is crucial for maintaining social harmony and ensuring that everyone can exercise their rights without infringing upon the rights of others

5.4. RIGHTS AND RESPONSIBILITIES OF INDIVIDUALS IN SOCIETY

5.4.1. Defining Individual Rights in a Societal Context

In any society, the relationship between individuals and their rights forms the foundation of a functional and just social order. The recognition and protection of individual rights are fundamental to maintaining a harmonious and balanced community where each member can flourish and contribute to the collective progress. As we explore the intricacies of defining individual rights in a societal context, it becomes crucial to understand the underlying principles and considerations that shape this framework (Arato, 2016).

First and foremost, individual rights are inherent and inalienable, grounded in the intrinsic dignity and worth of every human being. They are not granted or revoked by any external entity but are fundamental attributes in a person's existence. These rights are not contingent upon the whims of governments, societal norms, or cultural beliefs; they are universal and apply to all individuals, regardless of their race, gender, nationality, religion, or any other characteristic (Vom Saal, 2012).

In a societal context, individual rights are not absolute or unlimited. They must be balanced with the rights of others and the collective well-being of the community. This necessitates an understanding that exercising one's rights should not infringe upon the rights of others or jeopardize the more significant social fabric. This delicate balance often requires thoughtful deliberation, dialogue, and compromise to safeguard individual freedoms while promoting a harmonious coexistence.

Furthermore, recognizing individual rights goes hand in hand with acknowledging the corresponding responsibilities that come with them. Just as individuals are entitled to their rights, they also bear the burden of respecting and upholding the rights of others. This reciprocity forms the basis of a healthy and functioning society, where mutual respect and consideration are integral to fostering a sense of community and shared values.

The definition of individual rights extends beyond necessities such as freedom of speech, thought, and expression. It encompasses a broad range of rights, including but not limited to the right to life, liberty, and security of person; the right to privacy and protection of personal data; the right to equality and non-discrimination; the right to education, healthcare, and social services; and the right to participate in decision-making processes that affect one's life and community (Arato, 2016).

Moreover, the definition of individual rights should be dynamic and adaptable to society's changing needs and aspirations. As societal norms evolve, new challenges emerge, and technological advancements reshape our lives, the understanding and interpretation of individual rights must keep pace. It is imperative to regularly reassess and reinterpret these rights to ensure their relevance and effectiveness in addressing the concerns and aspirations of individuals within the societal context. Defining individual rights in a societal context requires a comprehensive approach that balances personal freedoms with social responsibility. It involves fostering a culture that recognizes and protects these rights and promotes their active exercise and engagement. Education and awareness play a vital role in instilling a deep understanding of individual rights and responsibilities from an early age, empowering individuals to navigate their roles as rights holders and responsible citizens (Vom Saal, 2012).

5.4.2. Balancing Individual Rights with Societal Interests

In any functioning society, the delicate balance between individual rights and societal interests is crucial in maintaining harmony and ensuring collective well-being. While individual rights empower citizens to exercise their freedoms and pursue their own goals, it is equally important to recognize that these rights must be balanced with the broader needs and objectives of society.

Balancing individual rights with societal interests requires a nuanced approach that acknowledges the fundamental value. Individual rights encompass a wide range of liberties and protections, including the freedom of speech, assembly, religion, privacy, and the right to a fair trial and equal treatment under the law. These rights are essential for upholding every individual's dignity, autonomy, and personal development.

However, it is crucial to recognize that no right is absolute. Certain circumstances may necessitate limitations or restrictions on individual rights when they conflict with society's greater welfare. This recognition stems from the understanding that societal interests are interconnected and multifaceted, encompassing public safety, health, environmental preservation, and social cohesion (Arato, 2016).

The challenge lies in finding the appropriate balance between individual rights and societal interests. This requires a thoughtful examination of the potential consequences and trade-offs associated with upholding certain rights in specific contexts. It is essential to consider the long-term implications and the potential impact on the broader community when individual actions or decisions have the potential to infringe upon societal well-being.

For example, freedom of speech is a fundamental individual right that allows individuals to express their opinions and ideas. However, there may be instances where hate speech, or misinformation can cause harm to individuals or incite violence, posing a threat to social cohesion. In such cases, restrictions on certain forms of speech may be necessary to safeguard the rights and well-being of all members of society (Vom Saal, 2012).

Similarly, the right to privacy safeguards personal autonomy and dignity. However, the balance between individual privacy and collective security has become more complex in the digital age. Balancing the need for confidentiality with measures aimed at countering terrorism, cybercrime, or ensuring public safety requires careful deliberation and the development of appropriate legal frameworks.

To balance individual rights and societal interests, societies often rely on democratic processes, the rule of law, and ethical frameworks. These mechanisms ensure that decisions regarding limiting or prioritizing certain rights are made through transparent, accountable, and inclusive processes. It is essential to foster public dialogue and engage in meaningful discussions to reach a consensus on navigating these complex issues.

Education and awareness also play a vital role in helping individuals understand the interplay between their rights and the greater societal context. By promoting a culture of responsibility and civic engagement, societies can encourage individuals to exercise their rights while considering the broader impact of their actions (Arato, 2016).

While rights ensure that individuals are granted certain freedoms and protections, they are not absolute and often come with ethical dilemmas and trade-offs that require careful consideration. Ethical dilemmas arise when the exercise of one individual's rights potentially infringes upon the rights or well-being of others. These situations can be complex and multifaceted, often requiring difficult decisions that balance conflicting interests. Society must grapple with such ethical dilemmas to strike a fair and just balance between individual rights and collective well-being.

5.4.3. Ethical Dilemmas and Trade-Offs in Upholding Individual Rights

Ethical dilemmas are common in the complex fabric of society, as the exercise of individual rights may conflict with the greater good or the rights of others. One common ethical dilemma is the right to privacy versus the need for security. Individuals have a fundamental right to privacy, encompassing personal information, communications, and autonomy. However, in the face of growing security threats, there is a need for enhanced surveillance measures to safeguard public safety. Balancing the preservation of individual privacy with the collective need for security presents a delicate trade-off that requires careful consideration and debate (Vom Saal, 2012). Another ethical dilemma emerges from the tension between freedom of expression and protection against hate speech. Freedom of expression is a fundamental right that allows individuals to voice their opinions and engage in open dialogue. However, when freedom of expression extends to hate speech or incitement of violence, it can cause harm and infringe upon the rights and well-being of others. Striking the right balance between upholding free speech and protecting individuals from damage is an ongoing societal challenge.

Furthermore, the right to property ownership often intersects with social justice issues and economic inequality. While individuals have the right to acquire and possess property, extreme concentration of wealth can lead to social disparities and marginalization of certain groups. Balancing the right to property with the goal of a more equitable society necessitates considering mechanisms such as progressive taxation and wealth redistribution, which may involve trade-offs that impact individual rights (Arato, 2016).

The principle of individual rights also intersects with issues such as healthcare access and resource allocation. Ensuring universal access to healthcare is a fundamental right, but allocating limited resources presents ethical dilemmas. Choices must be made regarding the distribution of resources, including prioritizing treatments, determining eligibility, and managing costs. These decisions often require weighing the individual's right to healthcare against societal considerations such as the population's overall well-being.

The right to religious freedom can also clash with other individual rights or societal norms. Spiritual practices and beliefs are deeply personal and deserve protection, but conflicts can arise when they infringe upon the rights of others or contradict prevailing ethical principles. Balancing religious freedoms with the rights and values of a diverse society necessitates nuanced discussions and compromises that respect both individual autonomy and societal cohesion (Vom Saal, 2012).

However, navigating these ethical dilemmas and trade-offs is not a one-size-fits-all process. Societies must engage in ongoing dialogue, debate, and reflection to develop frameworks and policies that promote the greatest good while upholding individual rights. Flexibility, adaptability, and a commitment to justice and fairness are essential in striking the delicate balance between individual rights and the collective well-being of society. In addition, striking a balance between the broader protection and upholding of individual rights and responsibilities determines a community's principles in upholding social harmony and effective conflict resolution (Arato, 2016).

5.5. SOCIAL HARMONY AND CONFLICT RESOLUTION

5.5.1. Promoting Social Harmony as a Foundation for Political Justice

Pursuing political justice and societal well-being in any society relies heavily on establishing social harmony and effective conflict-resolution mechanisms. Social connection can be understood as peaceful coexistence and cooperation among individuals, groups, and communities, leading to a stable and cohesive society. It encompasses many factors, including tolerance, mutual respect, empathy, and the ability to address conflicts constructively (Figure 5.4).

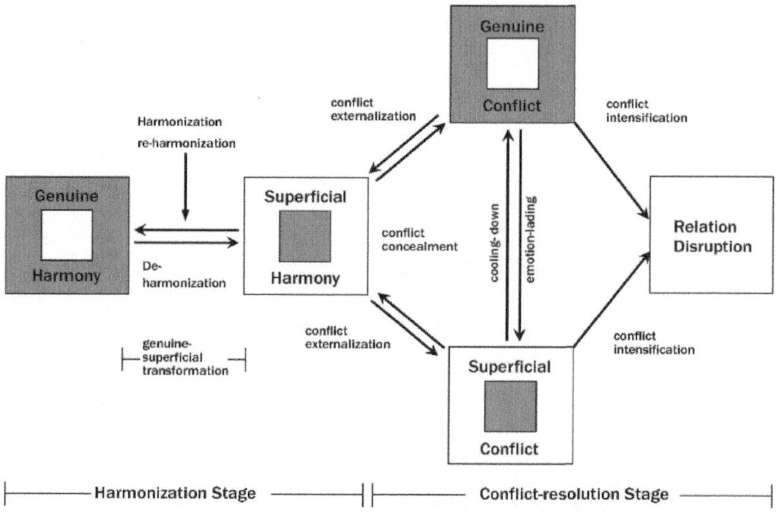

Figure 5.4. A dynamic model of interpersonal harmony and conflict (disharmony).

Source: Li-Li Huang, (2016), Interpersonal Harmony and Conflict for Chinese People: A Yin–Yang Perspective, Volume 7, https://doi.org/10.3389/fpsyg.2016.00847

Promoting social harmony is essential for creating a just and equitable political system. When individuals and communities live in peace, they are more likely to work together towards shared goals, fostering a sense of unity and solidarity. In such an environment, the principles of fairness, equality, and respect can flourish, allowing for the creation of laws and policies that reflect society's diverse needs and aspirations.

One fundamental aspect of promoting social harmony is cultivating a culture of inclusivity and diversity. Recognizing and celebrating the unique identities, perspectives, and contributions of all members of society is crucial for building bridges and fostering understanding. Embracing diversity not only enriches the cultural fabric of a society but also allows for the exploration of new ideas and the generation of innovative solutions to societal challenges (Vom Saal, 2012).

Education plays a pivotal role in promoting social harmony. Education equips individuals with the tools necessary to navigate complex social dynamics and resolve conflicts peacefully by imparting knowledge, nurturing critical thinking, and instilling values of empathy and cooperation. When individuals are empowered with the skills to understand and appreciate diverse viewpoints, they are more likely to engage in constructive dialogue, seek common ground, and find mutually beneficial solutions.

Effective conflict resolution mechanisms are integral to maintaining social harmony. Conflicts are inevitable in any society, arising from differences in opinions, interests, or resources. However, how conflicts are managed and resolved determines a community's overall stability and well-being. A just and fair conflict resolution process ensures that grievances are heard, disputes are addressed promptly, and solutions are reached through dialogue and negotiation rather than resorting to violence or coercion (Arato, 2016).

Societies can establish various mechanisms to promote effective conflict resolution, including impartial courts, mediation services, and community-based reconciliation processes. These mechanisms should be accessible to all community members, ensuring that justice is not only served but also perceived as fair and legitimate. Additionally, efforts should be made to promote restorative justice approaches, which focus on healing and rebuilding relationships rather than solely punitive measures.

5.5.2. Strategies for Conflict Resolution in Societal Contexts

Social harmony is a fundamental principle of any well-functioning society, as it promotes cooperation, understanding, and peaceful coexistence among its members. However, conflicts inevitably arise in human interactions due to differences in beliefs, values, interests, and perspectives. To maintain social harmony and address these conflicts effectively, societies employ various strategies for conflict resolution. These strategies aim to foster communication, empathy, negotiation, and compromise while ensuring the fair and just resolution of disputes. This section explores some key strategies employed in societal contexts for conflict resolution (Vom Saal, 2012).

- Dialogue and Communication: Effective communication lies at the heart of conflict resolution. Encouraging open and honest dialogue between conflicting parties allows them to express their concerns, perspectives, and emotions. This exchange of information can help build understanding and empathy, enabling the parties to find common ground and potential solutions..
- Mediation and Facilitation: Mediation involves the intervention of a neutral third party to facilitate communication and negotiation between conflicting parties. Mediators help parties identify underlying interests, explore options, and work towards mutually acceptable solutions. By creating a safe and non-adversarial environment, mediation empowers individuals to resolve conflicts while ensuring a fair process (Arato, 2016).
- Negotiation and Compromise: Negotiation involves a process of give and take, where conflicting parties attempt to find mutually agreeable solutions. It requires flexibility, active listening, and a willingness to consider alternative perspectives. Through negotiation, individuals can identify shared interests, explore creative options, and ultimately reach compromises that address the needs of all parties involved.
- Legal System and Rule of Law: Societies often establish legal systems to address conflicts and ensure justice. The rule of law provides a framework for resolving disputes through fair and impartial processes. Courts and legal institutions interpret and apply laws, providing an avenue for individuals to seek redress and have their conflicts adjudicated in a formal and transparent manner.
- Conflict Prevention and Early Intervention: An essential aspect of conflict resolution is preventing conflicts from escalating to a point where resolution becomes more challenging. Societies invest in conflict prevention strategies such as education, awareness campaigns, and community-building initiatives. Early intervention programs aim to address conflicts at their inception, providing resources and support to prevent further escalation.
- Restorative Justice: Restorative justice approaches focus on repairing the harm caused by conflicts and fostering healing and

reconciliation. Rather than emphasizing punishment, restorative justice processes involve bringing together the affected parties to discuss the impact of the conflict, seek understanding, and collectively determine how to address the harm caused and prevent future conflicts (Vom Saal, 2012).

- Empathy and Emotional Intelligence: Developing empathy and emotional intelligence plays a vital role in conflict resolution. Empathy allows individuals to understand and appreciate others' perspectives and emotions, fostering better communication and relationship-building. Emotional intelligence enables individuals to manage their own emotions and respond empathetically to others, facilitating conflict resolution through compassionate and constructive dialogue.
- Cultural Sensitivity and Respect for Diversity: In diverse societies, conflicts often arise from cultural, ethnic, or religious differences. Building cultural sensitivity and promoting respect for diversity helps mitigate conflicts and encourages inclusive dialogue. Recognizing and valuing different perspectives and traditions fosters a climate of acceptance and understanding, reducing the likelihood of conflicts based on misunderstandings or biases (Arato, 2016).

By employing these conflict resolution strategies, societies can effectively address conflicts, maintain social harmony, and promote a culture of peace and cooperation. It is essential to adapt and evolve these strategies to suit the specific needs and dynamics of different societal contexts, as conflicts vary in nature, complexity, and underlying causes. Ultimately, the goal of conflict resolution in societal contexts is to create an environment where individuals can coexist harmoniously, celebrate diversity, and work collectively towards the betterment of society. However, this can be achieved through mediation and dialogue.

5.5.3. The Role of Mediation and Dialogue in Building a Just Society

Conflicts and disagreements will inevitably arise in any society. People have different perspectives, values, and interests, often leading to tensions and disputes. However, a just society acknowledges and addresses these conflicts fairly and peacefully. Mediation and dialogue play crucial roles in fostering social harmony and resolving disputes, paving the way for a more equitable and inclusive society. Mediation, as a method of conflict resolution, involves the intervention of a neutral third party who facilitates communication and negotiation between conflicting parties. This impartial mediator helps create an environment where individuals can openly express their concerns, interests, and emotions without fear of judgment or retribution. Through active listening and empathy, the mediator enables the conflicting parties to understand each other's perspectives and motivations better, thus promoting mutual respect and kindness (Vom Saal, 2012).

One of the primary advantages of mediation is that it allows for creative problem-solving and the exploration of win-win solutions. Instead of relying on a rigid legal framework or adversarial processes, mediation encourages the parties involved to collaboratively find resolutions that satisfy everyone's needs to the greatest extent possible. This approach helps build a sense of ownership and commitment to the solutions reached, fostering long-lasting agreements and minimizing the likelihood of future conflicts.

Furthermore, mediation and dialogue contribute to developing a just society by promoting inclusivity and giving marginalized voices a platform to be heard. In traditional adversarial systems, power imbalances often prevent specific individuals or groups from effectively advocating for their interests. Mediation, however, provides a space where all participants are given equal opportunities to voice their concerns and contribute to the resolution process. This inclusivity helps ensure that decisions are not disproportionately influenced by those in positions of power, leading to more equitable outcomes that reflect the diverse needs and perspectives within society.

Moreover, the mediation process cultivates valuable skills and attitudes crucial for a just society. Active listening, empathy, and open-mindedness are essential for effective mediators and participants. By engaging in constructive dialogue, individuals develop a deeper appreciation for the complexities of social issues and learn to see beyond their own biases and preconceptions. This enhanced understanding strengthens social bonds and fosters a culture of cooperation, respect, and empathy, which are fundamental principles for building a just society (Arato, 2016).

Furthermore, mediation and dialogue uphold the significance of legal systems and the rule of law. Instead, they complement these systems by offering an alternative and often more accessible avenue for resolving conflicts. Mediation can be employed at various levels, from interpersonal disputes to community conflicts, workplace grievances, or even international diplomacy. By incorporating meditation into the fabric of society, we create an environment that values peaceful resolution and actively promotes social harmony.

Mediation fosters social harmony and minimizes the destructive effects of conflicts by providing a platform for open communication, understanding, and collaborative problem-solving. It promotes inclusivity, empowers marginalized voices, and encourages the development of critical skills and attitudes necessary for a fair and equitable society. Embracing mediation as a cornerstone of our social fabric allows us to navigate disagreements with compassion and respect, contributing to a more harmonious and just organization for all (Vom Saal, 2012).

Generally, the principles of society discussed in this chapter shed light on fundamental aspects that underpin the functioning and well-being of any community. Throughout history, philosophers and thinkers have contemplated the social contract theory, which forms the basis of the relationship between individuals and the society they belong to. The concept of a social contract emphasizes the mutual obligations and responsibilities between citizens and their governing institutions, highlighting the need for cooperation and collective decision-making.

Equality and justice are integral components of a just society. While equality strives to ensure fairness and impartiality among individuals, justice seeks to uphold moral and legal principles to address societal disparities. However, achieving true equality and justice is challenging. Societies grapple with complex social, economic, and cultural factors that impede the pursuit of equality. Discrimination, systemic biases, and uneven distribution of resources pose significant obstacles to a more equitable society (Arato, 2016).

The rights and responsibilities of individuals within a society play a crucial role in maintaining a harmonious coexistence. Individual rights, which encompass personal freedoms and protections, must be balanced with the interests and well-being of the broader society. This delicate equilibrium requires careful consideration of ethical dilemmas and trade-offs that may arise. Balancing individual rights with societal interests necessitates navigating complex situations where conflicts may emerge, necessitating conflict resolution mechanisms.

Promoting social harmony is vital for realizing political justice within a society. It involves fostering an inclusive and cohesive environment that respects diversity and promotes dialogue. Conflicts can be addressed and resolved peacefully by acknowledging different perspectives and engaging in constructive conversations. Strategies for conflict resolution, including negotiation, mediation, and dialogue, play a crucial role in addressing societal conflicts and finding mutually agreeable solutions. Societies can work towards reconciliation and sustainable peace by engaging in constructive dialogue and understanding one another's concerns (Vom Saal, 2012).

Therefore, the principles of society are not merely abstract concepts but rather the guiding principles that shape the fabric of our communities. Pursuing a just and harmonious society requires constant reflection, adaptation, and collective action. By upholding the principles of the social contract, equality and justice, individual rights and responsibilities, and social harmony and conflict resolution, we can strive towards building a society that values the dignity and well-being of every individual while fostering a sense of belonging and shared purpose for the betterment of all. While these principles provide a framework for creating a just and equitable society, they also present complex challenges and ethical dilemmas that must be navigated with wisdom and empathy. By upholding these principles and addressing the obstacles encountered, organizations can strive towards a more harmonious, fair, and inclusive future for all their members (Vom Saal, 2012).

CHAPTER 6

Legislative and Executive Power

Contents

6.1. INTRODUCTION

In a country with democracy, the power is divided among different parts of the government to ensure a fair system (Figure 6.1). Two essential parts of running a country are the legislative and executive branches. These branches have other powers and responsibilities that are very important for the political system. Legislative power is the ability given to a group of people who make laws to create rules representing what the people want and what is good for them. This branch is responsible for making rules, creating laws, and overseeing what the executive branch does. The legislative branch comprises chosen people who discuss, think about, and approve rules that control the country. This branch of the government ensures that it does what's best for the people and is responsible for its actions (Polborn, 2021)

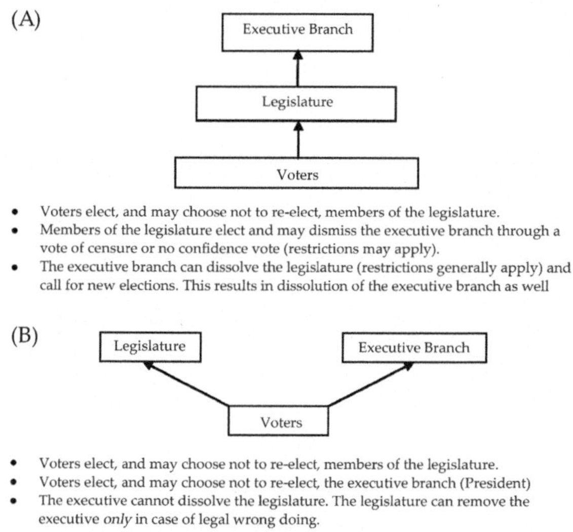

Figure 6.1. (A) Fused powers system. (B) Separation of powers system.

Source: Kreppel, Amie. (2011). Looking 'Up,' 'Down' and 'Sideways': Understanding EU Institutions in Context. West European Politics. 34. 167–179. Scientific Figure on ResearchGate. Available from: https://www.researchgate.net/figure/A-FUSED-POWERS-SYSTEM-B-SEPARATION-OF-POWERS-SYSTEM_fig1_233275393 (accessed on 22 September 2023)

On the other hand, the executive branch, which is led by the head of state or head of government, holds the power to make decisions. This may vary depending on the political structure of each country. This part of the government is responsible for following and enforcing laws, handling the government's daily tasks, and making crucial national security, foreign policy, and administration choices. The executive branch is responsible for putting into action and explaining laws made by the legislative branch. This brings the guidelines and instructions created by the legislature to life.

To understand how a country's political system works, learning how legislative and executive power is divided and used is essential. These two branches work together to ensure no one person or organization becomes too strong. This helps protect individuals' rights, promote democratic values, and stop any possible misuse of power. When we study how the government is organized and how it works, we can understand how it affects people's lives (Polborn, 2021).

6.2. LEGISLATIVE POWER

The legislative power is an essential part of a democratic society. It represents the people and makes the laws that govern the country (Figure 6.2). This power belongs to the group of people in the government who make laws. The citizens elect them; their job is to create, change, and remove regulations that represent what the people want and hope for. It is essential to understand how laws are made and why they are necessary in democratic countries. This knowledge helps us understand how governments work and how power is balanced (Power, 2011).

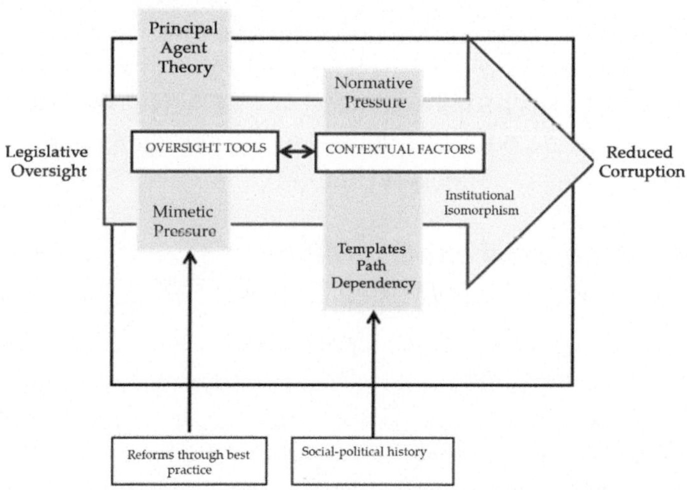

Figure 6.2. Conceptual synthesis of legislative oversight Pelizzo and Stapenhurst state that the understanding of all those theories and the empirical analysis form the explanation of what legislative oversight really is.

Source: Mohd Rosli, Rozaini & Quddus, S M Abdul. (2020). The Selangor

State Assembly Oversight and Government Accountability (Pengawasan dan Akauntabiliti Kerajaan di Dewan Negeri Selangor). Journal of Islam in Asia (E-ISSN 2289–8077). 17. 350–371. Scientific Figure on ResearchGate. Available from: https://www.researchgate.net/figure/Conceptual-Synthesis-of-Legislative-Oversight-Pelizzo-and-Stapenhurst-state-that-the_fig1_348157938 (accessed on 22 September 2023)

Legislative power is when a group of people can make, talk about, and approve laws. This means that it includes the beliefs of representation and discussion, making sure that the different ideas and views of the people are considered in making decisions. Legislative power gives elected representatives the authority to create laws. These laws help control how people behave in society, protect people's rights, and benefit everyone.

The origins of legislative power can be found in ancient democratic traditions, where groups of citizens would come together to make decisions and create laws. Over time this power has changed into modern groups that make laws, sometimes with two or one part, depending on the country's political system. These bodies are where people discuss politics, make agreements, and find a middle ground, which leads to making laws. The legislative branch does more than make laws. They help monitor the executive branch, ensuring it is accountable and not becoming too powerful (Power, 2011).

Legislative power helps democracy by allowing people to participate and have a say in making laws. This helps make the government more open, responsible and protects people's rights. The legislative branch is significant because it balances the power of the executive and judicial components. It helps prevent any misuse of power (Polborn, 2021).

Historical Background and Evolution

The past and changes in legislative power are essential to understand how democracy and the establishment of legislative bodies contribute to political systems. Understanding how legislative power has changed over time helps us see how important it is in shaping societies and ensuring that people are represented and participate in decision-making. Legislative power has existed since ancient times when groups gathered together to make decisions. In ancient Greece, the Athenian assembly was called the Ecclesia. It lets citizens take part in making choices directly. They could pass laws and policies by voting. In the Roman Republic, the Senate was a group that discussed and made decisions about laws. They also advised the people in charge. During the Enlightenment era, the idea of legislative power became more important. This was because thinkers like John Locke and Montesquieu discussed the importance of separating powers and creating institutions where people could be represented. The Magna Carta was an important document from 1215 that limited the monarchy's power and gave the people certain rights and privileges. This document set the foundation for future improvements in law-making authority (Power, 2011).

An essential thing that happened to help make legislative power stronger was the English Civil War in the 17th century. The disagreement between the king and Parliament, led by Oliver Cromwell, caused the king to be killed and a temporary government called the Commonwealth of England to be made. This period showed that groups of lawmakers could challenge and remove the power of monarchs, which led to more fair systems of government.

In the late 1700s, when the United States of America was created and its Constitution was written, it was a critical moment for how laws were made. The people who created the U. S.A.S.A. Constitution followed the idea of dividing power by creating different branches of government: the Congress, which makes laws; the executive branch, which enforces laws; and the judicial branch, which interprets laws. The U.S. has a bicameral structure, meaning there are two government houses. Congress, which is comprised of the House of Representatives and the Senate, wanted to ensure that the people and the states were represented fairly. They wanted to make sure that no one group had too much power.

During the 1800s and 1900s, laws continued to change, allowing more people to vote, political groups became more robust, and legislative groups became fairer and more inclusive. Many countries changed from having a king or queen to having a government with rules made by elected representatives. In this type of government, the primary way laws are made, and the country is run is through groups of people called legislatures (Polborn, 2021).

Today, the power to make laws is essential in democracies worldwide. Law-making groups come in different types, like ones with one group or two groups. Elected representatives are significant in making and passing laws. The history and changes of legislative power show how people have always wanted democratic government, understanding that citizens should have a say, and always trying to keep up with changes in society and politics. By learning about the history and changes in how laws are made, we can better understand how important they are in governing today. It helps us understand and acknowledge the advancements in promoting democratic beliefs. It emphasizes the importance of ensuring legislative bodies work well as crucial tools for community involvement and responsibility (Power, 2011).

Structure of the Legislative Branch

The legislative branch is an essential part of democracy. It is responsible for making, discussing, and passing laws. The leading organization represents and works on the people's behalf, ensuring their needs are addressed through creating and enforcing regulations. It is essential to learn how the legislative branch works to understand how democratic systems function and how decisions are made in government. The legislative branch usually consists of elected people who work together to make laws. How this branch is organized differs in each country, influenced by factors like history, culture, and regulations. When creating the legislative branch, it is essential to make sure that all groups of people have enough representation and that no one group has too much power (Power, 2011).

In many countries, the lawmaking part works by having two separate levels of legislation or houses. This system tries to have a fair process and give equal power to different groups. For example, in the United States, Congress has two parts. One part is called the House of Representatives, where the number of members is based on how many people live in each state. The other part is called the Senate, where every state has the same number of representatives.

On the other hand, some countries have a unicameral system with only one group of lawmakers. This system is commonly used in small countries, as they do not need or cannot have two separate groups to make laws. A unicameral legislature can have benefits like making decisions faster and being more efficient (Polborn, 2021).

The legislative branch has different groups called committees and subcommittees that are important in making laws. These committees are groups that focus on specific topics. They do research, propose rules, and work in their particular areas. They give a place for detailed examination, professional viewpoints, and input from the public, which improves the process of creating laws. In addition, parliamentary systems usually have a government and opposition set up. The majority party or coalition forms the government, while the opposition includes the smaller parties. This structure allows people to share ideas, have discussions, and examine what the government is doing, which helps keep the government accountable in a democratic way.

It is essential to understand how the legislative branch is set up to know how laws are made, how people are represented, and how the government works in a democratic system. By studying different aspects like the structure of lawmaking and the government's role, we can understand how laws are created, accountability is maintained, and people's opinions are considered.

The Bicameral System Versus Unicameral System

The bicameral and unicameral systems are two different ways of organizing the legislative branch in democratic systems. The bicameral system is when two chambers, called the upper house and the lower house, work separately. The upper house is responsible for representing regional or state interests. It acts as a way to balance and oversee the lower house, making sure that different areas are fairly represented. The people elect the lower house and represent them based on proportional representation. The bicameral system has some benefits. One benefit is that it helps balance power between the two places. Another advantage is that it allows for different interests to be represented by having members from other regions or states. Finally, it allows for in-depth discussions and input from members of both houses who know specific areas (Power, 2011).

The unicameral system is different because it only has one group in the government that makes the laws. This system is commonly seen in smaller countries or those with a single central government structure. Unicameral systems are simpler and more efficient because only one group of lawmakers is involved in making laws. They usually use proportional representation, meaning the population has a direct say in the picture. Unicameral systems are seen as less expensive and more adaptable, quickly adapting to changes in politics and society (Polborn, 2021).

The decision to have either a bicameral or unicameral system depends on different things, like how many people and areas there are, what they want, what has happened in the past, and how stable things are politically. While having two chambers, the bicameral system provides safeguards to prevent too much power in one place, giving a more comprehensive range of voices a say in the decision-making process and allowing for thorough discussions. On the other hand, the unicameral system offers a more straightforward representation of the people's interests, saves money by having only one chamber, and is more adaptable to change. In the end, the choice of which system to use should be customized to fit the specific needs and goals of the country. This will guarantee that representation is effective, there is accountability in the democratic process, and that the legislative branch operates efficiently (Power, 2011).

Composition and Organization of The Legislative Body

How the legislative body is organized is significant because it affects how the legislative branch works in a democratic system. The composition means the people who are part of the legislative body, while the organization refers to how it is structured and operates. The people vote in elections to choose their representatives in the legislative body. The number of representatives can change depending on how many people live in an area and how voting districts are set up. Political parties are essential because representatives usually belong to parties, and the number of seats they have in the government reflects the results of elections. Sometimes, specific seats are set aside for certain groups or communities to ensure they are included and represented in the legislative branch. This helps ensure everyone has a say and feels like they belong.

How the legislative body is organized includes choosing leaders like a speaker or President. These leaders run the sessions and speak on behalf of the legislative branch. These committees make legislative work better by having people who are experts in certain areas, doing research and listening to what the public has to say. In simple words, rules and procedures are made to control discussions, voting, and the process of making laws to ensure everything is fair and organized. Parliamentary support staff, like clerks and researchers, help lawmakers by providing specialized knowledge, research help, and administrative support (Power, 2011).

How the legislative body is put together and managed is critical to ensure that people are well-represented, decisions are made moderately, and the legislative branch works well. By showcasing the different types of people in society, making sure everyone feels welcome, and having clear rules, the group in charge of making laws can accurately represent what the people want, have thoughtful discussions, and create laws that match what the people need and want. A well-organized group of lawmakers helps make democracy work better and makes citizens feel more confident in their government representatives (Polborn, 2021).

Functions of the Legislative Branch

The part of the government that makes laws and watches over the other part of the government is essential in a democracy. They decide what should happen, make laws, and ensure the government does its job correctly. This part of the government speaks for the people and ensures their interests are considered and held responsible. The legislative branch has many jobs, including making laws, representing people, providing things are being done correctly, and controlling how money is spent. To understand how the legislative branch affects a country's governance, it is essential to understand these functions (Power, 2011).

Lawmaking Process and the Role of Legislators

Lawmaking is an essential task of the legislative branch. It's when lawmakers help create and pass laws that control and guide the country. The most important part of this process is when lawmakers come up with ideas for new rules, write them down, and suggest them to other lawmakers. These laws can help with problems or things that society needs. These bills form the basis for making laws.

After a bill is proposed, it goes through a careful examination by committees. These groups, made up of lawmakers who know a lot about specific topics, carefully check the bill, studying what it says, what it could mean, and how it might affect things. They do thorough research, have meetings, and gather information from experts, people involved, and the public. These hearings allow lawmakers to listen to opinions, understand the bill's strengths, and make knowledgeable choices.

While making laws, legislators are critical in deciding what goes into the bill. They suggest changes, have discussions, and work with other lawmakers to make the rules better. These discussions let us consider different opinions, include many interests, and find agreements or compromises. After carefully reviewing and discussing the bill, it is voted on. Lawmakers vote to show whether they are in favor or against a suggested law. If most people vote in favor of the bill, it will pass in the legislative body (Power, 2011).

Legislators have responsibilities that go beyond making laws. They are like messengers for the people, speaking up and fighting for what they want and need. They talk to the public, listen to what they want, and use their ideas to make new laws. Lawmakers also act as messengers between the government and the general population. They inform people about government decisions and activities and give reasons or clarifications when needed. In simple terms, the lawmaking process and the job of legislators are essential for how the legislative branch works. Legislators are crucial in ensuring laws are changed when society needs them, helping the community, and representing what the people want (Polborn, 2021).

Representation of the People's Interests

A critical job of the legislative branch is to represent the people's interests. Lawmakers speak up for the people they represent, ensuring that their worries, wants, and dreams are understood and considered when making laws. The people choose legislators to express their viewpoints and interests by voting or being selected for the job. They communicate with the people they represent by listening to their worries and talking to them regularly to understand the problems that affect them. This direct connection helps lawmakers understand the challenges faced by people personally and use their input when making decisions.

Lawmakers work to help the particular needs and desires of the people they represent by proposing and supporting new laws. They create rules to deal with problems in their area and help people who support them on issues that matter to those who elected them. By actively making laws, lawmakers ensure they listen to and think about what people want and need. Aside from making laws, legislators also participate in activities like going to community events, town hall meetings, and public hearings to connect with the public. These interactions allow citizens to speak their opinions, share their stories, and make sure lawmakers are responsible for what they do. These methods will enable the public to easily reach lawmakers, which helps to build trust and encourage an open and fair democratic system (Power, 2011).

Legislators are essential because they represent the people and help connect the government with the citizens. They bring together the people and the government by representing the people's concerns, needs, and dreams to the government and communicating the government's plans and actions to the people. This way of describing ensures that the government listens to and fulfils what the voters want and expect. The legislative branch is essential because it means what the people want. It helps democracy by getting more people involved and accountable. Legislators help make rules and decisions that the people want and benefit society (Polborn, 2021).

Oversight and Checks on the Executive Branch

The legislative branch has the essential job of watching and controlling the executive branch of government. This function helps ensure the government is responsible, honest, and working correctly. Legislators keep an eye on and check the things the executive branch does. They can ask questions, look into things, and have meetings to review how well laws and government programs are being done. Legislators ensure that government officials follow the law, respect the Constitution, and do what they should for the people they serve.

They can ask for papers, call government workers to speak in court, and ask for reasons for what the leaders do. This oversight function helps ensure that the executive branch does everything within its power and breaks the rules of having separate branches of government. In addition, lawmakers can say yes, or no to people the government selects to hold important positions, like those in charge of specific departments, agencies, or the court system. This power to confirm allows lawmakers to check if the people chosen by the government to fill essential jobs are qualified, skilled, and trustworthy enough to work in the public's best interest (Power, 2011).

Legislators can review and change the government's budget and spending plans as part of their oversight. They carefully examine how public money is spent and ensure it is done openly and responsibly, with taxpayers' best interests in mind. This mistake stops people from using or managing public resources incorrectly and provides the executive branch is responsible for their financial choices.

The job of the legislative branch is essential because it helps make sure that no one group or person has too much power. It also keeps things fair and follows democratic rules. Legislators observe the executive branch to ensure that the government follows the rules, respects people's rights, and stays responsible to the public. This function protects against possible misuse of power, strengthens the system of checks and balances, and helps the government work well for the people (Polborn, 2021).

Budgetary Powers and Appropriations

The legislative branch has important control over how money is spent in the government. They help decide how public funds are used and ensure the government spends appropriately. This function ensures that the government spends money wisely and keeps track of how it is used. It also provides that money is being put towards essential things for the country. The main job of the legislative branch regarding money is to make and approve the government's budget. Lawmakers have the power to look at, change, and agree to the budget plan provided by the government's top officials. This process includes closely looking at how much money the government thinks it will make, how it plans to spend it, and how it decides where to put the resources for different things the government does (Power, 2011).

Lawmakers thoroughly examine the budget plan to make sure it aligns with the needs and desires of the people they represent. They evaluate how well and fast proposed spending will work, considering the possible advantages and disadvantages for society. In this process, lawmakers can move money around, decide how much to spend on certain things, and give special attention to critical areas like schooling, healthcare, roads, and protection. Additionally, the branch of the government that makes laws has the authority to monitor and manage how the government uses its money by using the appropriations process. Lawmakers examine and agree to give money to certain parts of the government, like agencies, programs, and projects. They evaluate how well these organizations are doing and the results they achieve, making sure that public funds are used wisely and with good results (Polborn, 2021).

By controlling the money, the part of the government that makes laws helps ensure public money is used responsibly and with transparency. Lawmakers are allowed to ask for money reports, investigate money matters, and ask for explanations for decisions about how money is spent made by the government. This role helps to stop bad management, corruption, or careless spending and ensures that public money is used for the benefit of the people.

Lawmakers can create and back laws that involve money by using their authority to control budgets and allocate funds. They can suggest ways to make money, like changing taxes or creating new ways to bring money and decide where to use it, like for social programs, building things, or helping the economy. In simple terms, the legislative branch plays a vital role in managing money wisely, ensuring that resources are used to benefit society, and holding the government responsible for how it spends money. By doing this function, lawmakers help decide how to use public money, improve people's well-being, and ensure that the nation's finances are handled responsibly and honestly.

Limitations on Legislative Power

Restrictions on laws ensure that no one branch of government has too much power to stop people from misusing their power and keep democracy and fairness in place. Although the legislative branch has a lot of energy, it also has some restrictions (Power, 2011).

- Constitutional Constraints: The power of making laws is restricted by the rules and limitations stated in a country's Constitution. The authorities in the body say what the government can do, give people fundamental rights and freedoms, and explain how power is divided between different parts of the government. Lawmakers have to work within the rules set by the Constitution. They should protect people's rights and follow the principles outlined in the Constitution (Polborn, 2021).
- Judicial review means that the court has the power to review laws made by the government and decide if they are fair and follow the rules. This helps keep the government in check and ensures they are not abusing their power. Courts can understand and explain the Constitution and decide if laws made by the government are allowed or not. If a rule is considered against the rules of the country's body, the court system can cancel it or say it is invalid. This process makes sure that laws follow the important rules and rights in the constitution.
- In many democratic systems, the leader of the government, like the president or prime minister, can say "no" to new laws made by the lawmakers. This veto can be completed or to be changed if most of the legislators agree. Like the president, the executive can veto laws they disagree with. This stops the rules from being passed if they go against the government's goals or plans.
- Legislatures must follow and abide by international agreements and treaties that their country has agreed to and signed. These responsibilities might restrict the ability of the lawmaking branch to make laws that go against or break these international promises. Lawmakers need to ensure that their country's laws follow the rules and guidelines set by other countries. This helps maintain harmony and consistency with international standards and norms.
- Public Opinion and Accountability: Lawmakers are responsible and answerable to the people they represent. Public opinion and feedback can limit lawmakers' power because they listen to the views and preferences of the people they represent. They need to think about what the public wants and worries about and find a way to make both the public and themselves happy.
- Institutional Constraints: The power of making laws can be

limited by the rules, procedures, and structures within the part of the government that makes laws. These limitations are implemented to ensure fairness, ensure things run smoothly, and help make good decisions. For instance, lawmaking groups often have guidelines for discussing topics, taking votes, and creating small groups. These inside systems help ensure that the process of making laws is fair and transparent, even though it can be complicated (Power, 2011).

It is essential to understand these limits on lawmakers' power to keep democratic systems honest and fair. These limitations help prevent potential misuse of power, ensure fairness in the legal system, safeguard people's rights, and ensure that no branch of government becomes too powerful. Legislators must understand and accept their limitations to responsibly use their power and uphold democratic principles in governing a nation (Polborn, 2021).

6.3. EXECUTIVE POWER

Executive power is an essential part of any government, and it includes the authority and responsibilities given to the leaders of the government. This means it is responsible for ensuring that laws are followed, putting policies into action, and doing the everyday tasks needed to keep the state running smoothly. To understand how democratic systems work and the executive branch's role in government, it is essential to know about executive power. This power is usually given to the leader of a country, like the president or prime minister. They use this power to run the government, make important decisions, and make sure that laws and policies are carried out effectively.

Historical development and modern-day manifestations

Executive power has changed over time, showing how governments have changed, and different political systems have developed. Throughout history, executive power has changed in different ways and influenced the executive branch's role and tasks in present-day governance. In the past, people in charge were usually kings or leaders with complete control. These autocratic systems gave all the power to one person, allowing them to make decisions independently and control the whole country. Some examples are ancient Egypt, where pharaohs had a lot of energy, and the Roman Empire, where emperors had a lot of authority (Polborn, 2021). The executive power grew as constitutional monarchies and representative institutions were created.

The Magna Carta, written in 1215, was an important document that restricted kings' ability and gave regular people certain rights. This change formed the basis for making rules about how the government works, where the leader's power was shared or controlled. The Enlightenment era strongly impacted how executive power grew and developed. Philosophers such as John Locke and Montesquieu believed in separating the powers of government. They argued for a separate executive branch responsible for following the laws. These ideas formed how we think about executive power today. They highlight the need for the executive to have limited capacity and to follow the rules (Power, 2011).

Today, the power of the leaders is shown in different ways, depending on how the government works. In countries like the United States, the president is elected by the people and has much power. They ensure laws are followed, choose government officials, and control the armed forces. The president's power is set by the constitution's rules and maintained by other parts of the government.

In countries with parliamentary systems, the person in charge of the government, like the prime minister, can make decisions. The group of lawmakers usually chooses them. The prime minister controls the government and has to answer to the legislature. The cabinet, comprised of a group of people, collectively exercises the power to make decisions. This system combines the capabilities of making laws and running the government. This makes decisions more quickly and ensures the government is answerable to the parliament.

Executive power is also shown through administrative agencies and bureaucracies that carry out organizational tasks and implement policies. These groups are controlled and overseen by the part of the government that carries out the laws and rules, making sure they are put into action. The power of the person in charge has changed over time to include restrictions and limitations set by the Constitution and ways to prevent too much power. But people are still discussing and facing difficulties about how much power the person in charge should have. Finding the right balance between effective governing and democratic accountability is always important. Ways to achieve this include judicial review, legislative oversight, and public scrutiny, which help prevent potential abuses of power (Polborn, 2021).

Understanding how executive power has changed over time and how it is used today gives us a better understanding of how governments work and the importance of leadership that is both strong and respects democratic values.

Looking at the past and present, we can better understand the complicated and detailed aspects of executive power in today's society (Power, 2011).

Structure of the Executive Branch

How the executive branch is set up differs in different countries and political systems. However, it usually includes a few essential parts. The top leader of the executive branch is the head of state and head of government. They have the most power and act as the representative of the country. Like a president or king, this person has the authority and job of making important decisions and taking action. Helping the leader of a country is a group of essential people called the cabinet or council of ministers. The leader chooses these people, gives advice, and helps make decisions in their areas of knowledge.

Government departments and agencies are essential parts of the government that focus on specific areas like money, protection, health, and learning. These departments are led by ministers or officials who are responsible for implementing policies. The executive branch also depends on skilled employees and government workers to ensure government services run well. Furthermore, some separate organizations and groups work independently and without influence from politicians to supervise certain things like banking or rights for people. How the executive branch is set up helps make governing, carrying out policies, and using executive powers easier in a political system. The goal is good leadership, knowledge, and the ability to manage things effectively (Power, 2011).

Functions of the Executive Branch

The executive branch of government is significant. It does many important things to ensure the country is run well and policies are implemented (Figure 6.3). These functions do many different things, including police work, making laws, working with other countries, and managing money. The main job of the executive branch is to make sure laws are followed and carried out. Its position is to ensure that people and organizations correctly follow the rules made by the lawmaking branch. This function ensures that laws are followed and people stay safe and secure. It is essential for keeping public order, protecting people's rights, and maintaining safety within the country (Polborn, 2021).

Policy making and carrying out policies are essential tasks of the government's executive branch. The government's executive branch creates and puts into action plans to solve societal problems, keep campaign promises, and meet the needs and desires of the people. This means evaluating the effect and possibility of suggested rules, doing research, talking to experts and people interested in the issue, and supervising the actual putting of these rules into practice throughout different parts of the government. The executive branch also represents our country to the world and talks and works with other countries. The leader of a country works with other countries to make deals, agreements, and treaties that protect their country's interests, encourage working together globally, and achieve their foreign policy goals. They are helped by diplomats and officials who handle foreign affairs. The executive branch also works with other countries and international groups to solve problems that affect the whole world. They speak on behalf of our country and work together with other countries to find solutions (Polborn, 2021).

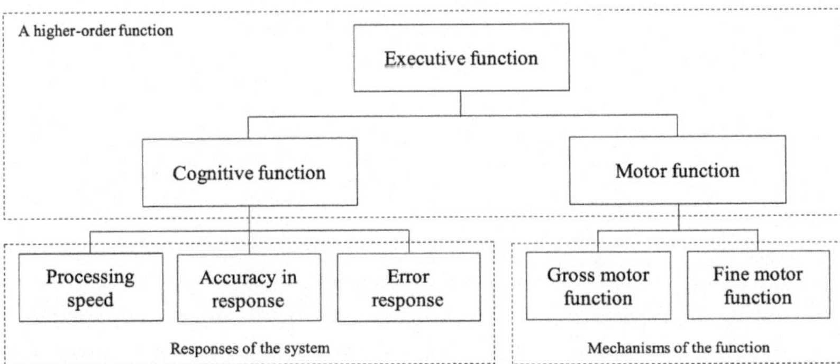

Figure 6.3. Flow diagram defining an overview of executive function.

Source: Chuangchai, Warawoot & Chanbenjapipu, Phumdecha & Thepmalee, Chutamas & Wongruck, Apiruck. (2023). A Review Article: Fall Incidents and Interior Architecture—Influence of Executive Function in Normal Ageing. Scientific Figure on ResearchGate. Available from: https://www.researchgate.net/figure/Flow-diagram-defining-an-overview-of-executive-function-in-the-article-Note-Adapted_fig1_355174449 (accessed on 22 September 2023)

In addition, the executive branch is in charge of handling the economy and making money decisions. This means creating plans for money, giving resources to different things, and looking over economic activities to make things better, steady, and successful. The executive branch of the government works with economic advisors, financial institutions, and relevant government departments to develop plans, control industries, and implement policies that help the economy grow and deal with economic problems (Power, 2011).

Moreover, the part of the government that handles decision-making has an essential job in handling crises and responding to emergencies. When nature causes significant problems, the government gathers tools and plans to help and keeps everyone safe. It works together with essential agencies, police, and emergency services to reduce risks, give help, and bring back normalcy.

The executive branch is in charge of choosing and supervising government officials and agencies. This means selecting people for essential government positions like the ones in the cabinet, the judges, the ambassadors, and other important officials. It also means watching how well they do their job and ensuring they are responsible for their actions. The executive branch can create administrative bodies or agencies to ensure specific policies are carried out and regulate certain activities.

The executive branch does many important things to ensure the government runs smoothly. The executive branch has important jobs like making laws and policies, representing the country abroad, managing money, handling crises, and overseeing government operations. They are responsible for taking care of the country and its people (Polborn, 2021).

Limitations on Executive Power

Restrictions on the power of leaders are essential to stop them from misusing their authority, safeguard people's rights, and keep a fair system of control in a democratic society. These limitations make sure that the executive branch follows specific rules and is responsible for what it does. There are many ways to control and balance the power of top leaders (Power, 2011).

Constitutional constraints are essential rules that limit the power of the leader. The laws in the Constitution explain what the president can and can't do, protect people's rights, and create a way to govern. These rules involve dividing power, ensuring fairness, and protecting fundamental rights and freedoms. The executive branch has to follow these constitutional rules and cannot go beyond its assigned capabilities. The idea of judicial review helps to restrict how much power the executive branch has. The judiciary can explain what the Constitution means and decide if the actions and policies of the government are legal and follow the Constitution. Courts have the power to stop efforts by the government that go against the Constitution or beyond what the law allows. This system ensures that the government follows the law and treats people fairly. Legislative oversight is a crucial way to keep the executive branch in check. The part of the government that makes laws uses committees, hearings, and investigations to keep an eye on what the part of the government that enforces laws does. Legislators cancan look over and assess the decisions made by the executive branch, create new rules, and put in place measures to limit and control the executive branch's authority. The legislative branch uses the money to control how the government spends it. This ensures the government is responsible for its actions and affects what the executive branch does (Power, 2011).

Public opinion and accountability serve as additional checks on the executive branch's power. The executive branch works in a democracy and is responsible to the people. Being watched and criticized by the public, media, and civil society is a way to ensure that government officials' actions are fair and responsible. Elections allow people to vote and pick the people representing them and leading their country. They also enable the public to show if they are happy or unhappy with how the leaders do their job (Polborn, 2021).

Independent institutions, like ombudsperson offices, human rights commissions, and anti-corruption bodies, also help to restrict the power of the government. These institutions protect people's rights by looking into complaints, ensuring things are fair and transparent, and ensuring the people in charge are responsible for what they do. Restrictions on the leader's power are essential for keeping the law, safeguarding people's rights, and avoiding too much power in one part of the government. They make sure that the part of the government that runs things follows the rules, treats everyone fairly, and is responsible to the people it serves (Power, 2011).

6.4. RELATIONSHIP BETWEEN LEGISLATIVE AND EXECUTIVE POWER

The connection between the law-making and decision-making parts of the government involves working together to ensure they're all doing their job correctly. The law-making part of the government creates laws, and the amount that puts them into action is called the executive branch. They ensure people are responsible, that the government works well, and doesn't have too much power (Polborn, 2021).

CHAPTER 7

Changes in the Structure of State Protection

Contents

7.1. INTRODUCTION

Legal procedures for political ends are a long-standing feature of the state's relationship with society. The law has been used to create and enforce social norms, regulate behavior and ensure that people adhere to specific standards. In many ways, this is an essential function of government to provide structure and stability to society. The way that it is done is by using the courts to help redistribute wealth. This can be done through lawsuits against corporations who have abused their power or by suing governments that are not doing enough to protect the public. This is done by using the legal system to intimidate companies into changing their behavior or by suing governments for not protecting people from harm caused by corporate actions (Hockings, 2014).

In the past, the state was responsible for ensuring social justice and treating all citizens fairly (Figure 7.1). However, as countries became industrialized and began to use legal procedures to gain an advantage over other countries, this changed. The state began to focus more on protecting business interests than on protecting its citizens or their rights. This has made it easier for corporations to gain access to government officials through bribery or other means. It also makes it possible for people who do not want to be part of society or wish to harm others by denying them access to resources or opportunities on a large scale, such as by creating pollution or restricting access to education, health care or water supplies (Taylor, 2011).

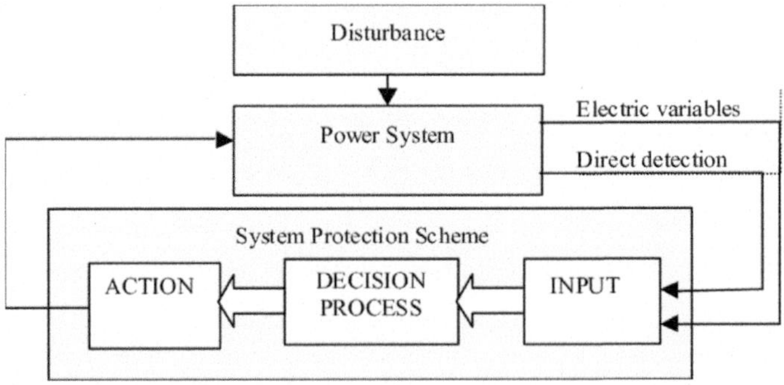

Figure 7.1. General structure of a system protection scheme.

Source: Mccalley, James & Olatujoye, Oluwaseyi & Krishnan, Venkat & Dai, Renchang & Singh, Chanan & Jiang, Kai. (2010). System Protection Schemes: Limitations, Risks, and Management. Scientific Figure on ResearchGate. Available from: https://www.researchgate.net/figure/General-structure-of-a-system-protection-scheme-According-to-their-control-variables-SPS_fig2_277330229 (accessed on 22 September 2023)

The structure of state protection is changing due to the growing influence of NGOs and academic researchers on legal systems. In particular, there has been a trend towards more rights-oriented legislation and legislation based on international human rights standards (Figure 7.2). In particular, new legislation has been introduced to protect the rights of Indigenous peoples (such as the Indigenous Peoples Act), child victims of violence (such as the Child Sexual Abuse Act), and people with disabilities. New laws also protect freedom of information and freedom of speech rights. For example, new regulations require public disclosure of political donations (Hockings, 2014).

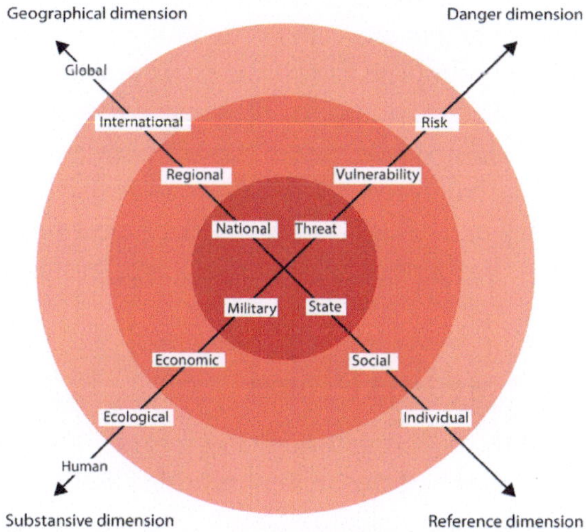

Figure 7.2. The extension of the concept of security.

Source: Hirsch Ballin, E., Dijstelbloem, H., de Goede, P. (2020). The Extension of the Concept of Security. In: Hirsch Ballin, E., Dijstelbloem, H., de Goede, P. (eds) Security in an Interconnected World. Research for Policy. Springer, Cham. https://doi.org/10.1007/978–3–030–37606–2_2

In periods of rapid political change, the state must often evolve quickly in order to avoid being overtaken by its adversaries. In this case, the state will be forced to use legal procedure for political ends. Political leaders will use legal procedure as a means of usurping power from their opponents. This can be done through a number of ways, by making laws that are impossible for any one party to overturn (such as creating an impenetrable bureaucracy), or by making laws that change so frequently that no party has time to react properly (such as changing laws every few years) (Taylor, 2011).

7.2. HISTORICAL EVOLUTION OF STATE PROTECTION MECHANISMS

State protection mechanisms have evolved significantly, shaped by changing political landscapes, technological advancements, and societal needs. The legal procedure for political ends is a controversial practice that governments have historically used to protect the ruling class's interests. This can lead to an erosion of democratic principles and civil liberties. The first use of legal procedure for political ends was during the French Revolution in 1789, when King Louis XVI tried to protect his interests by calling out the National Guard against rioters who were angry about high taxes. The king's actions sparked a series of events that led to his execution in 1793. In 1848, after the failure of Europe's revolutions, European governments began using legal procedures for political ends again. In response to an uprising by peasants in Germany, Austria-Hungary declared war on Serbia after Serbian troops fired against the Austrian forces; this declaration led to World War I. In 1917, during World War I, Russia used legal procedure for political ends when it suspended civil liberties to prevent antiwar protests from occurring (Hockings, 2014).

7.2.1. Ancient and Medieval Times

The establishment of Rome's Praetorian Guard is recognized as a significant turning point in the history of the ancient world. The Praetorian Guard was initially established by Augustus in the year 27 BCE to serve as the emperor's personal bodyguards. However, they evolved into influential political actors and were frequently involved in assassinations and political intrigues over time. During the time of feudalism in Europe, castle fortifications and feudal armies were developed to provide security for the ruling nobility and the lands they controlled. During this period, knights were an essential component of the feudal system, serving as personal guards for feudal lords and active participants in military operations (Taylor, 2011).

7.2.2. Enlightenment and the Birth of Modern State Protection

The period known as the Enlightenment saw a change in how states protected their citizens. As a result of the development of nation-states and the concept of the social contract theory, the responsibility of safeguarding the rights of citizens became an essential component of political administration. Consequently, more formalized structures for the protection of the state were established.

The French Revolution and the subsequent era of Napoleonic rule significantly influenced the growth of governmental safeguards. Maximilien Robespierre was chosen to head the Committee of Public Safety established in revolutionary France to consolidate power and suppress opposition. Nevertheless, the committee's actions, such as the Reign of Terror, demonstrated the perils of excessive state power and the necessity of having checks and balances in place (Hockings, 2014).

7.2.3 19th and 20th Century Developments

Industrialization, mass mobilization, and the rise of ideological conflicts all drove significant shifts in state protection mechanisms throughout the 19th and 20th centuries. These shifts occurred primarily in the United States. Establishing contemporary police forces, intelligence agencies, and military structures became necessary to preserve social order, defend national interests, and eliminate internal and external dangers. A significant turning point in the development of modern policing was the founding of the London Metropolitan Police Force in 1829, which Sir Robert Peel led. This event took place in London. Peel's theories on policing, which included the concept that officers should view themselves as public servants, are credited with laying the foundation for modern, professional police forces worldwide (Taylor, 2011).

The late 19th century also saw the rise of intelligence agencies like the British Secret Service Bureau (later MI6) and the French intelligence agency, the Deuxième Bureau. Both of these agencies were founded in the late 19th century. These agencies were primarily concerned with information gathering, counterintelligence, and the upkeep of state security. The two World Wars and the time period of the Cold War brought about additional shifts in state protection mechanisms. The activities of the intelligence agencies were expanded, and they played pivotal roles in espionage, sabotage, and deciphering enemy codes. The Central Intelligence Agency (CIA) in the United States and the KGB in the Soviet Union were established as examples of the growing significance of covert operations and intelligence gathering.

7.2.4. Technological Advancements and Contemporary State Protection

Rapid technological advancements that revolutionized state protection mechanisms occurred in the latter half of the 20th century and at the beginning of the 21st century. States were able to improve their monitoring capabilities and gather intelligence more efficiently due to the development of advanced surveillance systems, satellite technology, and computer network technology. The attacks on September 11, 2001, which terrorists carried out, marked a turning point in state protection and prompted a global focus on counter-terrorism efforts. To combat the changing nature of the threat landscape, governments worldwide have implemented increased security measures. These measures include tighter border controls, increased surveillance, and intelligence sharing.

The modern state's mechanisms for providing protection are becoming increasingly intricate and interconnected. State agencies can now analyze vast amounts of information, recognize patterns, and react more quickly to potential threats due to the use of artificial intelligence, facial recognition technology, and big data analytics (Taylor, 2011).

7.2.5. Challenges and Debates on the Historical Change of State Protection

The development of state protection mechanisms throughout history has not been without its share of challenges and heated debates. Finding a happy medium between the need for safety and protecting civil liberties and individual rights continues to be a concern. The use of legal processes for political ends, such as surveillance and monitoring of political dissidents, has raised questions about the erosion of privacy and potential abuses of power. These issues have been brought to light due to the use of legal procedures. These concerns have been brought to the forefront due to the revelations made by Edward Snowden in 2013 regarding the mass surveillance programs carried out by intelligence agencies. The discussion on successfully balancing security and privacy is ongoing, and recent developments have highlighted the significance of transparency, oversight, and accountability (Hockings, 2014).

7.3. TECHNOLOGICAL ADVANCEMENTS REVOLUTIONIZING STATE PROTECTION

Technological advancements have revolutionized state protection agencies, shaping their structure, capabilities, and operational strategies. These advancements help us gain insights into how technology has transformed the landscape of state security and the challenges it presents.

Surveillance Systems

Surveillance systems have developed into powerful tools that state protection agencies are utilizing. These tools enable comprehensive monitoring and the identification of potential threats. The capacity to recognize and keep tabs on individuals of interest has been significantly bolstered by the introduction of closed-circuit television (CCTV) cameras, advanced facial recognition technology, and other surveillance tools (Taylor, 2011).

The efficiency with which criminal investigations are carried out is one of the significant effects. The identification of suspects, the provision of evidence, and the facilitation of the arrest and prosecution of criminals are all significantly aided by using surveillance footage. A further benefit of real-time surveillance is that it enables law enforcement agencies to react promptly to developing incidents, which in turn helps to improve public safety.

Concerns have been raised, however, regarding potential violations of privacy rights and abuses of power brought on by the proliferation of surveillance systems. The extensive collection and storage of personally identifiable information raises concerns about the appropriate balance between individual privacy and national security. Maintaining a healthy equilibrium through implementing robust legal frameworks and effective monitoring systems is an ongoing challenge.

Artificial Intelligence

Implementing artificial intelligence (AI) has completely transformed the analytical capabilities of state protection agencies and the decision-making procedures they use. Algorithms powered by artificial intelligence cancan quickly analyze vast amounts of data and recognize patterns, enabling more effective threat assessment and intelligence gathering.

The application of AI in predictive policing is one of the most significant effects. The machine learning algorithms aim to analyze historical crime data to identify high-risk areas and patterns. This assists in effectively allocating resources and preventing criminal activities. Systems that AI powers can also explore online communication and social media platforms to identify potential threats, which is helpful for anti-terrorism efforts (Hockings, 2014).

Artificial intelligence (AI) has the potential to offer significant benefits; however, ethical concerns and biases must be addressed. The reliability of algorithms is only as good as the data they are trained on. If that data is biased or incomplete, the results of the algorithm's application could be discriminatory. It is essential to maintain public trust and fairness, ensure that AI systems are transparent and accountable, and address any inherent biases (Taylor, 2011).

Cybersecurity Measures

The level of sophistication of cyberattacks is growing in line with the advancement of technology (Figure 7.3). To protect vital infrastructure, sensitive information, and national security interests, state protection agencies have been forced to adapt and develop robust cybersecurity measures. Various strategies, such as network monitoring, encryption, intrusion detection systems, and incident response plans, are incorporated into the various cybersecurity measures taken. These precautions are designed to forestall cyberattacks, identify potential dangers, neutralize them, protect the integrity of classified information, and maintain its secrecy.

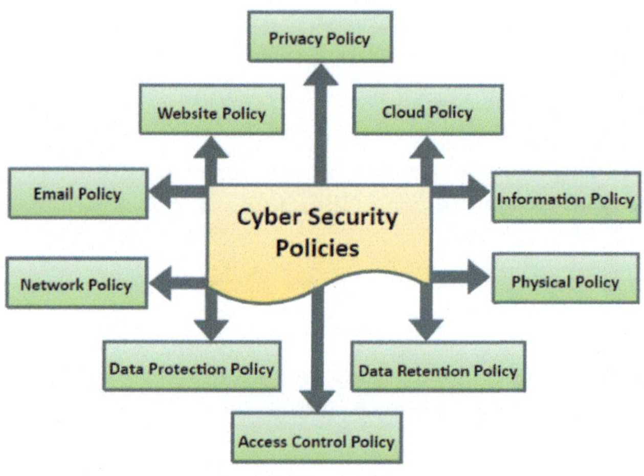

Figure 7.3. Cybersecurity policies.

Source: Mishra, A., Alzoubi, Y. I., Gill, A. Q., & Anwar, M. J. (2022). Cybersecurity Enterprises Policies: A Comparative Study. Sensors, 22(2), 538. MDPI AG. Retrieved from http://dx.doi.org/10.3390/s22020538

The effects of cyber-attacks are far-reaching and affect private businesses, public institutions, and individuals. The disruption of essential services, the compromise of national security, and invading individual privacy are potential outcomes of cyberattacks. To stay one step ahead of ever-evolving dangers and keep their resilience in the digital domain, state protection agencies need to upgrade their cybersecurity measures continuously (Taylor, 2011).

7.3.1. Interconnected Challenges

Technological advances' effect on state protection agencies is highly interconnected and multifaceted. Surveillance systems, artificial intelligence, and various cybersecurity measures frequently overlap and complement one another, creating an all-encompassing security ecosystem. For instance, artificial intelligence (AI)-powered surveillance systems can improve law enforcement agencies' efficiency by automating the process of analyzing surveillance footage and locating potential dangers. Concurrently, these systems are protected from cyber threats that aim to compromise the integrity of the data and disrupt operations by using stringent cybersecurity measures. However, these technological advances also bring about new problems. Because of our dependence on technology, we are more susceptible to cyber-attacks, which requires us to make ongoing efforts to improve our defences. In addition, the application of AI in surveillance raises concerns regarding invasive management, the possibility of bias, and the erosion of privacy rights. To effectively address these challenges, the appropriate regulatory, oversight, and accountability mechanisms must be put in place (Hockings, 2014).

7.3.2. International Implications

Because attacks and threats are not limited by national boundaries, technological advances in state protection have implications beyond the borders of individual nations. Cooperation between different government agencies and information sharing has become increasingly important in the fight against transnational threats such as terrorism, organized crime, and cyber warfare. The Five Eyes Alliance and Interpol are two examples of international agreements and alliances that make it easier for state protection agencies worldwide to work together. Sharing intelligence, identifying transnational criminal activity, and coordinating effective responses are more accessible with advanced surveillance systems, artificial intelligence capabilities, and cybersecurity precautions (Taylor, 2011).

Nevertheless, international cooperation also raises concerns regarding the appropriate balance between protecting national security interests while respecting other nations' sovereignty and the right of their citizens to personal privacy. In today's rapid technological advancement, achieving a healthy equilibrium by cultivating mutual trust, maintaining transparency, and adhering to international standards is still tricky.

7.4. LEGAL FRAMEWORKS GOVERNING STATE PROTECTION

Legal frameworks play a crucial role in regulating state protection activities, balancing safeguarding national security and protecting individual rights. Constitutional principles, international human rights norms, and domestic laws all served as the basis for developing the legal frameworks currently in place to govern state protection. The right to life, liberty, and security is frequently enshrined in a constitution, and international instruments like the Universal Declaration of Human Rights and regional conventions provide a framework for protecting individual rights. A significant turning point in the evolution of legal frameworks was the period immediately following World War II when nations worked to eliminate the possibility of future violations of human rights. The Nuremberg Trials and other subsequent international tribunals are responsible for establishing the principle of individual criminal responsibility. These trials also highlighted the importance of legal constraints on the state's power (Taylor, 2011).

As state protection agencies are entrusted with the responsibility of maintaining security while upholding the rule of law, their main challenge lies in striking a balance between the imperatives of national security and the rights of individuals. Checks and balances are built into legal frameworks to prevent power abuses and ensure accountable decisions are made. One of the most critical aspects of this equilibrium is the restriction of state powers through legal procedures, such as the mandated use of warrants, the right to due process, and the supervision of the judiciary. These safeguards aim to prevent the arbitrary exercise of power, protect individuals' rights to privacy, and preserve the presumption of innocence (Hockings, 2014).

7.4.1. Changes in Legal Frameworks

Legal frameworks that govern state protection have undergone significant changes over history to accommodate shifting security threats, moving societal values, and technological advances. The expansion of surveillance powers, the introduction of counterterrorism legislation, and the challenges posed by emerging digital environments are all notable changes that have taken place recently. Opportunities and difficulties have been brought about due to the growth of modern surveillance technologies. To combat ever-evolving dangers like terrorism, organized crime, and cyberattacks, existing legal frameworks have been modified to confer expanded surveillance authority on state protection agencies.

Following the attacks of September 11, many nations passed anti-terrorism legislation that broadened the scope of surveillance, intelligence gathering, and data storage. On the other hand, these expansions have raised concerns about the possibility of excessive state intrusion and the eroding of privacy rights. Finding a happy medium between protecting citizens' civil liberties and keeping them safe is still one of the most contentious issues in developing legal frameworks.

The rise of terrorist acts across the globe has resulted in the passage of specialized anti-terrorism legislation in several different jurisdictions. These laws provide state protection agencies with the resources necessary to stop terrorist activities and bring those responsible to justice. On the other hand, legislation intended to combat terrorism has come under fire for the possibility that it will violate the rights of individuals. Concerns have been raised regarding the potential for abuse and the erosion of civil liberties due to the expansion of law enforcement powers, the use of preventive detention, and the broadening of the definition of what constitutes terrorism (Taylor, 2011).

The growth of digital environments, such as the Internet and platforms for social media, has presented legal frameworks with a set of entirely new challenges. The complexities of digital surveillance, cybercrime, and the protection of digital privacy must be navigated by state protection agencies. In response to these challenges, legislation has been enacted to address issues such as data protection, encryption, and cybercrime, which has led to the evolution of legal frameworks. On the other hand, the rapid pace of technological progress makes it challenging to guarantee that existing legal frameworks will continue to be efficient and flexible in the face of new challenges.

Essential court cases and rulings have significantly impacted the development of the legal frameworks that govern state protection. Matters of historical significance, such as the decisions made by the United States Supreme Court in the 1960s and 1970s regarding the Fourth Amendment and electronic surveillance, have impacted the delicate balance between the powers of the state and the rights of individuals. In recent years, the European Court of Human Rights has been instrumental in examining the surveillance practices of conditions. It has issued decisions highlighting the significance of proportionality, necessity, and oversight in protecting individual rights (Taylor, 2011).

To ensure that state protection agencies function within the bounds of the law, legal frameworks typically include provisions for oversight mechanisms and accountability. Independent oversight bodies, parliamentary committees, and judicial review are mechanisms that could fall under this category. On the other hand, the efficiency of the various oversight mechanisms varies significantly between jurisdictions. To hold state protection agencies accountable and keep the public's trust, it is essential to ensure that they have complete autonomy, complete transparency, and access to all of the information they require (Hockings, 2014).

7.5. ROLE OF INTELLIGENCE AGENCIES IN CHANGING THE STRUCTURE OF STATE PROTECTION

Intelligence agencies are responsible for providing information to the government and its leaders (Figure 7.4). They have been involved in changing the structure of state protection. This role is to gather information and give it to the state and serve as an agent of change. This is because they have a direct relationship with the people and can influence them by pointing out their strengths and weaknesses. State protection agencies can help the government protect its citizens by gathering information about threats against them. They can also help prevent these threats by providing information about possible ways to avoid them. They can also protect individuals vulnerable to attacks because of their age, gender or other factors. They employ various methods, such as human intelligence (HUMINT), signals intelligence (SIGINT), and open-source intelligence (OSINT), to collect, analyze, and disseminate critical information. HUMINT involves agents infiltrating target organizations or regions to gather classified information. SIGINT focuses on intercepting and decoding communications, including electronic signals and digital data. OSINT leverages publicly available information from media, social networks, and academic research (Taylor, 2011).

However, these agencies sometimes have enough resources or workforce to accomplish all their tasks fully. In addition, they often need more knowledge to determine how best to respond in given situations; this makes it difficult for them to identify threats effectively or prevent them from happening. Intelligence agencies must work with other agencies involved in state protection so that each can fulfil its role effectively without interfering with another's ability to do so. For intelligence agencies to succeed, they must have a good relationship with government officials. This means that they must be able to communicate with them effectively and get their help when needed. Intelligence agencies also need to be able to investigate crimes within their jurisdiction to determine if anyone has committed any violations of their laws or regulations (Taylor, 2011).

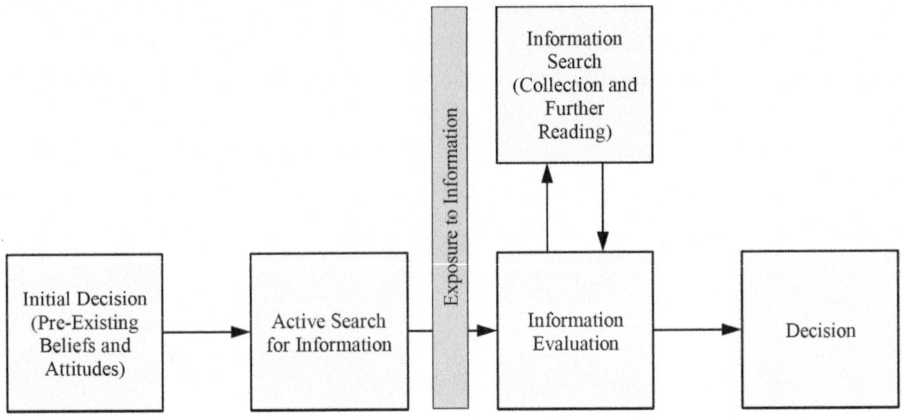

Figure 7.4. High-level model of activities in the intelligence cycle (HLMAIC).

Source: Winter, Lisa-Christina. (2017). Mitigation and Prediction of the Confirmation Bias in Intelligence Analysis. Scientific Figure on ResearchGate. Available from: https://www.researchgate.net/figure/High-Level-Model-of-Activities-in-the-Intelligence-Cycle-HLMAIC-Selective-Exposure_fig3_321309639 (accessed on 22 September 2023)

Intelligence agencies have several vital functions, including counterintelligence, which aims to uncover and foil any foreign intelligence operations directed against national interests. The activities that fall under the umbrella of "counterintelligence" include discovering and preventing attempts at espionage, locating "moles" or "double agents," and preventing unauthorized access to sensitive information. Counterintelligence operations almost always require close cooperation with other intelligence agencies, law enforcement agencies, and diplomatic channels. Information sharing and coordinating efforts on a domestic and international level are two of the most critical components of effective counterintelligence operations (Hockings, 2014).

7.5.1. Evolution of Intelligence Agencies

Early forms of intelligence gathering were utilized to gain a strategic advantage in ancient civilizations, which can be used to trace the origins of the evolution of intelligence agencies. Throughout history, intelligence agencies have evolved into highly specialized institutions that preserve national security. As a result of geopolitical competition, the two World Wars, and the period known as the Cold War, the structures and functions of intelligence agencies went through significant development in the 20th century. The increasing significance of intelligence in protecting states is demonstrated by the creation of organizations such as the British Secret Intelligence Service (MI6), the Central Intelligence Agency (CIA) of the United States, and the KGB of the Soviet Union (Taylor, 2011).

7.5.2. Impacts on Legal Procedures

Because their work frequently intersects with concerns regarding privacy, surveillance, and the delicate balance between security and civil liberties, the activities of intelligence agencies can have significant implications for the legal procedures carried out. Intelligence agencies in many different jurisdictions must operate within specific legal frameworks, which define the scope of their authority, the boundaries of their jurisdiction, and the mechanisms by which they are monitored. Legal frameworks for activities involving intelligence gathering are provided by legislation such as the Foreign Intelligence Surveillance Act (FISA) in the United States and the Regulation of Investigatory Powers Act (RIPA) in the United Kingdom, respectively.

However, using intelligence information in legal proceedings can present difficulties, mainly when issues about classified information, the protection of sources, and the guaranteeing of fair trials arise. The need to protect sensitive intelligence while ensuring that due process is followed is a complex and constantly evolving challenge, and finding the right balance between the two is difficult.

7.5.3. Political Ends and Intelligence

It is common practice for intelligence agencies to play a part in pursuing political ends, which can include defending national interests and supporting particular policies or political agendas. Both domestically and internationally, their evaluations and reports have the potential to impact the decision-making process. The potential for political influence on intelligence agencies to compromise their objectivity and independence is a concern that needs to be addressed. Intelligence agencies must keep their honesty and professionalism intact to ensure that their work serves the interests of national security rather than partisan politics. Covert operations, which may include sabotage, assassinations, or cyber warfare, are another area in which intelligence agencies are involved. These actions require careful consideration of their legitimacy, proportionality, and adherence to international standards, raising ethical and legal questions (Taylor, 2011).

7.5.4. Intelligence Sharing and International Cooperation

The constantly shifting architecture of state security has resulted in increased intelligence sharing and international cooperation among intelligence agencies. To effectively address transnational threats like terrorism, cybercrime, and organized crime, collaborative efforts and information sharing are required. The sharing of intelligence and the working together of law enforcement agencies are made more accessible by international organizations like Interpol and alliances like the Five Eyes, including the United States, the United Kingdom, Canada, Australia, and New Zealand. Despite this, there are still many obstacles to overcome when balancing the need to share sensitive information, protect national interests, and maintain trust among partner agencies (Hockings, 2014).

7.5.5. Oversight and Accountability

It is necessary to establish oversight and accountability mechanisms for intelligence agencies to prevent abuses of power and safeguard civil liberties. When it comes to monitoring intelligence activities and protecting against potential violations of rights or unethical behavior, independent oversight bodies, parliamentary committees, and judicial review play an essential part. On the other hand, due to the covert nature of intelligence work, it can take time to implement effective oversight and accountability measures successfully. It is essential to find the right balance between secrecy and transparency if one wishes to continue to enjoy the trust and confidence of the general public in intelligence agencies (Taylor, 2011).

7.6. INFLUENCE OF GLOBAL EVENTS ON STATE PROTECTION

Global events have a significant impact on the structure of state protection. This is because they affect the state's ability and willingness to protect people, property, and society. For example, suppose a country is suffering from a civil war. In that case, it may be forced to abandon some of its police or military forces to focus on protecting civilians. This will impact the protection of property and other aspects of society. The protection provided by the state should be fair, equitable, and just; however, this can take time to achieve when so many people need assistance from the state (Figure 7.5).

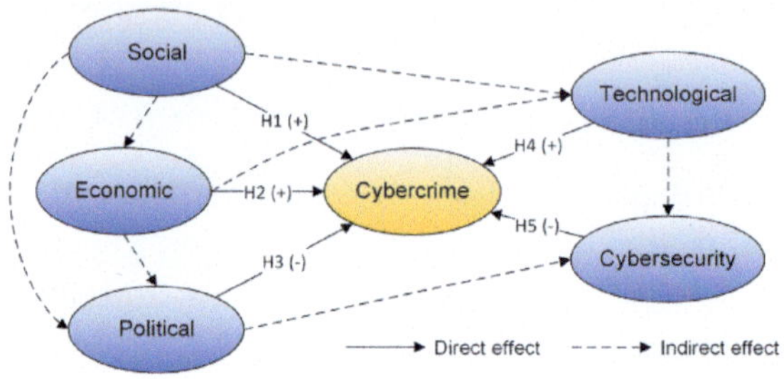

Figure 7.5. Exploring the global geography of cybercrime and its driving forces.

Source: Chen, S., Hao, M., Ding, F. et al. Exploring the global geography of cybercrime and its driving forces. *Humanit Soc Sci Commun* 10, 71 (2023). https://doi.org/10.1057/s41599–023–01560-x

- The Great Recession had a profound impact on state protection. States were forced to cut back on their spending on public works projects, as well as other social programs. This had a negative effect on the economy and led to an increase in unemployment rates. It also resulted in an increase in poverty levels for many individuals within these states (Hockings, 2014).
- The European migrant crisis also had an impact on state protection during this time period. In response to increased migration from Africa into Europe, some states enacted policies that restricted access to jobs within those countries while others enacted measures aimed at making it more difficult for migrants to gain citizenship within those states (Taylor, 2011).

In terms of state protection, there have been two major changes that have occurred as a result of these global events. The first is that states are becoming much more aggressive in their approach to protecting their citizens from threats and challenges. This can be seen through measures such as increased police presence at public venues or increased surveillance of public spaces by security forces. The second change is that states have begun to share information about threats and risks between themselves through organizations such as the World Trade Organization (WTO) or the

United Nations Security Council (UNSC).

7.6.1. Terrorist Attacks and State Protection

Attacks by terrorists have played a significant role in forming the organizational structures and operational strategies of state protection agencies worldwide. Significant shifts in counterterrorism measures and the overall approach to state protection have been brought about due to high-profile attacks such as 9/11, the London bombings in 2005, and the attacks in Paris in 2015. As a direct result of these attacks, state protection agencies have placed a greater emphasis on the exchange of intelligence, the enhancement of surveillance capabilities, and the improvement of international cooperation. As a direct result of the attacks, specialized counterterrorism units, expanded intelligence networks, and stringent security measures have been developed and implemented.

The legal system has also been significantly altered as a direct result of the terrorist attacks that have taken place. The USA PATRIOT Act in the United States and counterterrorism laws in various other countries expanded state powers in intelligence gathering, surveillance, and detention. These laws were enacted in response to the threat posed by terrorism. The purpose of these legislative amendments is to provide law enforcement with the resources necessary to detect and respond to potential terrorist attacks (Taylor, 2011).

7.6.2. Geopolitical Shifts and State Protection

Changes in geopolitical dynamics, such as shifts in alliances, emerging conflicts, or shifts in global power dynamics, directly impact the structure and strategies of state protection agencies. These shifts can be disputes, for example, or changes in global power dynamics. Due to these shifts, it is necessary to adjust how intelligence is gathered, threats are evaluated, and international cooperation is conducted.

For instance, the conclusion of the Cold War and the dissolution of the Soviet Union brought about a shift in the priorities placed on the protection of states. The intelligence community has redirected its attention to new types of danger, such as non-state actors, asymmetric warfare, and transnational criminal organizations. The structure of state protection has also been reshaped due to geopolitical conflicts such as the wars in Iraq and Afghanistan. Because of these conflicts, there needed to be a greater emphasis placed on the collection of intelligence in conflict zones, as well as the deployment of specialized military and intelligence units, and there needed to be enhanced collaboration between various agencies (Hockings, 2014).

7.6.3. Changes in Legal Procedures

Events on a global scale frequently prompt changes in legal procedures that govern state protection. The state's response to these events could result in introducing or modifying legislation to improve security measures, intelligence gathering, and efforts to combat terrorism. For instance, in the wake of the September 11, 2001 attacks, governments worldwide enacted significant legal reforms. The United States of America passed the USA PATRIOT Act, which enhanced the capabilities of surveillance, widened the scope of authority granted to intelligence agencies, and made it easier for agencies to share data (Taylor, 2011).

Similarly, the European Union (EU) responded to terrorist attacks by introducing directives and regulations to strengthen counterterrorism measures, improve intelligence sharing, and harmonize legal frameworks across member states. However, these changes in legal procedures are raising concerns about potential infringements on civil liberties, privacy rights, and the appropriate balance between security and individual freedoms. Although the changes are intended to empower state protection agencies to combat emerging threats, they also raise concerns about the right balance between safety and personal liberties.

7.6.4. Political Ends and State Protection

Events on a global scale also have political repercussions, which in turn influence the tactics and organizational structures utilized by state protection agencies. Alterations in political leadership, shifts in ideologies, or the pursuit of particular policy objectives can all have an effect on the path that state protection is headed down and the priorities that it prioritizes. It is possible for political ends to influence the distribution of resources, the concentration on particular dangers, and the priority placed on intelligence gathering in particular regions. It is possible for the influence of political actors on intelligence agencies to raise concerns about the potential for the intelligence to become politicized, which would compromise its objectivity and independence (Hockings, 2014).

7.7. MEDIA AND PUBLIC PERCEPTION OF STATE PROTECTION

The way the media portrays state protection agencies has a significant impact on how people feel about them. The role of the media as a conduit through which information about security threats, actions taken by state protection agencies, and the overall effectiveness of their efforts can be communicated to the general public is essential. The public's trust in state protection agencies can be increased through the positive coverage of successful operations, the foiling of attempted attacks, or the commitment of personnel in the media. On the other hand, unfavorable portrayals in the media, scandals, or controversies can erode public confidence and raise concerns about the abuse of power, infringements on civil liberties, or inadequate accountability mechanisms (Taylor, 2011).

In addition, the media is essential in uncovering possible misconduct or wrongdoing within state protection agencies. Investigative journalism can bring to light misconduct, flaws in a system, or violations of both legal and ethical norms. This kind of scrutiny from the media can result in policy changes, enhanced transparency, and more robust accountability mechanisms.

The state's policies and practices regarding protection are significantly impacted by public opinion. Policymakers frequently respond to public sentiment and concerns about security, civil liberties, and the balance between the two to maintain public support. This is because policymakers are aware of the need to maintain public support. Opinions expressed by members of the public have the potential to influence decisions made by policymakers regarding the implementation of counterterrorism strategies, the sharing of intelligence, and the distribution of resources among state protection agencies. To address the issues brought to the public's attention, governments may, in response to public sentiment, introduce new legislation, amend existing legislation, establish new oversight mechanisms, or launch general inquiries (Taylor, 2011).

The priorities that state protection agencies prioritize can also be influenced by public opinion. It is possible that changes in resource allocation, priorities for intelligence gathering, or the establishment of specialized units could be brought about due to public concerns regarding particular threats, such as terrorism or cybercrime. It is possible to observe the effect of public opinion on the structure and strategies of state protection agencies in how they respond to new threats, shifts in technological development, or developing geopolitical dynamics (Hockings, 2014). While the coverage provided by the media has a significant impact on how the general public views the state's role in protecting its citizens, it is also subject to several obstacles that could compromise its accuracy and objectivity. Balance and comprehensive reporting can be challenging when time constraints exist, a tendency toward sensationalism, restricted access to information, or the influence of commercial or political interests. The rapid pace at which news is disseminated in the digital age can result in the dissemination of needs to be more accurate or information insufficient. This could affect the public's understanding of essential issues and mold perceptions of state protection agencies. To ensure that they are providing accurate reporting, media organizations must prioritize upholding journalistic standards, fact-checking information, and providing context.

To shape public opinion and ensure the public's continued trust, state protection agencies engage in perception management on their own. Efforts in public relations and strategic communication, as well as proactive engagement with the media, are being taken to shape to shape the narrative surrounding state protection activities. State protection agencies may engage in public outreach, press conferences, or release statements to provide reassurance, explain policies, or address concerns. This engagement is essential for upholding transparency, effectively managing the public's expectations, and demonstrating accountability. Problems, on the other hand, arise whenever attempts at perception management work to undermine transparency and accountability. The erosion of public trust and raising questions regarding the independence and integrity of state protection agencies can be caused by excessive secrecy, the manipulation of information, or the suppression of voices that disagree with the status quo (Taylor, 2011).

The coverage of the media and the opinion of the public play an essential part in holding state protection agencies accountable. Encourages transparency, challenges abuses of power, and demands adherence to legal and ethical standards. Public scrutiny is made possible by reporting in the media and public discourse. Awareness and participation on the part of the public are essential factors in ensuring that state protection agencies work within the bounds of the law, protect civil liberties, and keep checks and balances in place. Investigations conducted by the media, public inquiries, and organizations representing civil society all provide avenues for accountability and oversight, holding state protection agencies responsible for their actions (Hockings, 2014).

The relationship between the media, public perception, and state protection agencies presents challenges and opportunities for state protection agencies. On the one hand, coverage in the media has the potential to help the public understand issues of accountability and reform. On the other hand, sensationalism, restricted access to information, or biased reporting can distort the public perception and undermine the relationship between the media and state protection agencies. To address these challenges, organizations that report the news should uphold journalistic integrity, work toward writing in a balanced manner, and fact-check information. Transparency must be embraced by state protection agencies, as well as engagement with the media and a willingness to respond to legitimate concerns raised by the public. Public education on state protection practices, civil liberties, and the complexities of national security can foster informed public discourse and a deeper understanding of state protection issues (Taylor, 2011).

7.8. TRANSNATIONAL COOPERATION IN STATE PROTECTION

The current international system is based on dividing countries into small, independent states. Due to their unequal economic development, this has led to an imbalance in power between developed and developing countries. Moreover, this system also needs help, such as under-development and corruption. As a result, there is an urgent need to create new models for cooperation among nations. In particular, transnational cooperation can be used as an effective method for promoting national development and improving the competitiveness of developing countries. It can also be used to reduce corruption and improve governance in developing countries.

Transnational cooperation can be used to facilitate changes in the structure of State protection. This would involve building platforms for dialogue and debate between stakeholders on both sides of the border, allowing them to share information and make decisions based on these inputs. The first thing to note about this phenomenon is that states can cooperate in many different ways. One way would be through extradition treaties or similar agreements where one form requests that another state extradite their citizens for prosecution in their courts. Another way would be through agreements on extradition between countries that do not have such a treaty but have other contracts, allowing for the transfer of people across borders at will (Hockings, 2014).

CHAPTER 8

Political Trial

Contents

8.1. INTRODUCTION

A political trial is a legal action with significant political consequences or goals. It is the legal system's use to take legal action against individuals or groups based on their political affiliations, actions, or ideas rather than actual criminal activity.

Charges against an individual in a political prosecution are typically political to stifle criticism, repress opposition, or consolidate authority. The procedures used were most likely prejudiced, unfair, or lacking due process, and political influences dictated or impacted the conclusion (Kirchheimer, 2015).

Political trials can take several shapes depending on the circumstances and the goals of those in power. They can range from deliberate show trials to those meant to seem legal while achieving political goals. Military or special tribunals may sometimes preside over trials, although ordinary courts may.

Numerous political trials have happened throughout history. Political opponents and dissenters, for example, were routinely punished through show trials in the Soviet Union under Joseph Stalin. Political dissidents and activists are often subjected to political courts in authoritarian regimes (Collingridge, 2019).

It's important to remember that the idea of a political trial is inherently subjective, with different political ideologies and points of view interpreting the trial's aims in different ways. The phrase has political overtones, and its use depends on the context and the speaker's point of view.

Political trials typically fit into one of four kinds; however, distinguishing them from traditional judicial processes can take time and effort. The most well-known kind of political persecution is partisan trials. It comprises the government's illegal legal operations to consolidate control, remove competitors, or project dominance. These political trials, even if they take place in a courtroom, have nothing to do with justice. Politicized practices, on the other hand, promote the interests of the strong.

Partisan trials are usually easy to spot since the government chooses judges, prosecutors, and defence counsel based on their political affiliation with the regime. In certain countries, the government may utilize subconscious pressure to influence tribunal and attorney judgments. In any case, these processes often offer a more realistic and unbiased alternative. Numerous judges, prosecutors, and defence lawyers participated in terror and propaganda operations for Adolf Hitler's Germany and Joseph Stalin's

Soviet Union (Collingridge, 2019). As a second type of political trial, political and religious dissidents are tried. Governments have been challenged throughout history by citizens who defy the law on moral grounds. Most governments find dealing with such disobedience, which can take the form of violent or quiet protest, difficult (Kirchheimer, 2015).

The government must sanction lawbreakers to maintain the integrity of the legal system. If the trial is held publicly, a political or religious dissident may doubt the existing government's legitimacy or competency and the constitutionality of specific legislation or policy. If the government secretly silenced a dissident, the legal system would be open to claims of persecution, undermining public trust in the rule of law.

By bringing dissidents before an impartial judge and juror, the American legal system seeks to balance the competing interests of the government and dissenters. In the past, numerous administrations still need to achieve this precise equilibrium. Socrates became a martyr when 500 Athenian jurors executed him in ancient Greece for corrupting the young and opposing authority. Pontius Pilate, the Roman governor, incited organized religious opposition to his administration by condemning Jesus of Nazareth for claiming to be the Jewish Messiah and Son of God. In 1735, British officials attempted and acquitted John Peter Zenger of seditious libel, sowing the seeds of rebellion in the American colonies (Kirchheimer, 2015).

The third most prevalent form of political trial involves nationalists challenging a government's authority to represent them. Nationalists are a distinct community of individuals who share a trait, such as race, religion, or ethnicity. Nationalists' struggles cast doubt on society's cohesion and a government's ability to voice for the people. Governments persecute nationalists to demonstrate their legitimacy as overlords of the people. To raise political awareness and document their battle for future generations, many nationalists continue to mount a valiant defence despite inevitable defeats (Collingridge, 2019).

For instance, the 1922 trial of Mohandas K. Gandhi ignited nationalism in India by uniting the populace against the oppressive British colonial government. Similarly, Nelson Mandela's treason trials in Pretoria during the late 1950s and early 1960s brought the apartheid state to the international community's attention. Even though the regimes they opposed temporarily suppressed them in both instances, their causes ultimately prevailed because their people had equal input in political decisions. The fourth category of political trials includes the indictment of entire administrations or their top administrators. The new administration must determine how to treat former government employees after a coup or revolution destabilizes the previous government. On occasion, compassion is shown to former government members, and efforts are made to integrate them into society. In other instances, former government officials lose their citizenship, are removed from office, and are denied entry into the country. In contrast, the new administration typically brings the previous regime to justice and prosecutes it for all infractions, no matter how minor (Kirchheimer, 2015).

These investigations could serve two distinct functions. They may initially concentrate on the negative characteristics of the deposed dictatorship. In the aftermath of a revolution, civil war, or other armed conflict, they can also help reduce calls for firing squad executions. This may highlight the strengths of the new leadership. Despite calls for their execution, members of a despised regime were granted a complete spectrum of legal privileges during the Nuremberg war crimes trials, in which the Allies convicted twenty-four prominent Nazis for war crimes following World War II (Collingridge, 2019).

In varying degrees, politics is prevalent in all legal proceedings. The judiciary is an essential component of the political system because it is one of the three pillars of government. In addition, every trial has political repercussions in the real world by establishing the duties and responsibilities of civil and criminal litigants. Because many judicial decisions are considered precedents, the legal principles established in one case may be applied to other members of society in a similar situation.

However, the scope of a political prosecution has expanded in the United States. When a trial exposes a topic with broader societal, cultural, or international significance than guilt or innocence, it is considered political. For instance, in the middle of the 1970s, the Watergate prosecutions centered on the legal issues of burglary, conspiracy, and obstruction of justice. However, these examples also illustrated the demise of a president and the consequences of abusing power.

Typically, political trials reveal fundamental dilemmas that ignite public debate. These concerns could force society to halt and even reconsider its actual values. Political problems, such as the Nuremberg and Watergate trials, have helped define an era or a nation (Kirchheimer, 2015).

8.2. THE TRIAL OF SOCRATES (399 BCE)

After Athens was defeated by Sparta in the Peloponnesian War (431–404 BCE), Socrates was prosecuted in 399 BCE. Not only were Athens and Sparta rivals in antiquity, but they also had vastly distinct political systems. Athens was a democracy: all of its adult male citizens were Assembly members; many of the city's positions were filled by lot (the election was viewed as undemocratic because it effectively declared some citizens to be more qualified than others); and its residents enjoyed a high degree of freedom to live and speak as they wished, so long as they obeyed the law and did not harm the democracy or the general welfare. On the other hand, Sparta had a mixed regime based on a sophisticated power-sharing arrangement between many aristocratic groups and ordinary people, and it exerted significantly more control over its citizens' daily life and education than Athens did (Collingridge, 2019).

Athenians revered certain aspects of Spartan life and government, especially the well-born, affluent, and young. These young men, who spent a great deal of time in the public gymnasia, took pride in their fortitude, wore simple clothing, and wore their hair long in imitation of Spartan customs. (Plato and Xenophon demonstrate that Socrates possessed a number of these qualities. Young people who declare their affection for Sparta are portrayed as "Socratizing" in Aristophanes' Birds. Athens, an empire-building city with vast resources and a large population, could not combat Sparta, a minuscule and impoverished rival state, and consequently lost its empire to Sparta. This likely increased the appeal of the Spartan political system and way of life.

The common Athenians, who had to work for a living and were not from aristocratic families, were proud of their democratic institutions and liberties. Still, they were also aware that their form of government had internal and external opponents. In addition, they made no distinction between civic and religious issues, believing that all citizens owed respect to the city's spiritual life, which democratic institutions governed, and that disrespecting the gods recognized by the municipality or violating traditional religious laws could have severe repercussions for the city (Kirchheimer, 2015).

8.2.1. Religious Scandal and the Coup of the Oligarchs

Several incidents during and immediately following the battle with Sparta revealed the extent to which Athenian democracy was threatened by citizens who disregarded local religious traditions, lacked allegiance to democratic institutions or applauded their city's adversaries. Several statues of Hermes, the deity of travel, were defaced one night in 415, just before the departure of a significant naval expedition to Sicily. Those guilty were individuals who desired to thwart the mission. During the investigation, several individuals, including one of Socrates' most ardent allies, Alcibiades, who sponsored and helped coordinate the Sicilian expedition, were accused of ridiculing a holy ceremony and divulging its sacred secrets. Several of them were put on trial and executed. Alcibiades, previously suspected of involvement in several church controversies, was summoned from Sicily to stand the test. However, due to his opponents' ferocity and the suspicion surrounding him, he chose to flee to Sparta instead of returning to Athens, where he would almost undoubtedly be executed. In his absence, he and his companions were murdered by Athens, but he continued to advise and lead Sparta in its battle against Athens. When he returned to Athens in 407, he was acquitted of all charges but never wholly regained the trust of the Democratic Party or its opponents. Alcibiades was only one of the numerous students of Socrates implicated in the 415 religious controversies mentioned by Plato in his works (Kirchheimer, 2015).

400 anti-democratic Athenians attempted to establish an oligarchy by staging a revolt in 411; however, they were overthrown the following year, and democracy was restored. Several of them, including some of Socrates' companions, retreated into exile after their revolt failed. Sparta installed the Thirty Tyrants in Athens in 404, shortly after the Athenians were defeated, to establish a government that was considerably less democratic. Charmides and Critias, the radical wing's commander, were both members of the Socratic circle. The following year, democracy was restored after many Democratic leaders fled Athens after gaining power. (In Plato's Apology, Socrates describes the oppression of the Thirty and their futile attempt to link him to their offenses) (Collingridge, 2019).

8.2.2. The Perceived fragility of Athenian Democracy

In the same year that Socrates was charged with impiety, 399, several other well-known individuals were also prosecuted in Athens on similar charges. This does not appear to be a coincidence; instead, it suggests that there was concern at the time regarding the potential political ramifications of theological heresy. People still remembered the religious crises of 415, and there had been two recent attempts to destabilize Athens' democracy. As a result of a general amnesty, no one could be punished for crimes committed before 403, when the 30 were defeated. However, this would not have precluded the prosecution of anyone who committed an offence after 403 days. Even the most ardent amnesty supporters would not have opposed placing Socrates on trial if, after 403, he had continued to engage in the same actions that characterized him throughout his adult life. In addition, once the problem had begun, it was typical for prosecutors to present any evidence that could be perceived as damaging to the defendant. No legal precedent or judge appointed by the court could have prevented Socrates' accusers from naming his supporters, including Alcibiades, Critias, Charmides, and others who had opposed democratic Athens or been embroiled in a religious scandal. Socrates was accused of violating a law prohibiting desecration and corrupting the youth. His jury may have viewed him as hazardous due to his associations with anti-democracy groups or individuals convicted of or accused of committing crimes motivated by religion (Kirchheimer, 2015).

Given that Anytus, one of those who participated in Socrates' prosecution and spoke against him, was a prominent democratic leader, it is much more likely that Socrates' trial was motivated by concerns for the survival of Athenian democracy. Even if Anytus and the other prosecutors (Meletus and Lycon) shared different problems, it is improbable that the individuals who heard his case did not. In any case, jurors would have had difficulty dismissing Socrates' membership in anti-democracy organizations, even if they were willing to do so, given that he expressed his anti-democratic views during his defence argument. In 399, the democracy of Athens must have appeared fragile. Only in hindsight do we realize that its institutions were robust enough to endure the remainder of the fourth century (Collingridge, 2019).

Alcibiades and Critias' statements during Socrates' trial were not recorded, and it is difficult to interpret the evidence they provided; therefore, it is unclear whether the individuals who prosecuted Socrates brought them up during his trial. Nonetheless, there is a high probability that specific identities were mentioned. In Plato's Apology, Socrates remarks that several accusers claimed to be his pupils. He weakly refutes this allegation by asserting that he has never attempted to educate anyone and, therefore, cannot have had any pupils. Alcibiades and Critias were Socrates' students, according to "the accuser," Xenophon's account in Memorabilia. Some scholars believe the term accuser refers to one of the three witnesses who testified against Socrates in 399. In contrast, others believe that Xenophon defended Socrates against allegations made in a treatise written by the rhetorical master Polycrates some years later. In any case, many years later, in the fourth century, the orator Aeschines explicitly stated in his speech

"Against Timarchus" that Socrates was found guilty because "it was demonstrated that he was the teacher of Critias, one of the thirty who had overthrown democracy."

However, while Socrates' relationship with Critias and Alcibiades was crucial to his trial and conviction, it was neither the primary nor the most critical element of the prosecution's case. Socrates was accused of breaking the law against impiety, and Plato's primary defence was that Socrates' life had been consumed by his unwavering devotion to the divine. In Plato's Apology, Socrates is convinced that he must refute the charge of impiety levied against him. There is no reason to believe this accusation is false and that Socrates was not convicted for his anti-democratic affiliations and views. Understanding the political context of his prosecution is essential, as it explains why he was never prosecuted in the 430s, 420s, or at any other time in his life. Everything we know about him suggests that he was the same person in both 399 and 423, the Year of the Clouds and that he led the same existence in both years. In 399, after so many years of his actions being tolerated, a change in the political climate led to his conviction. On the other hand, Socrates of Apology asserts that his purported religious heterodoxy troubled the prosecution and jury. Because of this, he is entirely intent on this accusation (Kirchheimer, 2015).

8.2.3. The Athenian Ideal of Free Speech by Socrates

The fact that Socrates was prosecuted for his political and religious beliefs demonstrates how quickly his fellow Athenians could abandon an ideal—the concept of free and open debate among citizens—when they felt insecure. Demosthenes's assertion that it is permissible to glorify the Spartan constitution in Athens but not in Sparta is a compelling demonstration of the relevance of this ideal in Athens. Aside from the Socrates trial, were other instances where an Athene was prosecuted for allegedly spreading harmful ideas? Protagoras, Anaxagoras, Damon, Aspasia, and Diagoras were exiled or prosecuted decades after Socrates' murder, according to several authors. According to some researchers, Athens' commitment to free expression weakened significantly in the second half of the fifth century. Some argue that authors fabricated the majority of the evidence for a period of persecution and harassment to support the claims of their favored philosophers, such as Socrates, that they, too, had been persecuted by the Athenians. What is certain is that the Socrates trial is the only instance in which an Athenian was tried under the law not for an overt act that directly harmed the public or a specific person, such as treason, corruption, or slander, but for alleged indirect harm caused by the expression and teaching of ideas (Collingridge, 2019).

According to Plato's Apology, the decision to convict Socrates was exceptionally close; if thirty of those who voted for conviction had voted differently, he would not have been convicted. Fifty-nine individuals voted to convict him. Assuming, as many scholars do, that his jury comprised 501 individuals, 280 individuals voted for conviction, and 221 individuals voted against it.). It is reasonable to assume that many of those who opposed Socrates' belief did so in part because, regardless of how little they cared about what he believed or how he lived, they valued the freedom of speech enjoyed by all Athenians and weighed it more heavily than any potential harm Socrates might have caused in the past or future. Socrates persuaded and criticized his fellow Athenians for the duration of his lengthy life due to the Athenians' respect for free speech. Still, it ultimately collapsed under severe stress, albeit just barely.

8.3. THE DREYFUS AFFAIR (1894–1906)

The Dreyfus controversy was a political crisis from 1894 to 1906 in France's Third Republic. The discussion centered on Army Captain Alfred Dreyfus, convicted of treason in December 1894 for purportedly selling military secrets to the Germans. People initially accepted Dreyfus's conviction and admitted that he, a Jew, was culpable. Early coverage of the case was dominated by anti-Semitic groups (most notably the newspaper La Libre Parole, led by Édouard Drumont), who used Dreyfus to symbolize the alleged betrayal of French Jews (Kirchheimer, 2015).

As evidence of the guilt of another French officer, Ferdinand Walsin-Esterhazy began to emerge in 1896, the pro-Dreyfus side gradually gained supporters, including journalists Joseph Reinach and Georges Clemenceau, who would eventually become the war's premier, and Senator Auguste Scheurer-Kestner. In January 1898, Esterhazy was absolved of treason charges at a court-martial. In a letter titled "J'accuse," published in Clemenceau's publication L'Aurore, Émile Zola expressed his displeasure with the decision. In it, he criticized the military for suppressing their erroneous verdict against Dreyfus, which led to his conviction for libel (Collingridge, 2019).

At the time of the Zola letter, the Dreyfus controversy had divided France into two opposing factions and generated widespread public outrage. The anti-Dreyfusards (those opposed to reopening the topic) viewed the conflict as an endeavor by France's adversaries to harm the nation and the army. The Dreyfusards (those who advocated for Captain Dreyfus' exoneration) viewed the issue as the notion of individual liberty giving way to the need for national security. They supported the army to be under parliamentary control and republicanization.

Between 1898 and 1899, the cause of Dreyfusard gathered momentum. In August 1898, it was determined that a crucial document implicating Dreyfus was forged. Major Hubert-Joseph Henry, commander of the intelligence division, confessed to fabricating the report to support the army's argument, which increased the likelihood of a change. During the same period, politicians began to take an active interest in the situation. The Republican parties in the Chamber of Deputies recognized that the legislative system was under attack from the nationalist right, which was becoming increasingly vocal. The Radicals were instrumental in forming a left-wing alliance. In June 1899, in response to the growing unrest and protests, a ministry commanded by the radical René Waldeck-Rousseau was established for the stated purpose of defending the republic, with the expectation that the judicial aspect of the Dreyfus case would be resolved as soon as feasible. The republic's president pardoned Dreyfus in September 1899 after a second court-martial in Rennes declared him guilty of ending the situation. In July 1906, a civilian appeals court (the Cour d'Appel) reversed the Rennes court's decision and restored Dreyfus' reputation. However, the army did not publicly declare his innocence until 1995 (Kirchheimer, 2015).

In the history of the Third Republic, the Dreyfusards' seizure of power marked the beginning of a new era. During this period, a succession of administrations led by the Radicals pursued an anti-clerical stance, culminating in the separation of church and state (1905). The case had a lasting effect on the French national consciousness, intensifying conflicts between the right and the left and compelling individuals to choose sides (Collingridge, 2019).

8.4. THE MOSCOW SHOW TRIALS (1936–1938)

In the 1930s, the counterrevolutionary bureaucracy of the Soviet Union, headed by Joseph Stalin, eliminated virtually the entire leadership of the October Revolution. Between 1936 and 1938, mock trials of Bolshevik leaders such as Zinoviev, Kamenev, Bukharin, and Rakovsky were staged. The execution of death sentences within hours marked the end of these abhorrent practices, in which prisoners were coerced into incriminating themselves after being falsely assured that doing so would save them and their families. As in the cases of Rakovsky and Radek, when the defendants were sentenced to prison, they were assassinated in secret. Only one aspect of an unprecedented campaign of mass murder was revealed to the public, with the remainder occurring behind closed doors.

Generations of Marxist intellectuals and laborers were wiped out, including hundreds of their finest Marxists. Between 1936 and 1939, a wave of counterrevolutionary violence claimed approximately one million lives. This liquidation shocked the revolutionary consciousness of the Soviet working class, from which the Soviet Union never fully recovered. It validated Trotsky's characterization of Stalin as the "gravedigger of the revolution." The history and evidence of these unprecedented crimes provide an irrefutable refutation of numerous bourgeois propagandists' claims that Marxism's theoretical and political foundations provided the basis for Stalinism, let alone the claim that Stalinism and Trotskyism were merely variations of the same Marxism. Trotsky stated that "a river of blood" separated Stalinism and Trotskyism, which is the best way to interpret his statement (Kirchheimer, 2015).

8.5. THE NUREMBERG TRIALS (1945–1946)

Nazi war criminals were tried in 13 trials in Nuremberg, Germany, between 1945 and 1949. Members of the Nazi Party, critical military commanders, German businesses, attorneys, and medics were accused of crimes against humanity and crimes against peace. Hitler, the Nazi Party's founder, committed suicide and was never convicted. Even though the Nuremberg Trials' legal justifications and procedural innovations were controversial at the time, they are now regarded as a significant step toward establishing a permanent international court and a precedent for future cases of genocide and other crimes against humanity.

After Adolf Hitler was elected Chancellor of Germany in 1933, he and the Nazi administration began adopting anti-Jewish and anti-state legislation. By the end of World War II (1939–1945), the state had killed an estimated 6 million European Jews and 4 to 6 million non-Jews (Collingridge, 2019).

The leaders of the Allies—Great Britain, the United States, and the Soviet Union—" issued the first joint declaration officially noting the mass murder of European Jewry and resolving to prosecute those responsible for violence against civilian populations" in December 1942, according to the United States Holocaust Memorial Museum (USHMM). Stalin (1878–1953) suggested killing 50,000 to 100,000 German staff officers. American officials convinced Winston Churchill (1874–1955), the United Kingdom's first prime minister, that a criminal trial would be preferable to summary execution (killing high-ranking Nazis without a problem). In addition to guaranteeing that the defendants' claimed infractions are documented, criminal processes would cease arguments that the defendants were penalized without adequate proof (Kirchheimer, 2015).

Several formal and legal objections were presented throughout the Nuremberg trials. There has never been a global prosecution for war crimes. Confederate army General Henry Wirz (1823–1865) was hanged during the American Civil War (186–185), and Turkish courts-martial were established in 1919–1920 to prosecute those in the leadership of the 1915–16 Armenian genocide. Unlike the Nuremberg trials, which were undertaken by four nations (France, the United Kingdom, the Soviet Union, and the United States), these trials were conducted by a single country.

On August 8, 1945, the Allies adopted the London Charter of the International Military Tribunal (IMT), which set the guiding principles and procedures for the Nuremberg trials. War crimes, often known as crimes against humanity, involve the death, slavery, or deportation of people and discrimination against persons based on their ethnicity, religion, or other repressive beliefs. War crimes include breaches of military traditions and regulations, as well as the treatment of civilians and prisoners of war inhumanely. It was found that both army and civilian officers might face war crimes charges (Collingridge, 2019).

The proceedings were conducted in the German city of Nuremberg (sometimes spelt Nurnberg) because it had a large prison complex and a Palace of Justice that had primarily survived the war's destruction. The postwar trials were conducted in Nuremberg because the city had previously hosted annual Nazi propaganda parades, which signified the collapse of Hitler's Third Reich.

The Most famous Nuremberg proceedings were the Trial of Major War Criminals, held between November 20, 1945, and October 1, 1946. As British and American law required, the prosecutor and defence attorney were present during the trial. However, a tribunal (a council of justices) rendered the verdicts and penalties instead of a single judge and jury. Robert H. Jackson (1892–1954), an associate justice on the United States Supreme Court, was the nation's leading prosecutor. Each ally contributed two judges, a primary and a reserve (Kirchheimer, 2015).

Six Nazi organizations, including the "Gestapo," or covert state police, and twenty-four individuals were charged with criminal activity. When a second individual appeared before the court, one of the defendants was deemed medically unfit to stand trial. Hitler and two of his closest associates, Heinrich Himmler (1900–1945) and Joseph Goebbels (1897–1945), committed suicide in the spring of 1945 to avoid punishment. The claims in the London Charter were frequently cited as an example of ex post facto legislation, or laws that penalized behavior that occurred before the rules were written. The defendants were free to select their attorneys. Another viewpoint held that the trial exemplified Victor's justice, in which the Allies harshly punished German crimes while mitigating those committed by their soldiers.

Instant translation, a feature of modern technology that is now prevalent, was introduced during the trial. Each defendant and the judge spoke their respective native tongues. IBM supplied the necessary technology and recruited employees from foreign phone exchanges to provide real-time English, French, German, and Russian translations while donning headphones (Collingridge, 2019).

Except for three defendants, the international court deemed them all guilty. One defendant was declared guilty in absentia; the remaining defendants were sentenced to prison terms varying from ten years to life. On October 16, 1946, ten individuals found guilty of offences were executed. Hermann Goring (1893–1966), Hitler's designated successor and Luftwaffe (German air force) commander, took a cyanide tablet disguised as skin lotion the night before his execution.

After the Major War Criminals Trial, 12 additional trials were conducted in Nuremberg. Because they occurred between December 1946 and April 1949, these court proceedings were known as the Subsequent Nuremberg hearings. They were prosecuted by US military justices as opposed to the international tribunal that ruled on the fate of senior Nazi officials in the first trial. The change was necessary because previous collaborative testing had become problematic due to increasing divisions between the four Allies. The succeeding tests were conducted at the Palace of Justice in Nuremberg.

The Doctors Trial lasted from December 9, 1946, to August 20, 1947, and involved 23 defendants accused of crimes against humanity, such as using war captives as test subjects in medical studies. In the Judges' Trial, which lasted from March 5 to December 4, 1947, sixteen attorneys and judges were accused of aiding the Third Reich's eugenics program to promote Nazi racial purity. Following trials, senior military commanders were held accountable for atrocities committed against concentration camp inmates, German industrialists for using slave labor and plundering conquered countries, and SS officials for crimes committed against prisoners of war. According to the USHMM, twelve of the 185 defendants in the subsequent Nuremberg trials were condemned to death, eight were sentenced to life in prison, and the remaining 77 were sentenced to varying prison terms. The authorities subsequently reduced some punishments (Kirchheimer, 2015).

8.6. THE TRIAL OF NELSON MANDELA (1963–1964)

In October 1963, in what became known as "the trial that changed South Africa," ten prominent opponents of apartheid were convicted of sabotage and sentenced to execution. The most shocking statement made by Nelson Mandela during his trial was when he called the court he was standing before "illegitimate." He continued by stating that existing laws were equally severe and that it was acceptable to disregard them.

The Rivonia Trial and the detention of the MK's top leadership shed light on a problem frequently encountered by participants in the liberation struggle: the conflict between justice and legality. Even if they disagreed with the legitimacy of the minority-racial state, liberation organizations were required to operate within the legal system; when activists were incarcerated, they could not do so (Collingridge, 2019).

The 'accused' in the Rivonia Trial utilized the courts as a battleground to circumvent this obstacle. They declared that because the legislation was enacted to ensure the continuation of an unjust system without the consent of the majority, they would strive to establish a new one, including a legal system based on the principles of a non-racial constitution that protected human rights.

The primary defence attorneys were George Bizos, Bram Fischer, Vernon Berrange, Arthur Chaskalson, and Joel Joffe. Justice Quartus de Wet presided over the trial, and Dr Percy Yutar was the prosecutor. The Verwoerd administration intended the most severe possible punishment for the accused: death. The defence team urged its clients to initiate contingency planning immediately. Eleven accused individuals submitted not-guilty pleas in response to the charges brought against them (Kirchheimer, 2015).

Regular court appearances by the accused attracted large audiences that filled the courthouse and surrounding streets, and the courtroom became a new battleground for the opponents. Numerous supporters breached numerous entry control barriers, and the courts became their new battlefield.

According to Yutar, who argued on behalf of the prosecution, all defendants were members of "a cabinet of the government soon after the overthrow of the state." In this cabinet, Govan Mbeki was the Minister of European Affairs, while Nelson Mandela was the Deputy Minister and Minister of Defense. The remaining defendants were government employees (Collingridge, 2019).

Bruno Mtolo, who deposed under the alias "Mr X," was compelled to be the state's main witness. Mtolo, who had a photographic memory, held prominent positions in the MK's Natal region. He implicated them by describing various instances and times when he was exposed to Mandela's and his co-accused's overthrow of the government's comments and plans. He stated that he intended to depose the state because he was outraged by the lavish lifestyles of Sisulu and other high officials and that he was not paid the ten pounds per week to which he was entitled to his position in the MK.

The most notable aspect of the trial was Mandela's comments while being questioned. He claimed that the courtroom where he was being tried was a farce. He continued by stating that existing laws were equally severe and that it was acceptable to disregard them.

On June 12, 1964, after the proceedings, eight of the defendants were sentenced to life in prison. Mandela, Sisulu, Mbeki, Motsoaledi, Mlangeni, and Goldberg were cleared of all four offences. Due to the lack of evidence connecting Mahlaba, Kathrada, and Bernstein to the conspiracy, the defence hoped to avoid conviction. In contrast to Kathrada, who was found guilty on only one count of conspiracy, Mhlaba was found guilty on all four counts. After being declared not guilty, Bernstein was detained, released on parole, and placed under house arrest. He left the country promptly. Following the prosecution's case, Kantor was the sole defendant to be acquitted (Kirchheimer, 2015).

Except for Goldberg, who was condemned to 22 years in prison, all accused were held at Pretoria Central Prison. Pretoria Central was the only South African security facility harboring white political detainees at the time.

Shortly after the trial, Bram Fischer, the defence attorney, was detained and charged with "supporting communists." Since the defendants in the Rivonia trial were not sentenced to death, many individuals believe the government singled out Fischer. As an Afrikaner contending against an Afrikaner dictatorship, Fischer's case received a great deal of public attention. His eventual release from life imprisonment did not occur until he was in dire condition (Collingridge, 2019).

8.7. THE TRIAL OF SADDAM HUSSEIN (2005–2006)

Iraq's interim government prosecuted Saddam Hussein for crimes against humanity committed while he was in power.

The Iraqi Special Tribunal (IST), comprising five Iraqi justices, was founded with the agreement of the Coalition Provisional Authority on December 9, 2003. From the 1980s, the IST would trial Saddam Hussein and his collaborators for alleged war crimes, crimes against humanity, and genocide.

American soldiers seized Hussein on December 13, 2003. He was still being held in Camp Cropper in Baghdad by American forces, along with eleven other key Ba'athist leaders. During the Iran-Iraq War, brutal attacks against Kurds in the north, Shiites in the south during disturbances in 1991 and 1999, and the response in Dujail to a failed assassination attempt on Saddam Hussein on July 8, 1982, drew particular attention. Saddam claimed in his defence that despite being dismissed from office, he was still president of Iraq (Kirchheimer, 2015).

On October 19, 2005, the first hearing before the Iraqi Special Tribunal began. In 1982, the Islamic Dawa Party attempted but failed to assassinate Dujail. In this case, Saddam Hussein and seven other defendants were charged with crimes against humanity (see also Saddam Hussein's breaches of human rights in Iraq). Saddam and six other defendants were accused of genocide on August 21, 2006, concerning the Anfal military attack on northern Iraqi Kurds.

Saddam Hussein was condemned to death by hanging on November 5, 2006. Saddam's appeal was refused on December 26, and the death penalty was restored. Saddam was sentenced to death in less than 30 days, with no more requests allowed. The location and timing of the execution were undisclosed before the execution. Saddam Hussein was executed on December 30, 2006. All allegations against him were withdrawn after his death (Kirchheimer, 2015).

The trial was condemned as a "show trial" that breached international law's fair trial rules. The problem was "unfair," according to Human Rights

Watch and Amnesty International, and Saddam Hussein's execution "follows a flawed trial and marks a significant step away from the rule of law in Iraq." Former Iraq Special Tribunal head Salem Chalabi accused Iyad Allawi of supporting a speedy show trial and execution, arguing that "show trials followed by speedy executions may help the interim government politically in the short term, but will be counterproductive for the development of democracy and the rule of law in Iraq in the long term."

President Saddam Hussein displayed confidence and defiance throughout the 46-minute talk. He waved and listened while the judge, Rizgar Mohammed Amin, questioned the jury convened for his trial. He referred to the scene on the court as a "play" meant to boost Bush's prospects of becoming President of the United States. He vehemently refuted the charges levelled against him. Every act is a performance. He claims that President Bush is the real culprit. He was compelled to identify himself when appearing before an Iraqi judge. Due to security reasons, the prosecutor and three of the five judges could not be recognized or photographed, but he stated, "You are an Iraqi; you know who I am."

Due to his backing for Iraq's invasion of Kuwait in August 1990, the judge chastised Saddam for using strong language in court, referring to Kuwaitis as "dogs" who intended to convert Iraqi women into "two-penny whores" during his arraignment. On July 1, Kuwait's communications minister, Abul-Hassan, indicated that disparaging words from Saddam were "expected." The pastor deduced, "This is how he was raised (Collingridge, 2019)."

Saddam's first wife, Sajida Talfah, formed an international legal team that included Libyan Ayesha Gaddafi, American Curtis Doebbler, French Emmanuel Ludot, and Swiss Marc Henzeler. Jordanian Mohammad Rashdan led the team. The former president declined to sign the court records at the end of the first court session, signaling his disagreement with the claims (Kirchheimer, 2015).

Bush declared his readiness to see Saddam prosecuted before the International Court of Justice in The Hague in a taped February 2003 discussion with Spanish Prime Minister Jose Aznar.

In a 50-page brief presented in December 2004, Clive Stafford Smith, a defence team member, contended that Saddam Hussein should be held responsible under US criminal law in the United States.

The London-based Arabic-language newspaper Al-Quds Al-Arabi stated in early May 2005 that Saddam Hussein rejected a proposal to be released in exchange for issuing a call to arms for a truce with allies during a meeting with Donald Rumsfeld that was "known only to a few Iraqi officials in Jordan. "The British tabloid The Daily Telegraph alleged two weeks ago, citing an unidentified senior UK government source, that Iraqi rebels had agreed to a "deal" in which the Iraqi president would face less severe punishment if the assaults stopped (Collingridge, 2019).

Former US Attorney General Ramsey Clark, former French Foreign Minister Roland Dumas, and former Algerian President Ahmed Ben Bella announced the creation of an international crisis council for Iraq on June 17, 2005. The committee's primary goal is to secure fair trials for Saddam and the other former Baath Party members on problems with him.

On July 18, 2005, the Special Tribunal accused Saddam of the first of several crimes linked to the mass murder of people in the hamlet of Dujail following a botched assassination attempt in 1982.

On August 8, 2005, the Saddam family declared that the legal team located in Jordan had been dismantled and that Khalil al-Duleimi, the only member with an Iraqi address, had been replaced. On September 6, 2005, Iraqi President Jalal Talabani stated on Iraqi television that he persuaded Saddam Hussein to admit that he had ordered mass homicides and other "crimes" while in power and that "he deserved to die." Saddam's legal representation contested his confession two days later.

To extend the proceedings, Saddam's defence regularly claimed that it had not been furnished with any evidence acquired by the prosecution and needed more time to review any prosecution documents. However, the court never addressed these concerns. According to international human rights organizations such as Human Rights Watch and Amnesty International, as well as United Nations organizations such as the Working Group on Arbitrary Detention and the High Commissioner for Human Rights, the Iraqi Special Tribunal's legal procedure and fair trial standards were not followed. The United Nations Secretary-General, Kofi Annan, declined to sanction the case for similar concerns of objectivity and the threat of the death sentence (Kirchheimer, 2015).

Iraqi authorities brought Saddam and seven other former cabinet officials to trial on October 19, 2005, four days after the new Iraqi constitution was enacted on October 15, 2005. The prosecution asserted unequivocally that the defendants engaged in the murder of 148 Shiites from Dujail in reprisal for the failed assassination attempt on July 8, 1982. Saddam's followers rallied in Tikrit against the indictment. After reading the accusations, the eight defendants entered a not-guilty plea. The trial was initially open to the public. Still, it was closed on March 15, 2006, after Saddam mentioned politics during his evidence, and an incident erupted between him and the presiding judge (Collingridge, 2019).

Saddam made a combative first impression at the start of the October 19 Trial, as he had previously. He questioned the tribunal's validity and impartiality. Respectfully, I will not react to this court and will continue to use my constitutional power as Iraq's president, as Saddam stated. "Neither do I recognize the body that designated and authorized you, nor do I recognize the aggression," he explained, "because everything that has been based on false foundations is false." Saddam said, "I am the President of Iraq." What sets you apart from the crowd? As a result, he approached Kurdish judge Rizgar Mohammed Amin. I'd want to learn more about you. When Amin referred to Saddam as "the former president," he reacted angrily, claiming he was still in command of the Republic of Iraq and had not been overthrown.

Saddam's first trial lasted three hours. The court postponed the trial until November 28, 2005, due to witness intimidation and to give the defence additional time to analyze the material. Saddam's eldest daughter, Raghad, told the Arab news website al-Arabiya that the trial was a "farce" and that her father acted like a "lion" throughout. Despite being confined, he worked like a lion. Everyone who knows Saddam Hussein characterizes him as a powerful and aggressive man (Kirchheimer, 2015).

Chief Judge Rizgar Mohammed Amin postponed the trial on November 28, 2005, so some defendants might obtain fresh legal representation. Saadoun Sughaiyer al-Janabi, Awad Hamed al-Bandar's defence counsel, was kidnapped from his office on October 20, 2005, and his gunshot-wounded body was discovered nearby. Three assassins assassinated Adel al-Zubeidi, a supporter of Vice President Taha Yassin Ramadan and Abdullah Kazim Ruwayyyid, on November 8, 2005. In the event, Thamer Hamoud al-Khuzaie, Barazan Ibrahim's attorney, was also hurt (Collingridge, 2019).

Throughout the trial, Saddam disobeyed the court's authority on numerous occasions. At one point, Saddam's legal team walked out of court, citing concerns about the constitutionality of the tribunal, the return of defence materials confiscated by US Army forces, and security concerns regarding the safety of the defence. Together with his co-defendants, Saddam criticized the tribunal and Chief Judge Amin. After listening to hours of testimony against him the next day, he became enraged with the court. He pleaded with them to "go to hell" because he was too exhausted to complete the trial. Later, on December 7, 2005, Saddam refused to enter court as a protest against the proceedings and his confinement conditions. Saddam complained that he had not been permitted to change his clothing for four days. On December 12, 2005, Saddam stated that instead of interrogating witnesses, his American captors subjected him to torture, saying, "I have been beaten in every part of my body, and the marks are everywhere."

On January 29, 2006, Saddam's half-brother Barzan Ibrahim al-Tikriti was dragged away by security, the defence team left the courtroom, and Saddam was ejected after a verbal altercation with chief judge Rauf Rashid Abd al-Rahman (Kirchheimer, 2015).

Saddam and four other defendants, including Saddam's half-brother Barzan al-Tikriti, former vice president Taha Yassin Ramadan, and former chief judge of Saddam's Revolutionary Court Awad Hamid al-Bander, demanded the death penalty and would have been executed if convicted and sentenced to death.

When Saddam's primary defence counsel, Khamis al-Obeidi, was murdered, he went on a hunger strike to protest the absence of international protection for lawyers. On June 23, 2006, Saddam reportedly terminated his starvation strike after missing only one meal (Collingridge, 2019).

CHAPTER 9

Handling Political Crimes and Punishments

Contents

9.1. INTRODUCTION

Handling political crimes and punishments is critical to maintaining social order and upholding the integrity of political systems. Political crimes are offences directed against a state's political order and institutions. These acts typically undermine the political system's stability, integrity, or functioning. Political crimes can take various forms, such as treason, sedition, subversion, political assassinations, and terrorism (Cohen, 2020).

Definition of political crimes: Defining political crimes is essential for identifying and addressing these offences effectively. Political crimes involve actions specifically intended to challenge or undermine the political system, influence power dynamics, or inflict harm upon individuals or the state. The definition of political crimes may vary depending on legal procedures and cultural contexts. It encompasses a wide range of acts, from plotting to overthrow a government to engaging in acts of violence against political leaders or institutions. Governments can develop appropriate legal frameworks and strategies to handle these crimes by defining political crimes. Addressing political crimes is significant in maintaining political stability and functioning democratic systems. Political crimes directly threaten democratic processes, governance structures, and social cohesion. By addressing political crimes effectively, governments can uphold the rule of law, protect national security, and preserve public trust in political institutions. Furthermore, addressing political crimes ensures that individuals who engage in such acts are held accountable for their actions, deterring future instances of these offences. Failure to address political crimes adequately can lead to political instability, erosion of public trust, and the perpetuation of a culture of impunity (Kollmann, 2012).

Political punishment refers to the penalties or sanctions imposed on individuals convicted of political crimes. These punishments provide a deterrent effect, uphold justice, and maintain social order. Political disciplines can take various forms, including imprisonment, capital punishment, exile, fines, and public shaming. The choice of punishment depends on factors such as the severity of the crime, legal considerations, and societal norms. Political discipline aims to hold offenders accountable, deter potential offenders, and protect the state's and its citizens' interests. Effective handling of political punishments requires balancing the rule of law and respecting individual rights and freedoms. Additionally, considerations such as rehabilitation and reintegration of political offenders into society play a role in shaping the approach to political punishment (Cohen, 2020).

9.2. HISTORICAL CONTEXT OF POLITICAL CRIMES AND PUNISHMENTS

Political crimes and punishments have existed throughout human history, with the understanding and handling of these offences evolving. Examining the historical context provides valuable insights into the development of political justice systems and the societal response to such crimes.

9.2.1. Early Examples of Political Crimes and Punishments

This highlights the significance placed on maintaining political stability and the authority of the ruling powers. In ancient Greece, acts of treason, betrayal, or rebellion threatened the very foundations of the city-state. They were treated as grave offences against the collective well-being. Exile, a severe punishment, removed the offender from society and served as a deterrent to others contemplating similar actions. Similarly, in ancient Rome, conspiracies against the Roman Republic or emperors were seen as direct threats to the established order. Punishments, such as public execution or banishment, were intended to discourage dissent and reinforce the ruling elite's authority. These early examples demonstrate the strong connection between political crimes and the preservation of power and control in ancient civilizations (Kollmann, 2012).

9.2.2. Evolution of Political Justice Systems

Over time, political justice systems underwent significant transformations, influenced by changing social, political, and philosophical ideologies. These changes shaped the approach to political crimes and the corresponding punishments (Cohen, 2020).

Ancient Civilizations and Political Punishments

In ancient civilizations such as Mesopotamia, Egypt, and Persia, political crimes were often seen as direct challenges to the ruling authority. Ancient civilizations viewed political crimes as acts that directly threatened the established ruling authority and social order. As such, the punishments for these offences were severe and intended to deter any form of dissent or rebellion. Public executions were a standard method of punishment, serving as a public spectacle to instill fear and discourage others from challenging the ruling power. Mutilations, such as amputations or branding, were also employed as means of physical punishment and as visible markers of the offender's transgressions. In some cases, political offenders were enslaved, further diminishing their social standing and reinforcing the authority of the ruling class. The Hammurabi Code, one of the earliest known legal codes from ancient Babylon, included specific provisions addressing political crimes and establishing guidelines for their punishments, reflecting the importance of maintaining political order in ancient societies (Kollmann, 2012).

Medieval Political Crimes and Punishments

Political crimes were intricately linked to religious and feudal structures during the Middle Ages. Treason against the monarchy or the church was considered a violation of secular authority and an offence against divine order. The punishments for such crimes were often brutal and served as a deterrent to potential dissenters. Public executions were prevalent, with methods such as beheadings or burnings at the stake being used to showcase the consequences of challenging political or religious authority publicly. Additionally, the establishment of tribunals, like the notorious Spanish Inquisition, played a significant role in identifying, prosecuting, and punishing individuals accused of political crimes, particularly those deemed heretical or seditious. These tribunals had far-reaching powers, often employing methods of interrogation and torture to extract confessions and maintain control over perceived threats to the established political and religious order (Cohen, 2020).

Modern Approaches to Political Justice

The Enlightenment period and the subsequent development of modern democratic principles influenced the approach to political crimes and punishments. Concepts of individual rights, due process, and the rule of law shaped how political crimes were addressed. Disciplines became more standardized, and the focus shifted towards rehabilitation and protecting individual liberties. Establishing legal systems and recognizing human rights formed the basis for modern approaches to political justice.

Today, modern democracies emphasize fair trials, the presumption of innocence, and proportionate punishments for political crimes. International legal frameworks, such as the Universal Declaration of Human Rights, provide guidelines for handling political crimes and protecting human rights. However, challenges remain in balancing the need for national security and individual freedoms in an increasingly interconnected world. Ongoing technological developments, globalization, and the emergence of new forms of political crimes pose new challenges for political justice systems. As societies evolve, the understanding and handling political crimes and their punishments will continue to adapt in response to changing circumstances (Kollmann, 2012).

9.3. TYPES OF POLITICAL CRIMES

Political crimes encompass a range of offences that target a state's political order and institutions. Understanding the different types of political crimes is crucial in effectively addressing and punishing these acts. This section explores three significant types: treason and betrayal of the state, sedition and subversion, and political assassinations and terrorism.

9.3.1. Treason and Betrayal of the State

Treason involves acts of betrayal or disloyalty against one's country or government. It typically entails actions aimed at overthrowing or undermining the established political order, often in favor of an external entity or ideology. The scope of treason varies across jurisdictions, but it commonly includes offences such as plotting against the government, espionage, or aiding enemies in times of war.

Historical cases of treason illustrate the severe consequences that have accompanied acts of betrayal against the state. The Gunpowder Plot of 1605 remains a significant example in English history, where a group of conspirators, including Guy Fawkes, planned to assassinate King James I and detonate explosives in Parliament. The discovery of the plot led to the execution of the conspirators, demonstrating the severe punishment imposed for their treasonous actions (Cohen, 2020).

The Julius and Ethel Rosenberg case in the United States during the Cold War also exemplifies the gravity of treason. The couple was accused and convicted of passing classified nuclear information to the Soviet Union, heightening fears of espionage and jeopardizing national security. The *Rosenbergs* were sentenced to death and executed, reflecting the severe consequences that can accompany acts of treason, particularly in cases involving the potential compromise of sensitive national interests (Kollmann, 2012).

These historical cases underscore the significance placed on preserving the integrity and stability of the state, leading to strict punishments for treason.

Such severe penalties deter individuals from engaging in acts threatening the government's security, sovereignty, and functioning. The enduring legacy of these cases serves as a reminder of the enduring importance placed on combatting treason and safeguarding the state's interests (Cohen, 2020).

9.3.2. Sedition and Subversion

Understanding sedition and subversion provides insights into how to challenge or undermine the established political order.

Sedition encompasses actions aimed at inciting resistance or rebellion against the governing authority. It involves disseminating seditious ideas, such as advocating for the overthrow of the government, promoting discontent among the population, or organizing activities that threaten public order. Sedition often seeks to erode the legitimacy of the ruling power and foster dissent among the populace (Figure 9.1).

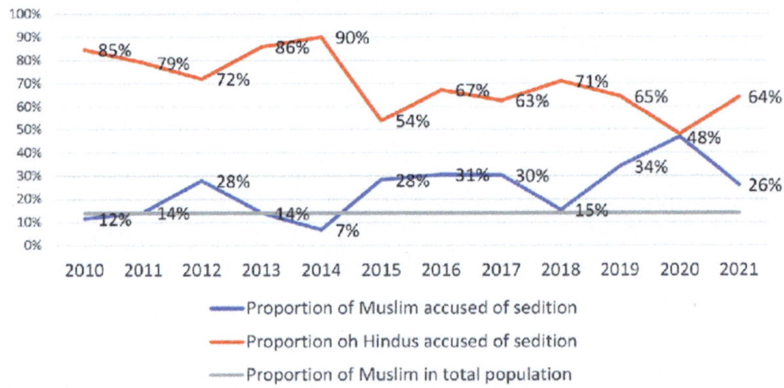

Figure 9.1. People accused of sedition by religion, 2010–21.

Source: Maiorano, Diego. (2023). INDIA AS AN ETHNOCRACY. Il Politico. 257. 59–75. 10.4081/ilpolitico.2022.766. Scientific Figure on ResearchGate. Available from: https://www.researchgate.net/figure/People-accused-of-sedition-by-religion-2010–21_fig1_367233757 (accessed on 22 September 2023)

Conversely, subversion involves more covert or secretive means of undermining the existing political order. It encompasses efforts to destabilize or weaken the government through activities intended to be subversive or clandestine. These activities may include espionage, infiltration, or sabotage to subvert the authority and functioning of the state (Cohen, 2020).

Both sedition and subversion pose significant challenges to political systems as they seek to erode the established order's stability, legitimacy, and authority. Governments often enact laws and regulations to address these threats, striking a balance between protecting national security and preserving individual freedoms, such as freedom of expression. The distinction between sedition and legitimate political dissent can be complex and vary depending on legal systems and cultural contexts (Kollmann, 2012).

Throughout history, various individuals and groups have used sedition and subversion to challenge existing political systems. One example is the French Revolution, where revolutionary factions used seditious propaganda and organized activities to incite the populace against the monarchy, leading to the overthrow of the French monarchy.

Another example is the activities of political extremists or separatist movements seeking to subvert the state's authority and establish an independent entity. The Irish Republican Army (IRA) in Ireland and the Basque separatist group ETA in Spain are notable examples of subversive movements that have engaged in violence and terrorism to further their political goals.

9.3.3. Political Assassinations and Terrorism

Political assassinations are defined as intentional and targeted killings of political leaders, influential figures, or individuals holding positions of power. These acts are carried out with the specific aim of achieving a political objective or influencing political outcomes. The motivations behind political assassinations can vary, including ideological, religious, or personal grievances, desire for power or control, or attempts to instigate social or political change.

Characteristics of political assassinations include their deliberate nature, as they are carefully planned and executed to eliminate specific individuals with significant political influence. These acts are intended to disrupt the government's functioning, alter political dynamics, or send a message to the broader population. Political assassinations can have far-reaching consequences, such as creating political instability, fueling social unrest, or shaping public opinion (Kollmann, 2012).

Political assassinations can be done by individuals acting alone, organized groups with shared objectives, or even state-sponsored entities. The methods employed can vary, including using firearms, explosives, or other means to carry out the assassination discreetly and maximize the act's impact. The choice of target often reflects the perceived importance of the individual's position or influence within the political landscape. The link between terrorism and political crimes is intricate and multifaceted (Figure 9.2). Terrorism can be seen as a specific form of political corruption that utilizes violence, intimidation, or coercion to achieve political, ideological, or religious objectives. Acts of terrorism are characterized by their intention to create fear, exert influence over a political system, and disrupt social order (Cohen, 2020).

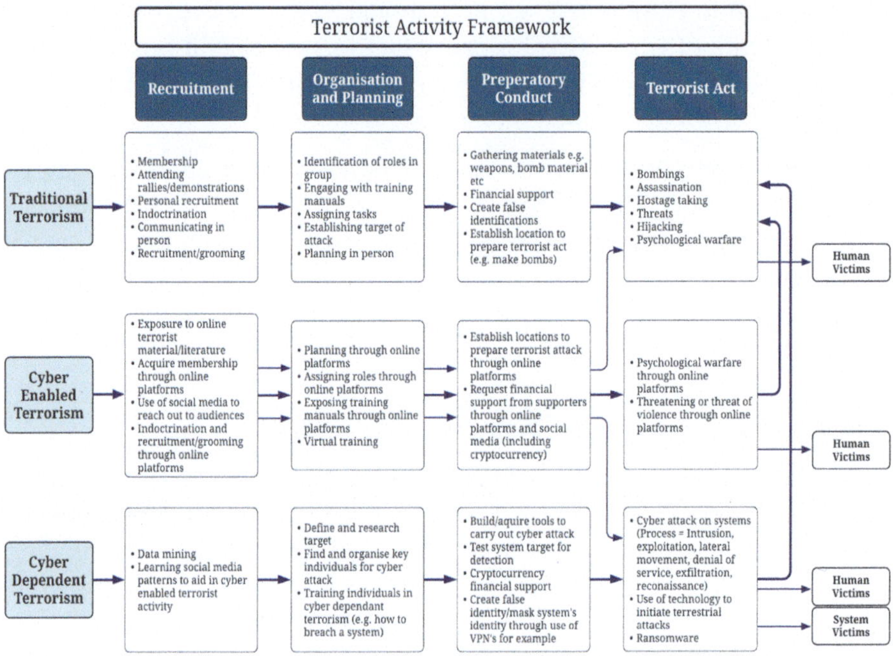

Figure 9.2. Terrorist activity framework entailing cyber terrorism.

Source: Correia, Victoria. (2022). An Explorative Study into the Importance of Defining and Classifying Cyber Terrorism in the United Kingdom. SN Computer Science. Scientific Figure on ResearchGate. Available from: https://www.researchgate.net/figure/Terrorist-activity-framework-entailing-cyber-terrorism-developed-from-7–16-This_fig2_356510214 (accessed on 22 September 2023)

Terrorism encompasses a range of activities, including bombings, assassinations, hostage-taking, and other acts of violence targeting civilians or political figures. These actions often challenge existing political structures, destabilize governments, or instigate social change. Terrorism seeks to achieve specific political outcomes by generating widespread fear and exerting pressure on political systems to meet the perpetrators' demands.

Political assassinations can also be employed as a tactic within broader terrorist campaigns. Targeting high-profile individuals, such as political leaders or influential figures, weakens the political system and undermines public confidence in the government's ability to maintain security. Assassinations can be strategically designed to disrupt governance, instigate social unrest, or further the agenda of the terrorist organization.

Numerous significant political assassinations have shaped the course of history. The assassination of Archduke Franz Ferdinand in 1914 triggered the start of World War I. The assassinations of leaders such as Mahatma Gandhi, Martin Luther King Jr., and Benazir Bhutto have had profound political and social impacts (Kollmann, 2012).

The aftermath of political assassinations often includes societal upheaval, political instability, and the reevaluation of security measures. These cases highlight the lasting consequences of political assassinations and the challenges in preventing and addressing such crimes.

9.4. POLITICAL PUNISHMENTS THROUGHOUT HISTORY

Throughout history, various forms of punishment have been employed to address political crimes. This section explores three significant types of political disciplines: capital punishment, imprisonment and exile, and public shaming and humiliation. Understanding the historical context, rationale, and impact of these punishments provides valuable insights into the evolution of political justice systems (Cohen, 2020).

9.4.1. Capital Punishment for Political Crimes

Capital punishment, or the death penalty, has been used for political offences throughout history. In ancient civilizations, such as Mesopotamia, Egypt, and Rome, political offenders faced public executions to deter and display the ruling power's authority. Methods of execution included crucifixion, beheading, or hanging, among others.

The death penalty for political crimes has been justified on various grounds. One rationale is to protect national security by eliminating individuals considered threats to the stability and functioning of the state. Capital punishment has been seen as a means to uphold the social order, sending a strong message that acts of treason or betrayal will not be tolerated. By imposing the ultimate penalty, societies sought to deter potential challengers and reinforce the authority of the ruling power. However, the use of the death penalty for political offences has been a topic of debate and controversy. Opponents argue that it violates fundamental human rights, such as the right to life and prohibiting cruel and unusual punishment. They emphasize the potential for wrongful convictions, the irreversibility of the sentence, and the risk of political motivations influencing judicial outcomes (Kollmann, 2012).

In contemporary times, the approach to capital punishment for political crimes varies across different jurisdictions. Some countries have abolished the death penalty altogether, while others retain it for specific offences. The trend has been towards a global decline in the use of the death penalty, with increasing recognition of the importance of human rights, due process, and proportionate punishment in political justice systems.

The use of capital punishment for political crimes has been debated and controversial. Arguments favor capital punishment emphasizing its deterrent effect, retribution for the offence, and the need to protect society from dangerous political offenders. Supporters argue that such disciplines send a strong message about the consequences of challenging political authority.

On the other hand, opponents of capital punishment argue that it violates human rights, including the right to life and the prohibition of cruel and unusual punishment. They highlight concerns about wrongful convictions, the irreversibility of the sentence, and the potential for political motivations to influence judicial outcomes. Additionally, critics argue that capital punishment fails to address the underlying causes of political crimes and may hinder prospects for rehabilitation (Cohen, 2020).

9.4.2. Imprisonment and Exile

Imprisonment has been a prevalent form of punishment for political crimes throughout history. Incarceration serves multiple purposes, including incapacitating offenders, protecting society, and promoting the concept of retribution or justice. Political imprisonment often involves the confinement of individuals engaged in acts of treason, sedition, or subversion against the state (Kollmann, 2012).

Imprisonment allows for the removal of political offenders from society, preventing further harm or disruptions to the political order. It also serves as a means of punishment and can be used to deter others from engaging in similar acts. Moreover, imprisonment may provide an opportunity for rehabilitation, reintegration, or gathering intelligence regarding other potential threats. Throughout history, political imprisonment and exile have been used to suppress dissent, maintain control, and punish individuals perceived as threats to the ruling powers. Examples from different eras illustrate how these punitive measures have been employed.

One prominent example is the exile of Napoleon Bonaparte following his defeat in 1815. After his reign as Emperor of France ended, Napoleon was exiled to the remote island of Saint Helena in the South Atlantic. This exile served the dual purpose of removing him from French soil and ensuring he posed no further political threat.

Totalitarian regimes of the 20th century also utilized political imprisonment and exile as tools of oppression. In the Soviet Union under Joseph Stalin, political dissidents and perceived enemies of the state were imprisoned in labor camps, such as the infamous Gulag system. Dissidents were stripped of their freedom and subjected to harsh conditions to suppress opposition to the ruling regime.

Similarly, during the Nazi regime in Germany, political opponents, including communists, socialists, and Jews, were targeted for imprisonment and eventual extermination in concentration camps. These camps served as instruments of political repression and genocide to eliminate perceived threats to Nazi ideology and maintain control over the population (Cohen, 2020).

These examples demonstrate how political imprisonment and exile have been used throughout history to silence dissent, punish the opposition, and maintain the authority of ruling powers. They highlight the grave human rights violations that can occur when these punitive measures are abused and serve as reminders of the importance of safeguarding individual liberties and protecting the rights of political prisoners (Kollmann, 2012).

9.4.3. Public Shaming and Humiliation

Public shaming has been used as a political punishment to publicly disgrace offenders and deter others from committing similar acts. This punishment aims to inflict psychological and social harm by subjecting individuals to public displays, physical disciplines, or symbolic gestures of humiliation. Examples include public floggings, parades of shame, or marking individuals with visible signs of their transgressions. Public shaming intends to create a strong deterrent effect and reinforce social norms, emphasizing the consequences of challenging political authority or committing political crimes. However, public shaming as a political punishment raises ethical concerns regarding human rights, dignity, and potential abuse. It is essential to balance addressing political offences and respecting individual rights, ensuring that punishment measures do not violate the principles of fairness, proportionality, and the preservation of human dignity.

Throughout history, numerous instances of public humiliation have been used as punishment for political crimes. For example, in ancient Rome, individuals convicted of treason or betrayal might be subjected to *damnation memoriae*, erasing their existence from historical records and public memory. Similarly, general "struggle sessions" were held publicly during the Chinese Cultural Revolution to shame and denounce individuals accused of political offences.

Public shaming and humiliation as punishments for political crimes raise ethical and human rights concerns. Critics argue that such practices can have long-lasting psychological effects, infringe upon an individual's dignity, and perpetuate a cycle of violence and retribution (Cohen, 2020).

Understanding the historical use of these political punishments provides valuable insights into the evolution of political justice systems, the rationale behind different forms of punishment, and the impact on individuals and society. Contemporary approaches to political disciplines often prioritize principles of fairness, proportionality, and the protection of human rights, reflecting an evolving understanding of justice and the need for a balanced response to political crimes (Kollmann, 2012).

9.5. THE ROLE OF INTERNATIONAL LAW IN HANDLING POLITICAL CRIMES

International law plays a crucial role in addressing political crimes and establishing a framework for holding individuals accountable for their actions. This section examines the critical aspects of international law that pertain to political crimes, including international legal frameworks, principles of extradition and political asylum, and the establishment of international criminal tribunals.

9.5.1. International Legal Frameworks for Addressing Political Crimes

International legal frameworks provide a basis for addressing political crimes and ensuring that individuals responsible for such offences are held accountable. Treaties and conventions, such as the International Covenant on Civil and Political Rights and the Geneva Conventions, outline the rights and protections afforded to individuals and establish the obligations of states in addressing political crimes. These legal instruments show principles of due process, fair trial, and prohibiting torture or cruel, inhuman, or degrading treatment.

Additionally, international legal frameworks encompass agreements related to specific political crimes, such as genocide, war crimes, crimes against humanity, and aggression. The Rome Statute, which established the International Criminal Court (ICC), is a significant treaty that provides a comprehensive legal framework for prosecuting individuals responsible for the most serious international crimes.

9.5.2. Principles of Extradition and Political Asylum

Extradition and political asylum are principles of international law that directly impact the handling of political crimes. Extradition is the legal process through which individuals charged with or convicted of political crimes in one country are transferred to another for prosecution or punishment. It involves cooperation between states and applying bilateral or multilateral extradition treaties (Cohen, 2020).

On the other hand, political asylum protects individuals who fear persecution or harm in their home country due to their political activities, beliefs, or affiliations. It allows individuals to seek refuge in another country and prohibits their return to their home country, where they may face persecution. Political asylum safeguards individuals who may be targeted for their involvement in political crimes or as a means of political repression (Kollmann, 2012).

9.5.3. The Establishment of International Criminal Tribunals

International criminal tribunals are specialized courts created to prosecute individuals responsible for severe political crimes. These tribunals operate within the framework of international law and aim to ensure justice, accountability, and the prevention of impunity.

The International Criminal Court (ICC)

The International Criminal Court (ICC) is the first permanent international tribunal with jurisdiction over individuals accused of genocide, crimes against humanity, war crimes, and aggression (Figure 9.3). It is designed to complement national criminal justice systems and step in when states can or unwillingly prosecute these crimes themselves. The ICC investigates and prosecutes individuals responsible for the most serious international crimes, irrespective of their official positions or nationalities (Cohen, 2020).

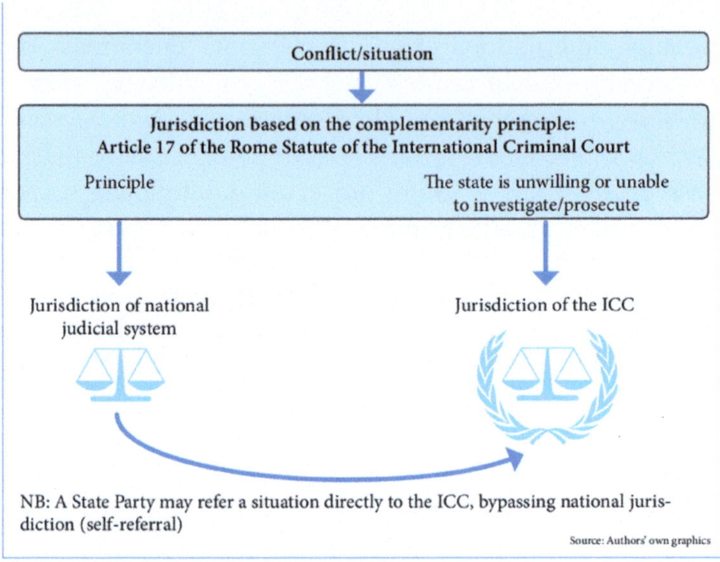

Figure 9.3. The International Criminal Court (ICC) is a court of last resort Complementarity and self-referrals.

Source: Roth, Michele & Ulbert, Cornelia & Debiel, Tobias. (2015). Global Trends 2015. Prospects for World Society. Scientific Figure on ResearchGate. Available from: https://www.researchgate.net/figure/The-International-Criminal-Court-ICC-is-a-court-of-last-resort-Complementarity-and_fig23_337473128 (accessed on 22 September 2023)

Ad Hoc Tribunals for Specific Political Crimes

Ad hoc tribunals, such as the International Criminal Tribunal for the former Yugoslavia (ICTY) and the International Criminal Tribunal for Rwanda (ICTR), were established to address specific political crimes committed during conflicts in the former Yugoslavia and Rwanda, respectively. These tribunals had temporal jurisdiction and were tasked with prosecuting individuals responsible for genocide, war crimes, and crimes against humanity.

These international criminal tribunals are crucial in ensuring victims' justice and holding those responsible for political crimes accountable. They contribute to developing international jurisprudence, establishing precedents, and fostering reconciliation and transitional justice in post-conflict societies (Kollmann, 2012).

International law provides a framework for addressing political crimes, encompassing legal frameworks, principles of extradition and political asylum, and the establishment of international criminal tribunals. These mechanisms aim to uphold human rights, promote accountability, and prevent impunity for individuals involved in political crimes. They contribute to developing a just and equitable global system that seeks to protect individuals, promote peace, and foster the rule of law in the face of political atrocities.

9.6. CHALLENGES IN INVESTIGATING AND PROSECUTING POLITICAL CRIMES

Investigating and prosecuting political crimes present numerous challenges due to the sensitive nature of these offences and the complexities involved. This section delves into the critical challenges encountered, including political interference and corruption, the lack of evidence and witness protection, balancing national security and individual rights, and overcoming jurisdictional hurdles in transnational cases (Cohen, 2020).

9.6.1. Political Interference and Corruption

One of the significant challenges in investigating and prosecuting political crimes is the potential for political interference and corruption. Political interference occurs when individuals in positions of power manipulate or obstruct investigations and prosecutions to protect their interests or those of their allies. This interference can impede the impartiality and independence of the justice system, hindering the pursuit of justice and accountability.

Corruption further compounds the challenge, as it undermines the integrity of law enforcement agencies, judicial systems, and institutions responsible for handling political crimes. Bribery, illicit influence, and the abuse of power can lead to the manipulation of evidence, the shielding of offenders, and the erosion of public trust in the justice system. Political interference and corruption are essential for fair and transparent investigations and prosecutions (Kollmann, 2012).

9.6.2. Lack of Evidence and Witness Protection

Obtaining sufficient evidence to establish guilt beyond a reasonable doubt is often challenging in political crime cases. Political crimes may involve covert activities, clandestine networks, and complex operations, making it difficult to gather concrete evidence. Additionally, witnesses may be reluctant to come forward due to fear of retaliation, intimidation, or potential harm to themselves or their families.

The lack of witness cooperation and protection presents a significant hurdle in investigating and prosecuting political crimes. Witnesses are crucial in providing testimony, corroborating evidence, and shedding light on the intricate networks involved. Ensuring their safety, confidentiality, and willingness to testify is vital for a successful investigation and prosecution. Implementing robust witness protection programs and creating a supportive environment is crucial in addressing this challenge (Kollmann, 2012).

9.6.3. Balancing National Security and Individual Rights

A critical challenge in handling political crimes lies in striking a balance between national security concerns and the protection of individual rights. Political crimes often intersect with matters of national security, as they may involve threats to the stability, sovereignty, or democratic processes of a state. This necessitates measures to safeguard national security interests, such as protecting classified information or intelligence sources.

However, upholding fundamental principles of justice, due process, and respect for human rights during investigations and prosecutions is essential. Safeguarding individual rights, including the right to a fair trial, the prohibition of torture, and the protection of privacy, is paramount in maintaining the justice system's integrity. Balancing national security and individual rights requires the development of legal frameworks, oversight mechanisms, and checks and balances that ensure accountability and transparency (Cohen, 2020).

9.6.4. Overcoming Jurisdictional Hurdles in Transnational Cases

Political crimes often transcend national boundaries, posing jurisdictional challenges in investigating and prosecuting perpetrators. Transnational cases involve multiple legal systems, varying laws, and complex extradition processes. Cooperation between different jurisdictions is vital to ensure effective investigations, the sharing of evidence, and the extradition of suspects. Differences in legal systems, extradition treaties, and political considerations can complicate pursuing justice in transnational cases. Harmonizing legal frameworks, enhancing international cooperation, and establishing mutual legal assistance agreements can help overcome these hurdles. International organizations, such as Interpol and Europol, play crucial roles in facilitating collaboration between law enforcement agencies and promoting coordination in transnational investigations and prosecutions.

Addressing the challenges in investigating and prosecuting political crimes requires robust institutional frameworks, transparency, accountability mechanisms, and international cooperation. Strengthening the rule of law, combating corruption, protecting witnesses, and upholding fundamental rights are essential in ensuring justice, accountability, and the prevention of impunity in political crime cases.

9.7. RESTORATIVE JUSTICE AND RECONCILIATION IN POLITICAL CRIMES

Restorative justice and reconciliation are alternative approaches to addressing political crimes that focus on healing, rebuilding relationships, and promoting long-term peace and stability. This section explores the concept of restorative justice, the role of truth and reconciliation commissions and provides case studies of successful reconciliation processes (Kollmann, 2012).

9.7.1. The Concept of Restorative Justice

Restorative justice goes beyond conventional criminal justice approaches by emphasizing the healing and restoration of individuals and communities affected by political crimes (Figure 9.4). It recognizes that the impacts of political crimes extend far beyond the immediate victims and offenders, affecting the fabric of society as a whole. By involving all stakeholders in the process, restorative justice promotes dialogue, empathy, and understanding, laying the foundation for genuine reconciliation (Cohen, 2020).

In the context of political crimes, restorative justice provides a space for acknowledging the pain and suffering endured by victims and communities. It allows victims to have their voices heard, share their experiences, and seek recognition for their pain. Offenders, in turn, are encouraged to take responsibility for their actions, confront the consequences of their behavior, and actively contribute to repairing the harm caused.

Figure 9.4. The most restorative processes involve the active participation of all three sets of primary stakeholders.

Source: McCold, Paul & WACHTEL, TED. (2003). In Pursuit of Paradigm: A Theory of Restorative Justice. Scientific Figure on ResearchGate. Available from: https://www.researchgate.net/figure/The-very-process-of-interacting-is-critical-to-meeting-stakeholders-emotional-needs-The_fig2_237314664 (accessed on 22 September 2023)

Restorative justice also recognizes the importance of addressing the underlying causes of political crimes, such as systemic inequalities, social divisions, or historical grievances. By fostering a deeper understanding of these factors, restorative justice seeks to address root causes, promote social cohesion, and prevent the recurrence of political crimes in the future (Kollmann, 2012).

Furthermore, restorative justice emphasizes the importance of reintegration and rehabilitation. It recognizes that offenders, too, have the potential to transform and contribute positively to society. By providing opportunities for offenders to understand the impact of their actions, make amends, and reintegrate into the community, restorative justice seeks to break cycles of violence and create conditions for sustainable peace (Cohen, 2020).

9.7.2. Truth and Reconciliation Commissions

Truth and reconciliation commissions (TRCs) are institutional mechanisms that facilitate healing, truth-seeking, and reconciliation in societies affected by political crimes or large-scale human rights abuses. TRCs provide a platform for victims and perpetrators to share their experiences, uncover the truth, and promote accountability while offering reparations and implementing systemic reforms to prevent future conflicts.

TRCs operate on the premise that the truth is essential for genuine reconciliation and restoring social harmony. By documenting human rights violations, providing a historical record, and fostering a culture of accountability, TRCs contribute to the healing process, address victims' grievances, and provide opportunities for societal transformation.

9.7.3. Case Studies of Successful Reconciliation Processes

Numerous case studies highlight successful reconciliation processes and their positive impact on post-conflict societies. One notable example is the Truth and Reconciliation Commission in South Africa, established after apartheid. The commission provided a platform for victims and perpetrators to share their stories, seek amnesty, and contribute to healing and reconciliation. While controversial, it was crucial in preventing widespread violence and laying the foundation for a more inclusive and democratic society.

Another case study is the reconciliation process in Rwanda following the 1994 genocide. The *Gacaca* courts, a community-based justice system, were established to address the immense caseload of perpetrators and facilitate the truth-telling process. These courts aimed to promote accountability, provide reparations and foster reconciliation at the grassroots level.

The success of these reconciliation processes was attributed to their inclusive nature, transparency, and commitment to addressing the needs of victims, promoting truth-telling, and holding perpetrators accountable. They demonstrated the transformative power of restorative justice in rebuilding social cohesion and preventing future conflicts (Kollmann, 2012). Restorative justice and reconciliation processes offer an alternative to traditional punitive approaches in addressing political crimes. They prioritize the healing and well-being of individuals and communities affected by conflicts, promote understanding, and lay the groundwork for sustainable peace and reconciliation. While challenges and limitations exist, their potential to promote justice, reconciliation, and societal healing makes them significant tools in the aftermath of political crimes.

9.8. CONTEMPORARY APPROACHES TO POLITICAL CRIMES AND PUNISHMENTS

In the modern era, addressing political crimes and punishments has evolved to adapt to the changing dynamics of society (Figure 9.5). This section explores contemporary approaches to political crimes, including a comparative analysis of political justice systems, innovations in handling political crimes through forensic technologies and psychological profiling, and the importance of rehabilitating and reintegrating political offenders (Cohen, 2020).

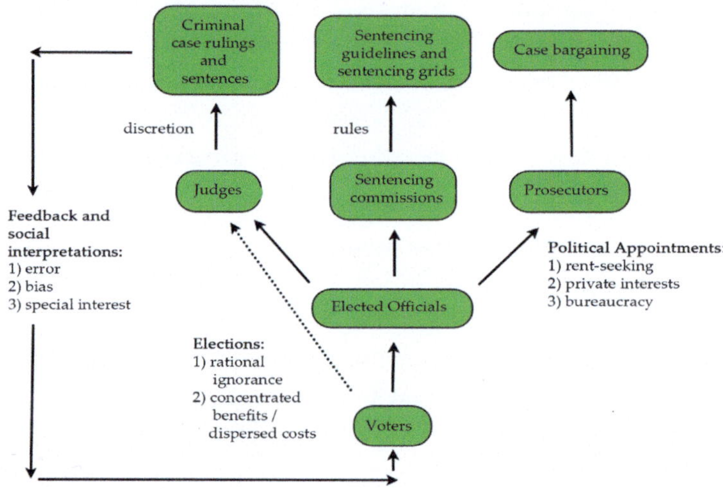

Figure 9.5. The structure of decision making within the criminal justice system.

Source: D'Amico, Daniel. (2023). The Imprisoner's Dilemma: The Political Economy of Proportionate Punishment A dissertation submitted in partial fulfillment of the requirements for the degree of Doctor of Philosophy at George Mason University. Scientific Figure on ResearchGate. Available from: https://www.researchgate.net/figure/The-structure-of-decision-making-within-the-criminal-justice-system_fig6_242672356 (accessed on 22 September 2023)

9.8.1. Comparative Analysis of Political Justice Systems

A comparative analysis of political justice systems allows for a comprehensive understanding of the various approaches taken by different countries in addressing political crimes. It examines the legal frameworks, judicial processes, and institutional structures governing the handling of these offences. By studying and comparing these systems, policymakers and practitioners can gain valuable insights into the strengths and weaknesses of different approaches (Cohen, 2020).

One crucial aspect to consider in comparative analysis is the historical context of political justice systems. Historical events, such as periods of political instability or transitions from authoritarian rule to democracy, can shape the development of legal frameworks and the approaches taken to address political crimes. Cultural norms and values also influence the design and implementation of these systems, as societies may have differing views on the balance between individual rights and collective security.

Legal traditions and political ideologies further contribute to the diversity of political justice systems. For example, common law and civil law traditions have distinct approaches to criminal justice and may prioritize different aspects, such as adversarial versus inquisitorial processes. Similarly, political ideologies can influence the emphasis on punishment, rehabilitation, or restorative justice in addressing political crimes (Kollmann, 2012).

Comparative analysis allows for the identification of best practices and areas for improvement. By examining the outcomes of different systems, policymakers can learn from successful approaches and implement reforms that align with the principles of fairness, justice, and human rights. It enables sharing of knowledge and ideas across jurisdictions, fostering a collaborative and evidence-based approach to addressing political crimes.

Furthermore, comparative analysis promotes accountability and transparency in political justice systems. It provides a basis for evaluating the effectiveness of measures taken to prevent political crimes, investigate offences, and hold perpetrators accountable. By assessing the strengths and weaknesses of different systems, policymakers can implement reforms that enhance their systems' integrity, efficiency, and fairness (Cohen, 2020).

9.8.2. Innovations in Handling Political Crimes

Advancements in technology and understanding human behavior have led to innovative approaches to handling political crimes (Figure 9.6).

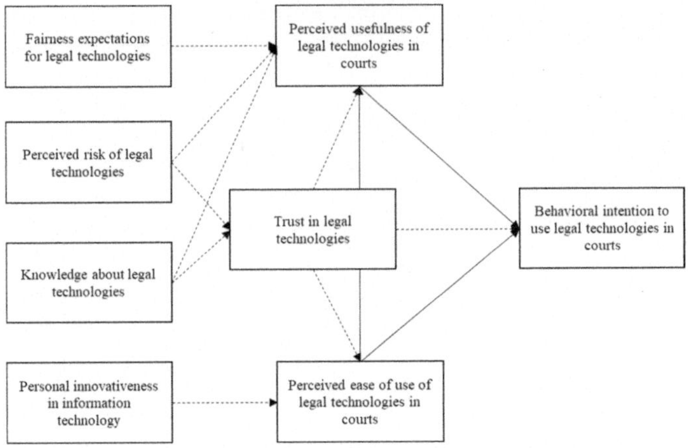

Figure 9.6. People's attitudes towards technologies in courts.

Source: Barysė, D. (2022). People's Attitudes towards Technologies in Courts. *Laws*, 11(5), 71. MDPI AG. Retrieved from http://dx.doi.org/10.3390/laws11050071

Two notable innovations are the utilization of forensic technologies and the application of psychological profiling.

Utilization of Forensic Technologies

Forensic technologies have revolutionized the investigation and prosecution of political crimes. DNA analysis, fingerprint identification, digital forensics, and surveillance technologies provide valuable evidence to establish links, identify perpetrators, and support legal proceedings. These technologies enable investigators to reconstruct events, gather critical evidence, and strengthen the case against those responsible for political crimes.

Using forensic technologies, such as advanced crime scene investigation techniques and digital analysis tools, improves the accuracy and reliability of evidence. It enhances the chances of identifying offenders, ensuring a more robust and scientific approach to investigating and prosecuting political crimes (Kollmann, 2012).

Application of Psychological Profiling

Psychological profiling is another innovative approach to handling political crimes. It involves analyzing the behavior, motivations, and psychological characteristics of individuals involved in political offences to gain insights into their actions and potential future behavior (Cohen, 2020). Psychological profiling can help investigators and law enforcement agencies identify patterns, understand the underlying motivations behind political crimes, and develop strategies to prevent and address such offences. By combining psychological analysis with other investigative techniques, authorities can create profiles that assist in identifying and apprehending individuals involved in political crimes.

9.8.3. Rehabilitation and Reintegration of Political Offenders

Rehabilitation and reintegration are essential to a comprehensive approach to addressing political crimes. While punishment and accountability play important roles, the ultimate goal is to reintegrate offenders into society and prevent the recurrence of political crimes.

Rehabilitation programs for political offenders focus on addressing the underlying causes that contribute to their engagement in political crimes. These programs may include educational opportunities, vocational training, counselling, and support services to promote personal growth, develop life skills, and foster empathy and non-violent conflict resolution (Kollmann, 2012).

Successful rehabilitation and reintegration require a multi-dimensional approach involving collaboration between criminal justice systems, social services, educational institutions, and the community. By addressing the root causes of political crimes and providing opportunities for personal transformation, rehabilitation programs reduce recidivism and promote long-term social stability.

Reintegrating political offenders into society is a delicate process that requires community support, forgiveness, and opportunities for them to contribute positively to society. Through programs facilitating their reintegration, political offenders can regain their sense of belonging, rebuild their lives, and contribute to developing peaceful and inclusive communities.

9.9. THE ROLE OF INTERNATIONAL ORGANIZATIONS IN ADDRESSING POLITICAL CRIMES

International organizations play a crucial role in addressing political crimes and promoting justice on a global scale. This section explores the part of the United Nations (UN) and its initiatives, as well as the contribution of regional organizations in promoting political justice (Kollmann, 2012).

9.9.1. United Nations and Its Initiatives

With its broad membership and global reach, the United Nations is a critical platform for addressing political crimes and fostering international cooperation. The UN promotes human rights, the rule of law, and the prevention of impunity through various initiatives and mechanisms (Cohen, 2020).

One significant initiative is the International Criminal Court (ICC), established by the Rome Statute in 1998. The ICC is the first permanent international criminal tribunal with jurisdiction over genocide, war crimes, crimes against humanity, and the crime of aggression. It investigates and prosecutes individuals responsible for the most serious international crimes, including political crimes, when national jurisdictions are unable or unwilling to do so (Kollmann, 2012).

The UN also supports the work of special rapporteurs, independent experts, and commissions of inquiry to investigate political crimes and human rights violations. These mechanisms gather evidence, document violations, and provide recommendations to member states and the international community.

Furthermore, the UN General Assembly and Security Council can establish ad hoc tribunals, such as the International Criminal Tribunal for the Former Yugoslavia (ICTY) and the International Criminal Tribunal for Rwanda (ICTR), to address specific political crimes committed during conflicts. These tribunals contribute to accountability, justice, and reconciliation in post-conflict societies.

9.9.2. Role of Regional Organizations in Promoting Political Justice

Regional organizations also play a vital role in addressing political crimes and promoting justice within their respective regions. These organizations have a deeper understanding of the local context and can collaborate closely with member states to address specific challenges and strengthen regional mechanisms for political justice (Cohen, 2020).

For example, the European Union (EU) has been instrumental in promoting human rights, democracy, and the rule of law among its member states. The EU provides financial and technical assistance and monitors compliance with these principles through the European Court of Human Rights and the European Commission (Kollmann, 2012).

In Africa, the African Union (AU) has established the African Court on Human and Peoples' Rights and the African Commission on Human and Peoples' Rights to address human rights violations, including political crimes, within the continent. The AU also supports peacekeeping missions and initiatives to prevent and resolve conflicts, which can contribute to addressing the root causes of political crimes.

In the Americas, the Organization of American States (OAS) has mechanisms to promote democracy, human rights, and the rule of law among its member states. The Inter-American Court of Human Rights and the Inter-American Commission on Human Rights work to investigate human rights violations and provide recommendations for justice and accountability (Cohen, 2020).

These regional organizations provide a platform for dialogue, collaboration, and the exchange of best practices in addressing political crimes. They are vital in supporting member states' efforts to strengthen their legal frameworks, enhance investigative capacities, and promote justice, reconciliation, and respect for human rights within their regions.

9.10. CONCLUSION

Throughout this chapter, we have explored the multifaceted topic of handling political crimes and punishments. We began by defining political crimes and understanding their significance in society. We delved into the historical context of political crimes, examining early examples and the evolution of political justice systems from ancient civilizations to modern approaches.

We then explored the various types of political crimes, including treason, sedition, subversion, and political assassinations, and discussed their definitions, historical cases, and characteristics. We examined the different forms of political punishments throughout history, such as capital punishment, imprisonment, exile, and public shaming (Kollmann, 2012).

The role of international law in handling political crimes was highlighted, including international legal frameworks, principles of extradition and political asylum, and the establishment of international criminal tribunals like the International Criminal Court (ICC) and ad hoc tribunals.

We also addressed the challenges in investigating and prosecuting political crimes, such as political interference, corruption, lack of evidence, witness protection, and balancing national security and individual rights. Additionally, we discussed the importance of restorative justice and reconciliation in addressing political crimes, including the concept of restorative justice, truth and reconciliation commissions, and successful case studies (Cohen, 2020).

Furthermore, we examined contemporary approaches to political crimes and punishments, such as the comparative analysis of political justice systems, innovations in handling political crimes through forensic technologies and psychological profiling, and the rehabilitation and reintegration of political offenders.

The effective handling of political crimes and punishments is of paramount importance for the maintenance of peace, justice, and societal stability. Political crimes threaten the functioning of political institutions, the rule of law, and the well-being of individuals and communities. By addressing political crimes effectively, societies can ensure accountability, deterrence, and the protection of human rights.

Addressing political crimes in a fair and just manner is crucial for the establishment of trust in political systems and institutions. It sends a message that no one is above the law, regardless of their position or influence. Effective handling of political crimes also promotes social cohesion, reconciliation, and healing of societies affected by past political atrocities (Cohen, 2020).

Moreover, the handling of political crimes sets precedents and influences future behavior. By providing appropriate punishments and rehabilitation opportunities, societies can prevent the recurrence of political crimes and promote a culture of peace, respect for human rights, and democratic governance.

Political justice systems will continue to face various challenges and opportunities. Technological advancements will present benefits and challenges in investigating and prosecuting political crimes. Forensic technologies, artificial intelligence, and data analytics will enhance investigative capabilities and raise concerns about privacy, ethics, and potential biases (Kollmann, 2012).

Globalization and the interconnectedness of societies will necessitate increased cooperation and collaboration between nations in addressing transnational political crimes. Overcoming jurisdictional hurdles and harmonizing legal frameworks will be crucial for practical international collaboration in addressing political crimes.

Additionally, political justice systems must adapt to new and emerging forms of political crimes, such as cybercrimes, digital propaganda, and online disinformation campaigns. Strengthening legal frameworks, developing specialized investigative units, and enhancing international cooperation will be essential in tackling these evolving challenges (Kollmann, 2012).

The future of political justice systems also lies in advancing restorative justice approaches, promoting reconciliation, and prioritizing the rehabilitation and reintegration of political offenders. Investing in educational programs, vocational training, and psychological support will contribute to breaking cycles of violence and promoting long-term peace and stability (Cohen, 2020).

CHAPTER 10

Challenges in Political Justice

Contents

In the realm of political justice, the pursuit of fairness and equality in the governance of societies faces numerous challenges. These challenges arise from a complex interplay of factors, including the inherent complexities of political systems, the influence of power dynamics, the evolving nature of social and cultural contexts, and the inherent biases and limitations of human decision-making. This chapter delves into the intricacies and obstacles that impede the realization of political justice, shedding light on the multifaceted challenges that societies encounter in their quest for equitable governance (Habermas, 2010).

10.1. CORRUPTION

Corruption is a multifaceted and pervasive challenge that undermines the principles of political justice. It is characterized by the misuse of public power, entrusted resources, or positions of authority for personal gain or to secure unfair advantages. Corruption erodes the foundations of democracy, distorts decision-making processes, and hampers socioeconomic development (Scoones, 2010).

Corruption in political justice encompasses a wide range of illicit activities, including bribery, embezzlement, nepotism, favoritism, fraud, and money laundering. It can manifest at different levels of government, from local to national, and can permeate various branches and institutions within the political system. Political corruption can involve politicians, public officials, civil servants, and even private individuals who collude with those in power to exploit their influence for personal gain (Habermas, 2010).

One key aspect of corruption in political justice is bribery. This occurs when individuals offer, promise, or give money, gifts, or other forms of inducement to public officials to influence their actions or decisions. Bribery compromises the integrity of public officials, undermines the fairness of policy-making processes, and distorts the allocation of resources. It creates an environment where decisions are driven by personal interests rather than the common good, leading to a loss of public trust and confidence in the political system (Scoones, 2010).

Embezzlement is another form of corruption when individuals entrusted with public funds or assets misappropriate them for personal enrichment. This misallocation of resources deprives society of much-needed investments in infrastructure, healthcare, education, and other essential services. It perpetuates social inequalities and hampers sustainable development by diverting resources away from the public good towards the pockets of the corrupt. Nepotism and favoritism represent yet another facet of corruption in political justice. These practices involve showing undue preference to family members, friends, or acquaintances in distributing positions, contracts, or public resources. By prioritizing personal connections over merit and competence, nepotism and favoritism undermine the principles of fairness, equality of opportunity, and transparency. They create a breeding ground for inefficiency and ineffectiveness within the political system, as individuals with the necessary qualifications and skills may be overlooked in favor of those with personal connections (Habermas, 2010).

The consequences of corruption in political justice are far-reaching and damaging. It weakens the rule of law, erodes public trust, and fosters a culture of impunity. When corrupt individuals go unpunished or receive lenient sentences, it conveys that integrity and accountability are not valued in society. This, in turn, perpetuates a vicious cycle of corruption, as potential wrongdoers are emboldened by the lack of consequences (Scoones, 2010).

One of the most significant impacts of corruption on political justice is the erosion of public trust. When citizens witness politicians and public officials engaging in corrupt practices, such as bribery, embezzlement, or nepotism, their faith in the political system's integrity is shaken. Corruption creates a perception that those in power prioritize personal gain over the common good, leading to disillusionment and apathy among the populace. This erosion of trust undermines the legitimacy of political institutions and weakens their ability to serve as effective vehicles for justice (Habermas, 2010).

Moreover, corruption diverts resources from essential public services, leading to inadequate healthcare, education, and infrastructure. It exacerbates poverty and inequality, as those with access to power and resources enrich themselves at the expense of the marginalized and disadvantaged. Furthermore, corruption undermines democratic processes by distorting electoral campaigns, manipulating public opinion, and stifling political competition. It diminishes citizens' voices as decisions are made to serve the interests of a few rather than the welfare of the entire society.

Furthermore, corruption distorts decision-making processes within the political sphere. Instead of policies and laws being formulated based on the needs and interests of the people, they are often influenced by bribery or other illicit exchanges. This leads to a skewed allocation of resources, favoring the corrupt few at the expense of the wider population. As a result, political justice, which demands equitable distribution of resources and opportunities, becomes compromised. The marginalized and vulnerable segments of society suffer disproportionately, as corruption perpetuates a cycle of poverty, exclusion, and social injustice (Habermas, 2010).

Corruption also exacerbates inequalities within societies. It creates a system in which wealth and influence, rather than merit and competency, determine access to political power and decision-making. This undermines the principles of fairness and equal representation and reinforces existing disparities in socioeconomic status. Marginalized groups often lack the means to engage in corrupt practices or secure political favors, their voices are silenced, and their interests are ignored. Consequently, political justice becomes an elusive ideal, with power concentrated in the hands of a privileged few (Scoones, 2010).

The impact of corruption on political justice extends beyond national borders. Corruption in politics can severely affect global justice and the pursuit of international cooperation. Illicit financial flows often facilitated through corrupt practices, drain resources from developing countries, hindering their progress and exacerbating poverty. Moreover, corruption can undermine efforts to combat transnational challenges such as climate change, terrorism, and human rights abuses, as it compromises the credibility and effectiveness of international institutions.

Addressing corruption in political justice requires a comprehensive approach that combines legal measures, institutional reforms, and public awareness campaigns. Strengthening anti-corruption legislation, establishing independent oversight bodies, and promoting transparency and accountability are crucial to combating corruption. Additionally, fostering a culture of integrity and ethics within society, promoting civic engagement, and encouraging the active participation of citizens in the political process can help reduce corruption's grip on political justice (Scoones, 2010).

As we have seen, corruption poses significant challenges to political justice by undermining public trust, distorting resource allocation, and eroding the rule of law. However, crime is one of many obstacles to political justice. Partisanship and political bias also present formidable challenges that must be addressed to ensure a just and equitable political system. In the following section, we will delve into the impact of partisanship and political bias on political justice and explore potential strategies to mitigate their detrimental effects (Habermas, 2010).

10.2. PARTISANSHIP AND POLITICAL BIAS

In any democratic society, pursuing political justice is essential for maintaining the integrity and fairness of the political system. However, partisanship and political bias present significant challenges to seeking political justice, often compromising the principles of fairness and impartiality. Partisanship refers to the solid and unwavering support for a particular political party or ideology, which can influence judgments and actions within political justice.

On the other hand, political bias refers to the inclination or prejudice towards a particular political ideology, party, or group. It manifests in various forms, such as biased media coverage, skewed policy formulation, and unequal treatment of individuals based on their political affiliations. These biases can undermine the principles of fairness and impartiality, leading to a distorted representation of the diverse range of views and interests within society (Scoones, 2010).

One of the significant influences of partisanship is decision-making within the political justice system. When individuals in positions of authority, such as judges, prosecutors, or law enforcement officials, harbor strong partisan affiliations, there is a risk that their judgments may be swayed by their ideological leanings. This bias can manifest in various ways, including favoritism towards members of their party or a predisposition to dismiss or undermine the claims of political opponents. Such biases compromise the impartiality and fairness crucial for upholding political justice (Habermas, 2010).

Subsequently, besides the concept of political justice revolves around the principles of impartiality and fairness, partisan influences can undermine these principles and lead to unequal treatment under the law. When political bias seeps into the decision-making processes, it can distort the interpretation and application of laws, resulting in disparate outcomes for individuals or groups based on their political affiliation. This erosion of impartiality threatens the foundation of political justice and weakens public trust in the system (Scoones, 2010).

In addition, partisanship and political bias can erode public trust and confidence in political institutions, which is essential for the public to have faith in their government. These factors can create the perception that the justice system is not impartial but is somewhat influenced by political affiliations. When people perceive that the outcomes of legal proceedings or investigations are predetermined based on political affiliation, it undermines their belief in the system's fairness. This loss of trust can have far-reaching consequences, including decreased civic participation, disillusionment with the political process, and increased societal polarization.

While political bias affects the justice system's fairness and impartiality, unequal access further compounds these concerns, disparities in access to justice encompass a range of factors, including economic, social, and geographic barriers that hinder individuals and communities from fully exercising their rights within the legal system (Habermas, 2010).

10.3. DISPARITIES IN ACCESS TO JUSTICE

In pursuing a just and fair political system, ensuring that every individual has equal access to justice is crucial. However, one of the significant challenges in political justice lies in disparities in access to this fundamental right. These disparities can significantly impact the ability of certain groups or individuals to participate fully in the political process and seek redress for their grievances. Disparities in access to political justice can manifest in various ways, including but not limited to legal barriers and facilitators, Socioeconomic, geographic, education and information, and discrimination and marginalization.

10.3.1. Legal Barriers and Facilitators

The existence of legal barriers creates disparities in access to justice. These barriers can hinder individuals, particularly those from marginalized and disadvantaged communities, from effectively navigating the legal system and obtaining the redress they deserve (Habermas, 2010).

One primary barrier is the complexity and intricacy of legal procedures and processes. The law is often intricate, requiring specialized knowledge and expertise to comprehend and apply effectively. Understanding and navigating the legal system can be daunting and overwhelming for individuals who need legal training or financial means to hire legal representation. This complexity places them at a distinct disadvantage, as they may need help to articulate their grievances or present their case convincingly, leading to unequal outcomes (Scoones, 2010).

Another legal barrier is the high cost associated with legal proceedings. Legal fees, court costs, and other expenses can quickly accumulate, placing a heavy financial burden on individuals seeking justice. This financial strain can deter individuals with limited financial resources from pursuing their legal rights, effectively denying them access to justice. The inability to afford legal representation or meet the financial requirements of the legal process further exacerbates existing social and economic disparities.

Moreover, disparities in access to legal aid and assistance further contribute to the barriers disadvantaged individuals face. Legal support, which provides free or low-cost legal services, ensures equal access to justice. However, more resources and adequate funding for legal aid organizations often result in unrestricted availability and eligibility criteria. Consequently, many individuals need the necessary support and guidance to afford legal representation, making it difficult to assert their rights effectively (Habermas, 2010).

Furthermore, language and cultural barriers also present significant challenges in accessing justice. Legal systems are often complex and language-dependent, requiring individuals to navigate legal proceedings in a language they may need help understanding. This poses a substantial disadvantage to those with limited proficiency in the official language of the legal system, impeding their ability to comprehend legal documents, communicate effectively, and assert their rights. Additionally, cultural differences and biases within the legal system can further alienate individuals from marginalized communities, hindering their access to justice. (Scoones, 2010).

10.3.2. Socioeconomic Factors

Socioeconomic factors encompass a range of interconnected elements, including income, education, employment, and social status. These factors influence an individual's ability to navigate the complex legal landscape, engage competent legal representation, and bear the costs of pursuing justice. Consequently, individuals from disadvantaged socioeconomic backgrounds often find themselves marginalized and unable to participate effectively in the justice system, exacerbating societal power imbalances.

Income inequality plays a prominent role in perpetuating disparities in access to justice. Legal services, such as attorney fees, court fees, and related expenses, can be prohibitively high for individuals with limited financial resources. As a result, those who cannot afford legal representation may be forced to navigate the complexities of the legal system alone, potentially compromising their ability to present a strong case and secure a just outcome. This economic disadvantage creates a distinct power imbalance, favoring those who can afford robust legal representation and impeding the ability of disadvantaged individuals to exercise their rights fully.

Education also plays a significant role in shaping access to justice. A lack of educational opportunities and legal literacy can hinder individuals from understanding their rights, navigating legal procedures, and effectively engaging with the justice system. Limited knowledge of legal processes, terminologies, and available resources further marginalizes disadvantaged individuals, making it challenging for them to effectively advocate for themselves or access the support and guidance needed to pursue justice (Scoones, 2010).

Moreover, employment instability and the absence of adequate social support networks can compound the disparities in accessing justice. Unstable employment may limit individuals' ability to take time off work for legal proceedings, seek legal advice, or gather necessary evidence. Lack of access to affordable healthcare, housing, and other necessities can also divert their attention and resources from pursuing justice, forcing them to prioritize immediate survival over long-term legal remedies (Habermas, 2010).

These socioeconomic disparities in access to justice are detrimental to individuals and erode the foundations of a just and equitable society. When certain groups face barriers in seeking justice, it undermines the principle of equal protection under the law and perpetuates systemic injustices. Addressing these disparities by implementing measures that promote equal access to justice, regardless of socioeconomic background, is essential.

10.3.3. Geographic Factors

Geographic factors play a significant role in disparities in access to justice within political systems. Access to justice refers to the ability of individuals and communities to effectively engage with the legal system and seek redress for grievances or violations of their rights. However, not all individuals and communities enjoy equal access to justice, and geographic factors often exacerbate these disparities.

One key geographic factor influencing access to justice is the distribution of legal resources and institutions. In many countries, legal resources such as courts, law firms, and legal aid organizations are concentrated in urban centers, while rural and remote areas are often underserved. This disparity in the distribution of legal resources creates significant challenges for individuals residing in isolated regions who may have to travel long distances to access legal assistance or attend court hearings. The financial burden and logistical difficulties associated with travel can pose substantial barriers, effectively limiting access to justice for marginalized communities

(Habermas, 2010). Moreover, legal professionals and expertise availability also varies across different geographic areas. Urban centers typically attract a larger pool of legal professionals, offering greater specialization and expertise in diverse areas of law. Conversely, rural areas may need more legal professionals, particularly those with specialized knowledge required for some instances, such as human rights or environmental law. This need for more legal expertise in rural areas can limit the ability of individuals to find competent legal representation or access specialized legal advice, further contributing to disparities in access to justice (Scoones, 2010).

Another geographic factor that impacts access to justice is the infrastructure and connectivity of a region. Inadequate infrastructure, such as poor road networks or limited access to communication technologies, can hinder individuals' ability to engage with the legal system. For example, suppose a rural community needs reliable internet access. In that case, it becomes easier for residents to access online legal resources, communicate with legal professionals remotely, or participate in virtual court proceedings. These infrastructure limitations create additional barriers, disproportionately affecting those in geographically disadvantaged areas and impeding their access to justice (Scoones, 2010).

Furthermore, geographic factors also intersect with socio-economic disparities, compounding the challenges faced by marginalized communities. Poverty rates tend to be higher in rural and remote areas, and individuals with limited financial resources often struggle to afford legal representation or navigate the complexities of the legal system. The combination of limited financial means and geographic barriers creates a significant hurdle for individuals seeking justice, leading to a disparity in outcomes based on where people live (Habermas, 2010).

10.3.4. Education and Information

Education is pivotal in empowering individuals to understand and assert their rights effectively. A solid foundation in legal literacy equips citizens with the necessary knowledge and skills to navigate complex legal processes, comprehend their rights and obligations, and engage with the justice system. However, access to quality legal education still needs to be evenly distributed across many societies. This imbalance perpetuates social inequality and contributes to disparities in access to justice.

Insufficient access to quality education can leave individuals marginalized, unaware of their legal rights, and ill-prepared to face legal challenges.

Without a basic understanding of legal principles, procedural rules, and the avenues available for seeking redress, marginalized communities and disadvantaged individuals often find themselves at a disadvantage when confronted with legal issues. This lack of knowledge exacerbates the power imbalance between those with access to legal resources and those without, hindering the realization of political justice.

Furthermore, the availability and dissemination of accurate and reliable information are crucial in addressing disparities in access to justice. In many cases, individuals seeking justice encounter significant hurdles due to a lack of awareness about their rights or the legal remedies available. Unequal access to information due to socioeconomic factors, language barriers, or limited outreach efforts can severely impede an individual's ability to assert their political rights (Scoones, 2010).

To bridge these gaps, efforts must be made to enhance legal education and improve the dissemination of legal information. Governments, civil society organizations, and educational institutions can collaborate to develop and implement comprehensive legal literacy programs targeting vulnerable and marginalized populations. These programs should focus on providing accessible and practical knowledge about the legal system, legal rights, and available avenues for seeking redress (Habermas, 2010).

Additionally, leveraging technology and digital platforms can be instrumental in widening access to legal education and information. Online resources, such as interactive websites, mobile applications, and educational videos, can facilitate self-learning and empower individuals to independently understand and navigate legal processes. Moreover, partnerships between legal aid organizations and technology companies can help create user-friendly platforms that offer legal information and resources to underserved communities.

However, more than improving education and information alone is required. Efforts should also be made to ensure that legal processes and systems are designed to promote inclusivity and equal access. Simplifying legal jargon, enhancing the availability of translation services, and providing legal aid to those unable to afford representation are critical steps in levelling the playing field (Habermas, 2010).

10.3.5. Discrimination and Marginalization

Discrimination, in its various forms, presents a significant barrier to justice. Members of marginalized groups such as racial and ethnic minorities, women, the LGBTQ+ community, individuals with disabilities, and religious minorities often face systemic biases that hinder their access to fair and impartial legal processes. Discrimination can manifest itself at multiple stages of the justice system, from law enforcement and arrest to trial and sentencing, leading to a disproportionate representation of marginalized individuals within the criminal justice system.

One aspect of discrimination in access to justice is racial profiling, whereby law enforcement officials target individuals based on their race or ethnicity, leading to an unequal application of the law. Racial profiling undermines the principles of fairness and equality and perpetuates negative stereotypes, reinforcing societal divisions and eroding trust in the justice system. Similarly, gender bias within the legal system can result in discriminatory practices, affecting the ability of women to seek justice for various issues, including gender-based violence, discrimination in the workplace, and reproductive rights.

Marginalized communities often face additional barriers that exacerbate their discrimination in accessing justice. Socioeconomic factors like poverty and limited educational opportunities can restrict individuals' ability to navigate complex legal processes and afford legal representation. Lack of legal literacy further compounds the problem, as disadvantaged individuals may need help understanding their rights, procedures, and available remedies. Furthermore, language barriers and limited access to translation services can hinder effective communication, impeding marginalized individuals' ability to participate effectively in legal proceedings (Scoones, 2010).

Discrimination and marginalization in access to justice affect individuals and have broader societal implications. When certain groups face barriers to justice, it undermines the principle of equality before the law and erodes public trust in the political system. Marginalized communities may develop a sense of disillusionment, perceiving the legal system as biased and unresponsive to their needs. This, in turn, can lead to social unrest, a breakdown of social cohesion, and diminished respect for the rule of law (Habermas, 2010).

10.4. THREATS TO RULE OF LAW AND ACCOUNTABILITY

In pursuing political justice, the rule of law is the foundation upon which democratic societies are built. It ensures that all individuals, including political elites, are subject to the same laws and held accountable for their actions. However, numerous threats to the rule of law, transparency, and accountability can undermine the essence of political justice.

One of the primary threats to the rule of law is the erosion of institutional independence. When the institutions responsible for upholding the rule of law, such as the judiciary and law enforcement agencies, are compromised or influenced by political elites, the impartiality and integrity of the legal system are jeopardized. This erosion can manifest in various forms, including political interference in judicial appointments, the manipulation of legal processes, and the subversion of checks and balances. Such actions erode public trust in the fairness of the legal system and hinder the pursuit of political justice.

Another significant threat to the rule of law is the prevalence of corruption within political circles. When political elites engage in corrupt practices, they undermine the principles of transparency and accountability. Breakdown allows those in power to manipulate the legal framework for personal gain, perpetuating inequality and injustice. This not only hampers the effective functioning of democratic institutions but also impedes the ability of the justice system to hold individuals accountable, as corruption can undermine investigations, prosecutions, and the enforcement of penalties.

Lack of transparency further compounds the challenges in upholding the rule of law and achieving political justice. When decision-making processes and the allocation of resources remain opaque, political elites can exploit their positions of power for personal or partisan interests. The absence of transparency enables hidden agendas, favoritism, and the potential for abuse of power, all undermining the principles of fairness and justice. In a transparent system, citizens are empowered to scrutinize the actions of their leaders and demand accountability, thereby ensuring that the rule of law prevails (Habermas, 2010).

The implications of these threats to the rule of law are far-reaching. They weaken democratic institutions, erode public trust, and foster an environment of impunity. When political elites evade accountability for their actions, the fundamental principles of justice are compromised. The lack of consequences for those who violate the rule of law perpetuates inequality and undermines the legitimacy of the political system as a whole (Scoones, 2010).

While threats to the rule of law, transparency, and accountability instigated by political elites pose significant challenges to the pursuit of political justice, another critical factor that hinders the achievement of a just and equitable political system is political polarization. Political polarization refers to the increasing ideological divide and deepening partisan animosity within a society, forming distinct and opposing political factions. This growing division has far-reaching implications for political processes, decision-making, and governance, as it undermines cooperation, fosters hostility, and hampers the ability to address pressing societal issues.

10.5. POLITICAL POLARIZATION

Political polarization is a significant challenge that threatens the foundations of political justice in contemporary societies. It refers to the deepening divide and ideological fragmentation within a political system characterized by increasing hostility, mistrust, and a lack of willingness to engage in meaningful dialogue across differing viewpoints. This phenomenon has become particularly prominent in recent years, impacting democracies worldwide and posing substantial obstacles to pursuing fair and equitable governance (Habermas, 2010).

One of the primary causes of political polarization is the rise of extreme ideologies and the increasing influence of partisan media. In the digital age, individuals have unprecedented access to many news sources, creating echo chambers where people are exposed only to information that aligns with their pre-existing beliefs. This selective exposure reinforces biases and fosters an "us versus them" mentality, making finding common ground and compromising solutions challenging. The result is a society divided into ideological factions, vehemently defending their perspectives while dismissing alternative viewpoints.

The impact of political polarization on political justice is multifaceted. First and foremost, it hampers the functioning of democratic institutions. When political debates become fiercely partisan and polarized, the focus often shifts from policy discussions and pursuing the common good to winning ideological battles and maintaining power. This undermines the principles of transparency, accountability, and responsiveness essential for a just and effective political system (Habermas, 2010).

Furthermore, political polarization undermines social cohesion and exacerbates social inequalities. As people retreat into their ideological bubbles, empathy and understanding for those with different beliefs diminish, leading to increased social fragmentation. This division can perpetuate discrimination, marginalization, and a lack of representation for specific groups, impeding progress towards a more equitable and inclusive community.

The influence of political polarization is not limited to the political realm; it spills over into public discourse, media, and interpersonal relationships. Social media platforms, in particular, have played a significant role in exacerbating polarization. Online platforms, designed to maximize user engagement, often prioritize content reinforcing existing beliefs, contributing to a feedback loop perpetuating polarization. It is agreed that media influence greatly influences political polarization and its implications for political justice. The result is a society where individuals are more likely to interact with like-minded individuals and less exposed to diverse perspectives, hindering the potential for constructive dialogue and compromise (Scoones, 2010).

10.6. MEDIA INFLUENCE AND MANIPULATION

In contemporary society, the media plays a significant role in shaping political justice and influencing public opinion. Media outlets, including television, radio, print, and online platforms, act as intermediaries between political actors and the public, disseminating information, and shaping public discourse. However, the power and influence wielded by the media can also present challenges in pursuing political justice. This section explores the multifaceted role of the media in political justice, examining both its positive contributions and the challenges posed by media manipulation and disinformation (Habermas, 2010).

The media serves as a critical source of information in a democratic society, providing citizens with the knowledge necessary for political participation and decision-making. Through investigative journalism, media outlets uncover corruption, abuse of power, and other injustices, holding those in positions of authority accountable. By exposing wrongdoing, the media plays a crucial role in maintaining transparency and upholding the principles of political justice.

Furthermore, the media acts as a platform for public debate and discussion, facilitating the exchange of diverse perspectives. It provides a voice to marginalized groups, amplifying their concerns and advocating for their rights. In this way, the media can contribute to a more inclusive and equitable political system by challenging power imbalances and promoting social justice.

However, despite its potential for positive impact, the media also faces significant challenges in its role as a guardian of political justice. One such challenge is media manipulation and the spread of disinformation. In the digital age, where information flows rapidly and is easily accessible, false narratives and misleading content can be disseminated quickly, muddying the waters of public discourse. Political actors and interest groups often exploit this environment, using media platforms to spread misinformation, shape public opinion, and advance their agendas (Habermas, 2010).

The rise of social media platforms has further intensified this challenge. With the exponential growth of social media users, information can spread rapidly and widely, often needing proper fact-checking or verification. This creates fertile ground for disseminating false or misleading information, leading to the distortion of public discourse and public opinion. The sheer volume and speed of information shared on social media make it difficult for individuals to discern what is true and what is not, further exacerbating the challenge of media manipulation (Scoones, 2010).

Another significant challenge lies in the monetization of media platforms. In pursuing profitability, media organizations may prioritize sensationalism, clickbait, and the amplification of divisive content. This can contribute to the polarization of society and hinder the objective understanding of complex political issues. The need for revenue can create a conflict of interest, where media outlets may prioritize capturing audiences' attention over providing accurate and balanced information. Such practices erode the trust between the media and the public and hinder the pursuit of justice by distorting public perception.

The lack of media literacy among the general population poses yet another challenge. Many individuals need to be equipped with the critical thinking skills necessary to assess the credibility of information sources and discern between factual news and opinion-based content. Furthermore, the rapid proliferation of digital media platforms and the ease of creating and sharing content have made it increasingly harder to distinguish between reliable information and falsehoods. The abundance of fake news, clickbait headlines, and viral misinformation campaigns can confuse and mislead audiences. Hence, this deficiency makes people vulnerable to manipulation, as they may unknowingly consume and share misleading or false information. Therefore, educating individuals about the importance of fact-checking, source verification, and critical analysis becomes crucial (Habermas, 2010). In addition to media literacy and critical thinking, policy challenges also arise in political justice. Governments and regulatory bodies face balancing freedom of the press with the need for responsible journalism. Striking the right balance requires establishing clear guidelines and ethical standards for media organizations. However, implementing such policies without infringing upon freedom of speech and expression can be a delicate process. Policymakers must navigate the complexities of protecting the public interest while respecting journalistic independence.

Furthermore, the concentration of media ownership in the hands of a few powerful entities can contribute to biased reporting and limited diversity of perspectives. When a few corporations or individuals control a significant portion of media outlets, the potential for agenda-setting and the suppression of dissenting voices becomes a genuine concern. This consolidation of media power not only hampers the democratic ideals of pluralism and freedom of expression but also undermines the pursuit of political justice by limiting the dissemination of accurate and unbiased information (Scoones, 2010).

The influence and manipulation of media in the realm of political justice raise significant concerns about the functioning of democratic systems and the fairness of decision-making processes. As individuals increasingly rely on media sources for information and news, media literacy and critical thinking skills become vital in discerning the veracity and biases present within media narratives. However, while addressing media influence and manipulation is crucial, it is equally important to recognize that political justice challenges extend beyond national borders. In an era of globalization, where the world is more interconnected than ever, transnational challenges arise that have profound implications for political justice. Exploring the complexities of globalization and global challenges within the context of political justice provides a comprehensive understanding of the multifaceted obstacles faced in achieving fairness, equity, and accountability (Habermas, 2010).

10.7. GLOBALIZATION AND TRANSNATIONAL CHALLENGES

Globalization has transformed the world into an interconnected and interdependent network where one nation's actions can have far-reaching consequences on others. This increased connectivity and integration of economies, societies, and cultures across borders have given rise to many transnational issues that pose significant challenges in pursuing political justice. In this section, we will delve into the impact of globalization, global issues, and national interests, exploring their complexity and influence on the quest for political justice.

One of the critical impacts of globalization on political justice is the blurring of national boundaries. Traditional notions of sovereignty and territoriality are being challenged as global challenges such as climate change, terrorism, infectious diseases, and cyber threats transcend national borders. These transnational issues require coordinated efforts and cooperation among nations to address them effectively. However, pursuing political justice becomes complex when countries prioritize their national interests over collective action, resulting in a fragmented response to global challenges (Scoones, 2010).

The diverse interests of nations further compound the complexity of transnational challenges. Each country has its own set of priorities, shaped by its unique political, economic, and social context. While some governments may be more concerned with economic growth and development, others may prioritize human rights or environmental sustainability. These differing national interests can hinder the pursuit of political justice, as they often lead to conflicting agendas and a need for more consensus on addressing transnational issues.

Moreover, globalization has given rise to a power shift in international relations. Emerging economies are gaining influence and challenging the dominance of traditional global powers. This shift in power dynamics adds another layer of complexity to the pursuit of political justice, as competing interests and aspirations of various nations come into play. Struggles for power and influence can undermine efforts to promote justice, as powerful nations may use their leverage to advance their interests at the expense of others.

The interconnectedness of the global economy also poses challenges for political justice. Economic globalization has created an intricate web of trade and investment flows, making countries economically interdependent. However, this interdependence can create vulnerabilities and inequalities, where powerful nations exploit weaker ones or multinational corporations prioritize profit over social justice. Balancing economic interests with the pursuit of political justice becomes a delicate task, as policies and decisions often involve trade-offs and compromises (Habermas, 2010).

Furthermore, the rise of digital technologies and the internet has revolutionized communication and information sharing, enabling transnational activism and mobilization. Online platforms have provided a voice to marginalized groups and facilitated the spread of ideas and movements across borders. However, the digital realm also presents challenges in regulating online spaces, countering misinformation, and protecting individual rights and privacy. Striking a balance between fostering free expression and ensuring political justice in the digital age is a pressing concern (Scoones, 2010).

10.8. CONCLUSION

The challenges in achieving political justice are multifaceted and require concerted efforts from individuals, communities, and governments. This chapter has highlighted several key challenges that impede political justice, including corruption, partisanship, disparities in access to justice, threats to the rule of law, political polarization, media influence, and globalization.

Corruption remains a pervasive problem in many political systems worldwide. It undermines the principles of justice, fairness, and accountability, eroding public trust in institutions. Efforts to combat corruption must be prioritized through solid legal frameworks, robust enforcement mechanisms, and a culture of transparency and integrity.

Partisanship and political bias pose significant challenges to political justice. Political decisions driven by partisan interests rather than the common good can lead to policies perpetuating inequality and undermining fairness. Promoting impartiality and fostering a constructive dialogue and compromise culture is crucial to overcoming these challenges.

Disparities in access to justice present barriers for marginalized communities and individuals. Legal, socioeconomic, geographic, educational, and discriminatory factors contribute to these disparities. Addressing these challenges requires reforms ensuring equal access to legal representation, promoting legal literacy, bridging socioeconomic gaps, and eradicating discrimination (Habermas, 2010).

Threats to the rule of law and accountability further hinder political justice. When institutions fail to uphold the principles of justice, the rights and freedoms of individuals are compromised. Safeguarding the rule of law and holding those who violate it accountable is essential for political justice.

Fueled by ideological divisions and identity politics, political polarization creates an environment where the pursuit of justice becomes increasingly challenging. Overcoming polarization requires promoting inclusive and empathetic dialogue, respecting diverse perspectives, and prioritizing the common good over partisan interests (Scoones, 2010). Media influence and manipulation play a significant role in shaping public opinion and political discourse. Misinformation, propaganda, and biased reporting can distort the truth and undermine justice. Building media literacy, supporting independent journalism, and encouraging critical thinking is crucial in mitigating media manipulation's adverse effects (Habermas, 2010).

Globalization and transnational challenges add complexity to the pursuit of political justice. Climate change, migration, and global governance require cooperation and collective action. Developing mechanisms for effective global control, promoting multilateralism, and addressing global inequalities are vital to achieving political justice in an interconnected world.

In conclusion, addressing the challenges in political justice requires a holistic approach that encompasses legal reforms, institutional strengthening, public awareness, and societal transformation. It demands the active participation and collaboration of citizens, civil society organizations, governments, and international entities. By recognizing and confronting these challenges head-on, we can strive towards a more just and equitable political system that upholds the principles of democracy, fairness, and accountability for all (Habermas, 2010).

Bibliography

1. Almer, C., & Goeschl, T. (2010). Environmental crime and punishment: Empirical evidence from the German penal code. *Land Economics*, *86*(4), 707–726.
2. Amaral, S., Bhalotra, S., & Prakash, N. (2021). *Gender, Crime and Punishment: Evidence from Women Police Stations in India*. 5(2), 78–81.
3. Anderson, P. M., Henville, C. F., Rifaat, R., Johnson, B., & Meliopoulos, S. (2022). *Power System Protection*. John Wiley & Sons. *6*(4), 90–96.
4. Anthony, T. (2013). *Indigenous People, Crime and Punishment*. Routledge. *9*(7), 77–79.
5. Besley, T., & Persson, T. (2011). *Pillars of Prosperity: The Political Economics of Development Clusters*. Princeton University Press. *8*(7), 80–85.
6. Blake, M., & Smith, P. T. (2013). *International Distributive Justice*. *7*(5), 97–102.
7. Chemerinsky, E. (2019). *Constitutional Law: Principles and Policies*. Aspen Publishing. *3*(2), 27–34.
8. Chen, X., Gu, Z. C., Liu, Z. X., & Wen, X. G. (2013). Symmetry protected topological orders and the group cohomology of their symmetry group. *Physical Review B*, *87*(15), 155114.
9. Cohen, J. L., & Arato, A. (2016). Civil society and political theory. In *Democracy: A Reader* (pp. 370–374). Columbia University Press.
10. Cook, T. E. (2012). *Governing with the News: The News Media as a*

Political Institution. University of Chicago Press. *6*(2), 107–111.

11. Cooray, A., Dutta, N., & Mallick, S. (2017). Trade openness and labor force participation in Africa: the role of political institutions. *Industrial Relations: A Journal of Economy and Society*, *56*(2), 319–350.
12. Ergun, A. (2010). Post-Soviet political transformation in Azerbaijan: Political elite, civil society and the trials of democratization. *Uluslararası İlişkiler Dergisi*, *7*(26), 67–85.
13. Eriksen, E. O. (2016). Three conceptions of global political justice. *GLOBUS Research Paper*, *1*.
14. Floridi, L., Cowls, J., Beltrametti, M., Chatila, R., Chazerand, P., Dignum, V., ... & Vayena, E. (2021). An ethical framework for a good AI society: Opportunities, risks, principles, and recommendations. *Ethics, Governance, and Policies in Artificial Intelligence*, 19–39.
15. Fox, J., & Polborn, M. (2021). On the separation of executive and legislative powers: Executive independence, liberty, and social welfare. *Journal of Theoretical Politics*, *33*(4), 430–454.
16. Gilabert, P. (2012). Comparative assessments of justice, political feasibility, and ideal theory. *Ethical Theory and Moral Practice*, *15*, 39–56.
17. Gourevitch, P. A., & Shinn, J. (2010). *Political Power and Corporate Control: The New Global Politics of Corporate Governance*. Princeton University Press.
18. Habermas, J. (2010). Religion, law and politics. On political justice in a multicultural World-Society. *Polis. Political Studies*, *2*(2), 7–21.
19. Hafezi, M., Demler, E. A., Lukin, M. D., & Taylor, J. M. (2011). Robust optical delay lines with topological protection. *Nature Physics*, *7*(11), 907–912.
20. Hallegatte, S., Rentschler, J., & Rozenberg, J. (2020). *Adaptation Principles*. *11*(3), 101–107.
21. Harvey, D. (2010). *Social Justice and the City* (Vol. 1). University of Georgia Press. *5*(3), 60–64.
22. Hayner, P. B. (2010). *Unspeakable Truths 2e: Transitional Justice and the Challenge of Truth Commissions*. Routledge. *4*(5), 51–59.
23. Jay Olshansky, S., Biggs, S., Andrew Achenbaum, W., Davison, G. C., Fried, L., Gutman, G., & Butler, R. N. (2011). The global agenda council on the ageing society: policy principles. *Global Policy*, *2*(1), 97–105.

24. Jones, A. T. (2017). Government. *3*(1), 20–23.

25. Kapur, R. (2013). *Erotic Justice: Law and the New Politics of Postcolonialism*. Routledge. *4*(4), 32–38.

26. Kirchheimer, O. (2015). *Political Justice: The Use of Legal Procedure for Political Ends* (Vol. 2303). Princeton University Press. *15*(7), 105–111.

27. Kollmann, N. (2012). *Crime and Punishment in Early Modern Russia*. Cambridge University Press. *12*(4), 90–95.

28. Konow, J., & Schwettmann, L. (2016). The economics of justice. *Handbook of Social Justice Theory and Research*, 83–106.

29. Leach, M., Stirling, A. C., & Scoones, I. (2010). *Dynamic Sustainabilities: Technology, Environment, Social Justice* (p. 232). Taylor & Francis.

30. Martineau, H. (2020). *Society in America*. e-artnow. *2*(1), 10–14.

31. Okin, S. M. (2015). Justice, gender, and the family. In *Justice, Politics, and the Family* (pp. 63–87). Routledge.

32. O'neill, M. (2012). Free (and fair) markets without capitalism: political values, principles of justice, and property-owning democracy. *Property□Owning Democracy: Rawls and Beyond*, 75–100.

33. O'Reilly, T. (2011). Government as a Platform. *Innovations: technology, governance, globalization*, *6*(1), 13–40.

34. Power, T. J. (2010). Optimism, pessimism, and coalitional presidentialism: Debating the institutional design of Brazilian democracy. *Bulletin of Latin American Research*, *29*(1), 18–33.

35. Prost, A., Binik, A., Abubakar, I., Roy, A., De Allegri, M., Mouchoux, C., ... & Osrin, D. (2015). Logistic, ethical, and political dimensions of stepped wedge trials: critical review and case studies. *Trials*, *16*(1), 1–11.

36. Raile, E. D., Pereira, C., & Power, T. J. (2011). The executive toolbox: building legislative support in a multiparty presidential regime. *Political Research Quarterly*, *64*(2), 323–334.

37. Reinstein, R. J. (2010). Recognition: A Case Study on the Original Understanding of Executive Power. *U. Rich. L. Rev.*, *45*, 801.

38. Resh, N., & Sabbagh, C. (2016). Justice and education. *Handbook of Social Justice Theory and Research*, 349–367.

39. Roberts, J. T. (2011). *Athens on Trial: The Antidemocratic Tradition in*

Western Thought. Princeton University Press. *20*(5), 65–69.

40. Schmoller, G. (2016). The idea of justice in political economy. *Journal of Contextual Economics–Schmollers Jahrbuch, 136*(4), 335–360.
41. Schwarz, S., Baum, M. A., & Cohen, D. K. (2020). (Sex) crime and punishment in the# MeToo era: How the public views rape. *Political Behavior*, 1–30.
42. Selznick, P. (2020). *Law, Society, and Industrial Justice* (Vol. 30). Quid Pro Books.
43. Stieglitz, S., & Dang-Xuan, L. (2013). Social media and political communication: a social media analytics framework. *Social Network Analysis and Mining, 3*, 1277–1291.
44. Ullmann, W. (2010). *Principles of Government and Politics in the Middle Ages (Routledge Revivals)*. Routledge.
45. Voigt, P., & Von dem Bussche, A. (2017). The EU general data protection regulation (GDPR). *A Practical Guide, 1st Ed.,* Cham: Springer International Publishing, *10*(3152676), 10–55.
46. Waldron, J. (2013). Separation of powers in thought and practice. *BCL Rev., 54*, 433.
47. Walker, G. (2012). *Environmental Justice: Concepts, Evidence and Politics*. Routledge. *4*(2), 97–102.
48. Watson, J. E., Dudley, N., Segan, D. B., & Hockings, M. (2014). The performance and potential of protected areas. *Nature, 515*(7525), 67–73.
49. Woodhouse, E. J., & Collingridge, D. (2019). Incrementalism, intelligent trial-and-error, and the future of political decision theory. In *An Heretical Heir of the Enlightenment* (pp. 131–154). Routledge.
50. Zoeller, R. T., Brown, T. R., Doan, L. L., Gore, A. C., Skakkebaek, N. E., Soto, A. M., ... & Vom Saal, F. S. (2012). Endocrine-disrupting chemicals and public health protection: a statement of principles from The Endocrine Society. *Endocrinology, 153*(9), 4097–4110.

INDEX

N

O

P

T

U

V

W